FROM PILGRIMAGE TO HISTORY
The Renaissance
and Global Historicism

AMS STUDIES IN THE RENAISSANCE
ISSN 0195-8011

Number 41
John G. Demaray, FROM PILGRIMAGE TO HISTORY:
The Renaissance and Global Historicism

FROM PILGRIMAGE TO HISTORY
The Renaissance
and Global Historicism

by

John G. Demaray

AMS Press, Inc.
New York

Library of Congress Cataloging-in-Publication Data

Demaray, John G.
  From Pilgrimage to History: The Renaissance and Global
Historicism / John G. Demaray.
    p. cm. – (AMS Studies in the Renaissance ; no. 41)
    Includes bibliographical references and index.
    ISBN-10: 0-404-62341-7
    ISBN-13: 978-0-404-62341-8 (alk. paper)
    1. Historiography—History. 2. Historicism—History.
    I. Title. II. Series.
D13.D396   2006
907'.2'04—dc22   2004046226
                                                       CIP

All AMS Books are printed on acid-free paper that meets the guidelines
for performance and durability of the Committee on Production
Guidelines for Book Longevity of the Council on Library Resources.

AMS Press, Inc.
Brooklyn Navy Yard, 63 Flushing Ave – Unit #221
Brooklyn, NY 11205-1005, USA

MANUFACTURED IN THE UNITED STATES OF AMERICA

CONTENTS

ILLUSTRATIONS

Illustrations following page 55

Fig. 1. Henry More, etching by W. Faithorne, n.d. Courtesy of the Syndics of Cambridge University Library.

Fig. 2. Americus Vespuccius with astrolabe. Engraving by Johannes Collaert, n.d. Courtesy of the New York Public Library.

Fig. 3. Walter Ralegh, supposedly after his release from the Tower. Artist unknown, n.d.

Fig. 4. Mythic El Dorado, from Hulsius's German edition of Ralegh's *Discoverie*. Courtesy of the Henry E. Huntington Library and Art Gallery.

Fig. 5. The monstrous Ewaiepanenema race, from Hulsius's edition of Ralegh's *Discoverie*. Courtesy of the Henry E. Huntington Library and Art Gallery.

Fig. 6. Amazons slaughtering male invaders in Guiana, from Hulsius's edition of Ralegh's *Discoverie*. Courtesy of the Henry E. Huntington Library and Art Gallery.

Fig. 7. Providential eye of God surveying globular earth. Frontispiece for Ralegh's *History of the World* (1614). Courtesy of the Henry E. Huntington Library.

Fig. 8. Pilgrimage iconographic world, Christ as the Logos, Chartres Cathedral. Photograph: Painton Cowen.

Fig. 9. *Mappaemundi* (ca. 1285) in Hereford Cathedral, attributed to Richard of Haldingham, used as pilgrim guide to Jerusalem. Courtesy of the Dean and Chapter of Hereford Cathedral.

Fig. 10. Stone urn marking medieval geographic "center" of the world, in Constantine's Church of the Holy Sepulcher, Jerusalem. Photograph: author.

Fig. 11. Jerusalem map from Itinera Hierosolymitana Cruesignatorum (ca. 1180) depicting some of the medieval Stations of the Redemption. From *Zeitschrift des Deutschen Palästina-Vereins*, BD XV, fo. 5 (Leipzig, 1892).

Fig. 12. Exodus icon from Cosmos Indicoplenstes's ninth-century *Topographia Christiana* showing Moses (right) in the Sinai, Aaron (center), hand of God (upper right). Courtesy of Bibliotèca Medicea Laurenziana.

Fig. 13. Icon of Mt. Sinai "ring" of stations, from eleventh-century ms of Bishop John Climacus's *Scala Paradisi* in monastery at Patmos, Cod. 122, fo. Av-Br.

Fig. 14. Monastery of St. Catherine, 12th Station of the Exodus at foot of Mt. Sinai, is starting point for travelers ascending on the pathway "ring," seen veering behind the rear wall. Photograph: author.

Fig. 15. Mt. Sinai from pilgrimage pathway of Gebel St. Catherine pathway. Photograph: author.

Fig. 16. Stone stairs and Gate of Confession, Mt. Sinai. A second stone gate of St. Stephen also spans this section of the pilgrimage ring. Photograph: O. F. A. Meinardus.

Fig. 17. The Gebel Musa "ring" of stations in Jacobo di Verona's *Liber Peregrinationis* (1335). Pictured from bottom: Church of St. Catherine, checkered Church of St. Mary of the Apparition, plain, and Church of Elijah (with crosses on roof), pathway of purgation (dotted lines), summit buildings where Moses received the Laws, and repentance garden between Gabel Musa and Gebel St. Catherine at right.

Fig. 18. The 42 pilgrimage stations of the Exodus, rendered in Ortelius's *Theatrum Orbis Terrarum* (1606). Courtesy of the Henry. E. Huntington Library.

Illustrations following page 102

Fig. 19. Estimated route of Columbus's first two voyages west to the "end of the East" in Asia. Reconstruction by Ravenstein using the Behain globe.

Fig. 20. Pilgrimage motifs with those of global discovery on frontispiece of Purchas's *Hakluytus Posthumus* (1625). Top center: Israelite pilgrims to New Jerusalem; Elizabeth I (right) and James I (left). Circular icons depict supposed pilgrims, voyagers, and monarchs, including Noah, Abraham, Solomon, British King Edward the Navigator. Courtesy of the Henry E. Huntington Library.

Fig. 21. Earthly Paradise on map by Mercator in *Purchas* (1625). Courtesy of the Henry E. Huntington Library.

Fig. 22. Hondius's map of the "articke pole" depicting an imaginary sea and a land mass ("California"). From Purchas's *Hakluytus Posthumus* (1625). Courtesy of the Henry E. Huntington Library.

Fig. 23. View of London's Chelsea College, earlier known as King's College, where Purchas wrote major parts of *Purchas His Pilgrimes*. Frontispiece of John Darley's *Glory of Chelsea College Revived* (1662). Courtesy of the British Library.

Fig. 24. Map of Europe, Africa, and Asia showing the five traditional climatic zones, with two zones near the equator long thought too warm to be habitable, published by Ortelius in 1590. Courtesy of the New York Public Library.

Fig. 25. The Angel Uriel in Milton's *Paradise Lost* watches Satan journeying from the sun to Eden. Engraving by Bromley after painting by Fuseli. Courtesy of the Henry E. Huntington Library.

Fig. 26. Frontispiece for Thomas Fuller's *Historie of the Holy War* (1636), a work that denounces crusades and Moslem jihads while confirming the traditional relationship of the Temple of the Holy Sepulcher and the European cathedral. Courtesy of the Henry E. Huntington Library.

Fig. 27. Late Greek lithograph (ca. 1778) after an early Icon of Mt. Sinai, showing the monastery and the mountain "ring" of holy stations. Photograph: George W. Allen in Heinz Skroucha's *Sinai*. Courtesy of Oxford University Press.

Fig. 28. Iconographic *Ebstorf mappaemundi* (ca. 1235-84) believed to have been produced to accompany Otia Imperiala (ca. 1211) by British-born Gervaise of Tilsbury. Courtesy of the New York Public Library.

ACKNOWLEDGEMENTS

Grateful acknowledgement is made of a National Endowment for the Humanities Fellowship to the University of Cambridge and to the Huntington Library in support of this book, and to Rutgers University and its Research Council for subsequent travel and incidental grants. Special thanks are also due the Research Division of the New York Public Library for use of the Frederick Lewis Allen Room and access to rich collections.

Because this work had a long genesis, my debts to numerous unnamed students and colleagues are many and deep. At the Huntington Library, I owe particular thanks for past assistance to Stanley Stewart, J. Kent Clark, Martin Ridge, and Peter Mancall. Perceptive Milton criticism was offered in the past by John M. Steadman, Barbara Lewalski, S. K. Henniger, and Michael Lieb; aid and support were kindly provided by Edward Tayler, William Elton, and Albert Labriola. My long term debts are to Marjorie Hope Nicolson for her early analysis of my Milton work and her encouragement of overseas research in literature and history. Any inadequacies in the present book are my own.

Assistance overseas was generously provided by Giuseppe Galigani of the University of Florence; Archivist Henry Button of Christ's College, Cambridge; Sabino de Sandoli of the Franciscan Biblical Library, Jerusalem; and Geoffrey Ashe of Glastonbury, United Kingdom. I am also obligated for valuable research help to individual staff members of the University of Cambridge Library; Henry E. Huntington Library; British Library; Franciscan Biblical Library, Jerusalem; and the Bibliotèca Medicea Laurenziana, Florence. John Hopper, Ashlie K. Sponenberg, and Turid Weingartz of AMS Press deserves thanks for their dedicated editorial assistance. Still, my deepest debts are to Hannah Disinger Demaray who, on medieval pilgrimage chains in the East and in research libraries of the West, provided constant encouragement and scholarly–critical insight.

PREFACE

Today when parochial views of current world events often dominate public discussion, rarely have events of the distant past seemed so irrelevant to global understanding. In our own period instant opinions and superficial analyses have all too often become substitutes for long-term awareness of the patterns and forms of world cultures. Still, what took place centuries ago sometimes affords better insights into present problems than occurrences in our own time.

The contemporary European split between East and West, serious historians have pointed out, has origins not just in the present, but in events going back to the fourth century. In AD 325 following Constantine's conversion to Christianity and his movement of the seat of the Roman Empire to Constantinople, Greek Byzantine Orthodox Christianity and Western Latin Christianity divided at the Council of Nicaea, a division made lasting after a further Orthodox-Catholic breach in the eleventh century. In the East, Islam later overran many Orthodox territories; and in the West, Latin Christianity broke into Catholic and Protestant denominations. Today the depth of these East-West separations makes them especially difficult to overcome.

In taking a long-term view, I have sought to illumine the manner in which a medieval iconographic-historiography, having origins largely in the fourth century in the Byzantine East and disseminated by Latin pilgrims and others returning from the Holy Land, ultimately clashed with the developing empirical and naturalist historiography of the West. The cultural rift that followed has been long in unfolding.

Here is an account of how Renaissance historiographers and other writers, generally accepting but also revolting against an ancient biblical historicism, produced transforming theories and structures in their attempts at universal histories of a changing globe. Examined are the partially suppressed or openly acknowledged assumptions and practices governing Early Modern approaches to world cultural historiography.

To uncover this sweep of past outlooks, I have interpreted massive and complex global historicist productions in terms of their developing forms and discontinuities; for example, giving attention to Samuel Purchas's evolution of his historicist "method" in six radically altering versions from 1613 through 1626 of *Purchas his pilgrimage*; and in discussing John Milton's development of world historicist views in empirical and imaginative writings over some fifty-five years; that is, in his epic in miniature *On The Fifth of November*; his unfinished chronicle *History of Britain* and his experimental, empirical *A Brief History of Moscovia*; his outlines for planned works in the 1630s, and finally his 10–book and then 12–book versions of *Paradise Lost*. Contemporary historicists and cultural critics of varied persuasions are generally relegated to notes and insets: figures such as R. G. Collingwood, Irwin Panofsky, Hayden White, Christopher Hill, Stephen Greenblatt, Michel Foucault, Erich Auerbach, and many others.

There is no question about the present work's being interdisciplinary. Late medieval and Early Modern representations in art, literature, history, cosmography, and architecture unselfconsciously merged disciplines. But a fundamental difference between influential past and present outlooks remains. Today's interdisciplinary postmodernist criticism, often concerned with a supposed universal existential "present," frequently proclaims little epistemological relationship between historicist representations and the supposed external "reality" signified. By contrast, earlier historicist representations, arising from accounts of world discovery, were assumed to have grasped and to have effectively revealed the nature of the external world and many of its peoples. It was this deeply experienced belief that gave shape to a new global cultural cosmographical-historicism which in turn had a general impact upon later historicist views.

Although I have sought to avoid the fallacy of misplaced contemporaneity: the unmerited reading of the past in the light of the present, long-term historicist perspectives do provide points of reference. Early Modern historicism, in first responding to a dramatic new global vision, and in seeking new ways to represent and to interpret world civilizations, is accordingly seen as a generic wellspring for a range in later centuries of divergent scientific, philosophic, environmental, and even comparative-religious global historicist works.

New York City   J.G.D.
April 8, 2005

INTRODUCTION

People must come to see more and more
that all history is really the history of history,
that in stating what we take to be past facts
we are really and only and always recounting
and summarizing our own and other people's
investigations concerning the past.

R. G. Collingwood
"Lectures on the Philosophy of History,"
Oxford, Hilary Term, 1926

A new kind of world history arose in the fifteenth through the seventeenth centuries from the transformed remnants of the disintegrating medieval pilgrimage tradition. It was a mode of history that had distant antecedents in the works of Herodotus, Claudius Ptolemy, and wider classical and other sources; but a mode of history that in the West developed in part from attempts to understand biblical events in an empirical way. In its methods this reformist history finally centered upon gaining an empirical historical and geographic knowledge of the earth and its peoples.

This form of global historicism has been traced in its Western resurgence to the eighteenth-century cosmopolitan world outlook of Voltaire, Kant, and the French encyclopediests.[1] It is a fundamental premise of this book, however, that the most basic and varied roots of this historicism in its Western phase rest with the authors and theorists of the Continental and English Renaissance, many of whom have been neglected as reformist historiographers because never examined in that role. In this earlier period before the eighteenth-century enlightenment, historiographers and writers experienced a jolt when, as Holy Land pilgrimages to Jerusalem gave way to world-wide voyages of discovery, the largely Byzantine iconography of a medieval globe with Jerusalem at its supposed geographic "center" fragmented before accounts of a vast earth with no discernible "middle" point. This new, enlarged, irregular earth, still viewed by traditionalists as some kind of puzzling iconographic "Book of God's Works" supplementing the Bible as the "Book of God's Words," teemed with strange peoples and had a confusing and seemingly ever-expanding past.

This startling change in world views took place at a pivotal point in historiography: when medieval faith intermeshed with Renaissance empiricism; when the term "universal history" began to change in meaning; when currents of philosophy, cosmology, poetry, and religion mixed in strange combinations; and when accounts of "all things" transmuted into accounts of differing cultures. These revolutionary alterations were such that forms and echoes of this Early Modern historicism in its global reach appear reflected in historicist works of following centuries.

This book accordingly grew almost of its own accord over a period of years from my publications on structure and cosmography in the heroic poetry of Dante Alighieri, Edmund Spenser, and John Milton, publications based on studies in the Near East, Continental Europe, and England into early pilgrimage and later global voyage sources.[2] Central to these earlier studies were on-site inspections of the Egypt-Jerusalem-Rome and other European and English pilgrimage "chains" and "stations"; together with corresponding examinations of typal imitations of these "chains" and "stops" in medieval art works, literature, maps, and churches. I was acutely aware that between 1320, when Dante completed his sequential pilgrimage poem the *Commedia*, and 1674, when Milton published a final version beginning in medias res of his dramatic epic *Paradise Lost*, representations of the earth and its past both in imaginative literature and in new philosophical, historicist and travel writings had in fact changed profoundly. The ordered pilgrimage cosmos known to Dante, brilliantly mirrored in his long processional poem, had mutated into the irregular, spacious, and confounding new cosmos known to Milton. Roman pilgrimages to Jerusalem and to lesser holy shrines had in fact been largely replaced by hazardous voyages over the great ocean-seas to

2

unknown lands. The implications of this revolutionary historiography, when viewed in the perspective of the earlier pilgrimage tradition, could not be ignored; and they were subsequently pursued under a National Endowment for the Humanities fellowship to Cambridge University and the Henry E. Huntington Library.

The Renaissance authors who contributed to the new history— from Walter Ralegh and Richard Hakluyt through Peter Heylyn and Samuel Purchas—were fired by the extraordinary cosmological and cultural revelations of the Renaissance voyages of global discovery. Although the voyages were launched in a search for gold, natural resources, trading outposts, and lands open to colonization, they were also motivated by a deep curiosity about the nature and history of the world and the human race. The historiographers in their revisionist works continued to cite medieval pilgrim tracts recording journeys to the supposed center of the world at Jerusalem, a city allegedly located at the "end of the East," at the summit and middle of the earth's circular land mass in the northern hemisphere. They regularly included passages on the location and nature of the Garden of Eden. Similarly, the traditional structuring of Christian universal history into biblical "epochs"—among them, the Creation, the Fall, the Flood, the Redemption, the future Second Coming, and the future Kingdom of Eternal Bliss—became intervolved with different time-frames derived from empirical knowledge. As the earth's past grew ever more ancient and mysterious, and the earth's surface ever larger and more irregular, perplexing problems loomed in representing the world as ordered in some divine iconographic configuration. How was the new historiography to be given form? And would this form be truly universal and include an inevitable end of history?

Fascinated by Renaissance accounts by voyagers to unexplored lands and to the edges of the mysterious northern and southern polar caps, these new historiographers at first compiled journey tracts, and then strove to find new ways and methods objectively to interpret past and present societies, regions, peoples, and cultures.

3

Their massive publications serve collectively as a bridge between medieval biblical, pilgrimage, and iconographic outlooks, and a new empirical naturalism that radically altered historiography. A concluding chapter briefly recalls Renaissance contributions to empirical historicism following a passing, selective overview of later structured designs for world history, and especially for history's supposed "end," by, among others, Georg Wilhelm Friedrich Hegel, Karl Marx, and "globalist" Francis Fukuyama.

Over the past thirty years, an outpouring of books and articles have plumbed the economic and political conditions driving the interlaced Early Modern movements of exploration, colonization, alleged incipient capitalism, and imperialism. Another stream of publications on Early Modern discoveries has meticulously recorded what was found and reported by successive explorers— region by region, shoreline by shoreline, voyage by voyage.[3] Still, the vexing problem of how Renaissance writers and artists struggled to make historical sense of conflicting iconographic and naturalist outlooks is still very much in need of consideration.

Examined here are the wavering intellectual efforts of late Renaissance historians, compilers, and cartographers, torn between a belief in literal views of the Bible and eyewitness reports of new geographical discoveries, to find novel approaches and methods for an innovative world cultural historiography coalescing, in so far as possible, cosmography, climate, politics, religion, social organization, and customs. I am therefore concerned, not so much with history or globalization as such, but with what is here referred to as the global "historiography" or "historicism" of mainly the Early Modern period: that is, the structures, approaches, practices, and methods governing the composition of both actual histories and, given the interpenetration of Renaissance disciplines, mimetic and imaginative histories in literary works. Major primary texts are directly confronted and read, edition by edition when necessary, with a range of lesser texts cited in passing to provide perspective. Addressed in all instances are the pressing issues of how history might be understood and interpreted, and how history, if not

4

random or discontinuous, might possibly be seen to manifest some underlying pattern or form.

Opening chapters set out illustrations of the clash and intermingling of biblical and naturalist outlooks.

The discordant perspectives of Walter Ralegh, who imaginatively encompassed apparently paradoxical medieval iconographic and Renaissance attitudes, are first explicated. The pilgrimage writings of Ralegh, his eloquent *History of the World*, and his bizarre account of the search for mythic El Dorado, are discussed with reference to medieval historicist publications as well as Alexander Ross's *The Marrow of History*, a unique early "pocket book" condensation of Ralegh's history.

As background to Renaissance cultural dissociations, visual and written depictions of the earlier, ordered, medieval iconographic Book of the World are next investigated with attention to ancient pilgrimage routes and "stations," and to the curious global icons functioning as maps. The difficulties caused by the later survival of world book outlooks are then traced in the wit of poets and the confusions of historians.

As early as the fifteenth century, Christopher Columbus juxtaposed pilgrimage and biblical lore with then recent geographic findings, and so like almost all cosmographers of his era, misplaced Asia. He insisted until his death that in sailing to distant shores he had reached the "end of the East"; and in his Prophetic Books Columbus suggestively presented himself as a fulfilled type of a prophetic leader, a militant pilgrim commander ready to direct an armed force which would liberate Jerusalem, thus introducing an anticipated earthly Millennium.

Middle chapters confront problems in sixteenth and seventeenth-century theory, methodology, and visionary representation, often through edition-by-edition allusions to developing works.

Examined are Richard Hakluyt's conflicted use of pilgrimage as well as contemporaneous English voyage sources in his seminal *Principal Navigations*; Francis Bacon's rejection of pilgrimage materials in the *Novum Organum* in favor of plans for a new

5

"mixed" history resting on outlined but unrealized empirical theories; and Abraham Ortelius's presentations of splendid Modernist maps, complete with critical commentary on the old and new historicism, in *Theatrum Orbis Terrarum*, so named to celebrate an emerging, dramatic "Theatre" rather than a receding Book of the World.

Neglected historicist methodology is then retrieved from the editions of historical "Architect" Samuel Purchas's voluminous assembly of ancient and recent travel writings, *Purchas his pilgrimage*; and from two works by John Milton produced under the influence of Purchas's historicist method; that is, Milton's empirical *A Brief History of Moscovia* and the poet's biblical epic *Paradise Lost* with its rich empirical allusions.

In his early editions Purchas had struggled to find ways to overcome bias and intellectually to "grasp" the metamorphosed and, he believed, undeniably existent external world. But in 1619 Purchas, like a radical modern relativist, grew skeptical of all historical theories and narratives. He confessed to an extravagant metaphysical-historical cynicism comparable, it will be shown, to that captured in the verse conceits of John Donne's *The Progresse of the Soule* of 1601. Yet by 1625 Purchas had recovered his historicist convictions and was again developing the empirical method that Milton, Purchas's one-time Bread St. neighbor in London, sought to emulate and improve.

By taking notice of writers as different as Purchas and Milton in their seemingly incongruous but deserved roles as new historicists, insight is gained into how Milton, leaning primarily upon the Bible but also upon the "building blocks" of Purchas's method and the outlooks of Bacon, Ortelius, Galileo and others, eventually produced a theatrical epic of universal history ending with an earthly Millennium and eternal bliss. Combined prophetic biblical and empirical historicist elements will be found ingeniously structured by Milton in his deployment of counterbalanced cosmic voyages of discovery through a vast "Theatre" of the new universe as well as the world.

A final chapter affords an overview of largely secular historicist constructions from the eighteenth century to the present, ranging from the rationalist and dogmatic to the cyclical and progressive that reflect certain formalist elements in Renaissance works. Special light is cast upon dialectical or "period" histories with different kinds of supposedly inevitable, utopian, earthly "ends": those of philosophical idealist Georg Friedrich Hegel; dialectical materialists Karl Marx (of the later period) and Friedrich Engels; evolutionary socialist Roger Owen; and political and economic "globalist" Francis Fukuyama. In discussing the generic nature of cultural and world histories, I have cited in passing publications as varied as Auguste Comte's *Cours de philosophie positive*, Oswald Spengler's *The Decline of the West*, Philip Toynbee's religiously-orientated *A Study of History*, and Felipe Fernández-Armesto's environmental, world cultural history *Civilizations*. The origin of comparative, cultural, global historiography in its early empirical phase, it will become apparent, has been pressed back from the eighteenth to the seventeenth century. For Renaissance authors in their published attempts at encompassing empirical coverage prefigure writings by eighteenth-century French encyclopediests and theorists: namely, Jacques Bossuet's *Discours sur l'histoire universelle* (1679), Voltaire's *Philosophie de l'histoire* (1765), and Denis Diderot's famed editions of the *Encyclopédie* (1772-78), the last finally produced in twenty-four volumes with eleven additional volumes of plates. The text of the *Encyclopédie*, however, is only somewhat longer than that of Samuel Purchas's earlier four-folio world history of 1625, a work recently republished in twenty volumes.

Under the influence of recent critical currents appearing amid the waves of historicist theory, contemporary attempts to adjust old historical experience to present outlooks have been so concerted that past perspectives, often reviewed in isolated excerpts, are sometimes unnecessarily blurred or distorted. Yet the problems of the past when directly engaged often mirror and provide insight into those of the present. I have accordingly sought to uncover a complex, often-misunderstood mélange of beliefs, attitudes, source materials and issues, in themselves fascinating and frequently surprising, that shattered iconographic pilgrimage outlooks and eventually converged in the multiple forms of contemporary cultural historicism. These are the components of that remarkable, early "mixed" historiography that in its scope and attempted empirical embrace of the earth's regions and peoples, according to Francis Bacon in *The Advancement of Learning*, at last proved the Moderns superior to the Ancients.

1

WALTER RALEGH'S HISTORICIST INHERITANCE

God's Providential World and Marvelous El Dorado

Sometime before his execution for sedition against King James I, Walter Ralegh penned a deeply-felt allegorical verse comparing death and the afterlife to the centuries-old experience of pilgrimage to a holy shrine. This intensely personal meditation upon mortality, first published anonymously in 1604, was reprinted in 1681 under Ralegh's name as *The Pilgrimage* with a subtitle dramatically placing the supposed time of composition "the Day before" the poet-courtier's death.[1] Although written earlier probably during Ralegh's long imprisonment, this caustic poem, capturing the reflections of a courtier contemplating his end, rings with the spiritual passions, images, and themes of the ancient pilgrimage tradition. The narrator in the persona of a pilgrim takes up the traditional scallop-shell and other allegorical pilgrimage devices in preparation for a holy journey to the tomb of the Apostle St. James in Compostella.

> Give me my Scallop-Shell of Quiet,
> My Staff of Faith to lean upon;
> My Scrip of Joy, Immortal Diet,
> My Bottle of Salvation;
> My Gown of Glory, Hopes True Gage:
> And thus I'll go my Pilgrimage

This physical and spiritual journey, an apparent reflection of the political and legal dangers faced by the author in later life, first leads not to a sacred shrine but to an allegorical hall of judgment, a type of a venal royal court on earth that has its anti-type in a divine court in "Heav'ns Bribeless Hall." In oblique allusions bitterly denouncing the hypocrisy and depravity of the worldly tribunal, the pilgrim extols the ideal court in Heaven,

> Where no *Corrupted Voices bawl*;
>> No *Conscience* molded into *Gold*;
> No *Forg'd Accuser* Bought nor Sold;
>> No *Cause* Deferr'd, no vain-spent Journey:
> For CHRIST Himself's the Kings Attorney,
>> Who Pleads for All, without Degrees;

A flash of macabre wit marks the pilgrim's supplication:

> And this shall be my Eternal Plea,
>> To Him that made Heav'n, Earth, and Sea,
> That since my Flesh must Die so soon,
>> And want a Head to Dine next Noon;
> Even at the Stroke when my Veins spread,
>> *Set on my Soul an Everlasting Head.*

As the moment of mortal death approaches following judgment, the pilgrim climactically shifts the terminus of his mundane journey from the tomb of St. James in Compostella in Spain to the tomb of the Son in the Holy City of Jerusalem, the last a type for the Eternal City of Heaven.

> Then am I Ready, like a Palmer fit,
>> To Tread those Paths that I before have Writ

Suddenly invoking the famed long pilgrimage beyond the sea, the narrator proclaims himself spiritually "fit" to approach the most sacred of pilgrimage shrines on earth. The regenerated pilgrim—having by tradition converted his soul from sin to grace on the Sinai Exodus pathway, and then having entered the Holy Land by crossing the River Jordan—has "taken the palm" near Jericho, thus becoming a Palmer, and is at last spiritually ready for entrance into Jerusalem. This is the medieval spiritual journey, central to the personal and historical concerns of Ralegh, of which he also wrote in his monumental and very popular *The History of the World*,[2] a book first published in 1614 and then in nine subsequent printings in the seventeenth century. The work's continuing popularity stirred Alexander Ross in 1662 to publish *The Marrow of Historie*, a pocket-size "epitome" or condensation of Ralegh's volume apparently aimed at an audience of students and guildsmen.[3]

In the last twenty-three years of his life, Ralegh had careened chaotically back and forth between passionate secular and spiritual interests stirred by the confusions of the old and new cosmographic historicism. From 1595 when he voyaged to Guiana in modern-day Brazil impelled by stories of an earthly city of gold, he had engaged in speculations on a tangle of medieval and empirical geographical problems involving biblical texts, classical cosmology, New World geography, and Spanish romance mythology.

His cosmographical views led him to the 1596 publication of his essentially secular *The Discoverie of the large, rich, and bewtiful Empire of Guianna, with a relation of the great and Golden Citie of Manoa (which the Spanyards call El Dorado)*. Yet in dedicating the work to Charles Howard, he again displays his emotionally charged sense of mortality, noting that his sufferings from "labor, hunger, heat, sicknesse, & peril" gave to his journey "the construction of a painful pilgrimage."[4] When some years later in 1614 he published his very different *The History of the World* with its pronounced religious themes, he introduced learned statements on the literal positioning of biblical and ancient sites associated with historical events, all the while engaging the conflicting cosmological opinions of, to mention only a few, Plato, Macrobius, St. Augustine, Thomas Aquinas, Strabo, Justin Martyr, Ambrose, Avicenna, and Tertullian.

In what today appears a strange worldview, Ralegh in these late publications presented contrasting, imaginatively-elaborated descriptions of two wondrous cities and regions that had become the locus of his final hopes and dreams. In his *The Discoverie*, he spun out tales of tropical Guiana and its supposed gleaming city El Dorado, the so-called "gilded man," in a New World of untold earthly wealth. In *The History of the World*, with its strong pilgrimage and religious overtones, he wrote of the sacred East and the Holy Land in the Old World, with Jerusalem and an imagined Eden at the core, as a region of great fecundity and spiritual virtue.

Ralegh's *Discoverie* and *History* are remarkable exemplars of transitional, Renaissance historicist interpretations and structural designs of a kind variously evident in lesser historicist works by Peter Heylyn, Thomas Lanquet, Alexander Ross, and others. Meaning devolves in these works, not only from forthright religious and secular declarations, and from the suggestiveness of facts, legends, and symbolic components, but also significantly from containing historicist forms. The special structuring of these historicist compositions shows a movement from medieval biblical time-frames and ordered iconography toward Renaissance naturalist and empiricist paradigms.

Driven by a desire for preferment as well as fortune, and by genuine cosmographical fascination, Ralegh in the *Discoverie* sublimated his spiritual concerns to the romantic exaggeration of Guiana's natural beauty and material wealth. The narrative of his 1595 exploration of the Orinoco River area, and of the nearby coastal region and inhabited islands, contains much valuable factual information; but his book is most notable as a modest generic literary contribution to romance travel tales of distant world marvels.

Ralegh stresses throughout the *Discoverie* that he is looking for gold. He was obviously in competition with the Spanish who had plundered the New World treasures of Mexico and were seeking further native wealth in Guiana. Ralegh had preyed upon gold-laden Spanish ships in the Caribbean. In now writing of what he has recently heard from "such of the *Spanyardes* as haue seene *Manoa* the emperiall Citie of *Guianna*," he claims that this golden city "which the Spanyardes cal el Dorado" is located on a lake near an upper Orinoco River tributary; and that "for riches, and for the excellent seate, it farre exceedeth any of the world" (10). Ralegh may well have been influenced by Renaissance notions that the heat in regions near the equator produced chemical-alchemical reactions transmuting baser elements into silver and gold. But unable during his journey to find a golden city, a nearby gold mine, or even suitable samples of gold, Ralegh is reduced to insisting that in Guiana "all the rocks, mountaines, all stones in the plaines, in woodes, and by the riuers sides are in effect thorow shining, and appeare marueylous rich" (17).

The Guiana interior with its huge rivers and dense, tropical forests had long been a subject of myth. Tales had been circulated by the Spanish, after their long marches inland, about the headwaters of the Orinoco River rising from an ideal realm uplifted high above the surrounding jungle. In the fifteenth century Christopher Columbus had named this elevated region, a supposed source of the earth's greatest rivers, as the site of the Garden of Eden. In the sixteenth century the Spanish explorer Francisco de Orellana claimed that he had fought light-skinned female "Amazon" warriors, traditional mythic guardians of Eden, inland on the River Mara, later called the Amazon possibly after the Indian word amasona meaning "boat destroyer." According to other local stories having obvious origins in ancient legend and medieval pilgrimage accounts, the region was also said to be protected by a fierce, humanoid race of monstrous people.

Commentators regularly stress Ralegh's assertion in the *Discoverie* that he heard about but did not see Amazons or monstrous people, thus implying a degree of incredulity; but the courtier spurred by the pilgrimage tradition constantly affirms his personal belief in these accounts being "resolued that so many people did not all combine, or forthinke to make the report" (70).

The Amazons, Ralegh states in presenting his understanding of "the trueth of those warlike women," regularly attack intruders who invade their territory. If they take any male prisoners, he asserts, they first sleep with them but "in the end for certaine they put them to death: for they are said to be very cruell and bloodthirsty." Ralegh gives verisimilitude to such "truths" by professing just a touch of skepticism: "that they cut of the right dug of the brest I do not find to be true" (pp. 23-24). He eventually returns to a materialist theme, noting that the Amazons have "great store of plates of golde" (24).

Later in the *Discoverie* Ralegh foregoes even a modicum of skepticism, avowing that on an inland branch of the Coara river "are a nation of people, whose heades appeare not aboue their shoulders, which though it may be thought a meere fable, yet for mine owne part I am resolued it is true, because euery child in the prouinces of *Arromaia* and *Canuri* affirme the same: they are called the *Ewaipanoma*." Ralegh states that he learned from an older native that the Ewaipanoma warriors "are the most mightie men of all the lande, and use bowes, arrowes, and clubs thrice as bigge as any of Guiana." Explaining that an "honest" Spaniard actually had seen the Ewaipanoma, Ralegh, citing the medieval pilgrimage *Book of Sir John Maundeville* (ca. 1322-56) which contains tales about Amazons and monstrous races, observes that "Such a nation was written of by *Maundeuile*, whose reportes was holden for fables for many yeres, and yet since the East Indies were discouered, wee finde his relations true of such things as heretofore were held incredible" (69-70).

For Ralegh living a century after Columbus, the dream of a New World earthly paradise somewhere near the source of the Orinoco River had transformed into the dream of a New World gold mine and city near the source of the same river in a realm inhabited by extraordinary races. With El Dorado as discussed in *The Discoverie* presumed to be in Guiana in an equinoctial climatic zone, Ralegh in Chapter 3 of *The History* argues that Eden, which he believed to be only partially destroyed by the Flood and still identifiable, was positioned in the same zone but in a different part of the world (Sec. V, 86).

Ralegh pursues this subject at length because the literal location of Eden, and the literal location of events occurring to the First Parents' descendants in the first generations after the Fall, are crucial to the content and narrative organizational structure of his opening book. "It is necessary to discover the true place of Paradise," Ralegh insists, for "by knowing this place, we shall the better judge of the beginning of nations, and of the world's inhabitation; for near unto this did the sons of Noah also disperse themselves after the flood, into all other remote regions and countries..." (Sec. IV, 85). He concludes with modernist navigational specificity that the earthly paradise is seated in the lower part of the region of Eden, afterwards called Aram fluviorum, or Mesopotamia, which "taketh into it also a portion of Shinar and Armenia; this region standing 35 degrees from the equinoctial, and 55 from the north-pole"; in which climate "the most excellent wines, fruits, oil, grain of all sorts, are to this day found in abundance" (Sec. XV, 138).

The old and new cosmography here becomes entangled. Pilgrim tracts through the centuries had traditionally placed Eden at the point of the morning sunrise at the end of the East, the orientation point of what was generally considered a globular earth. In the fourteenth century the author calling himself John Maundeville, reporting on what he had "heard say of wise men," stated that Eden is in the East "at the beginning of the earth," and that it is on the summit of a mountain "so high that it nearly touches the circle of the moon." Maundeville adds that "when the sun is east in those parts towards Terrestrial Paradise, it is then midnight in our parts of this half, on account of the roundness of the earth." Maundeville humbly adds, "I repent not going there, but I was not worthy."[5]

Also in the fourteenth century, Dante Alighieri in the *Commedia* precisely positions Eden by reference to Jerusalem, imaginatively elaborating his account under the influence of biblical passages, medieval circular maps, and medieval encyclopedias such as Brunetto Latini's *Tresor*. Dante places the providence, as the fulfilled type of Jerusalem, on the summit of the globular earth's highest mountain at the antipodes or navel of the southern hemisphere. The foreshadowing type of Eden, the Holy City of Jerusalem, is then located in the opposite side of the globe at the exact center or navel of the northern hemisphere. Dante repeatedly calls attention to the twelve-hour time difference between these two holy places.[6]

In fifteen long sections of Book I of *The History of the World*, Ralegh discounts sites for Eden such as the whole world, or a mountain nearly as high as or higher than the sphere of the moon. He holds to the belief that, just as the remains of Eden are situated at ground level in the salutary equinoctial zone of the old world, so El Dorado is located in a counterpoised, beneficent equinoctial position in the new world. Ralegh's coordinates for Eden move the earthly paradise from its former location at the Ultimate East—that is at the apex of circular medieval maps oriented to the East—over and down to the off-center site in Mesopotamia, the place it occupies on the *History's* frontispiece map, which in seemingly tipsy fashion is oriented to the north. However, Ralegh, using the traditional language applied to medieval iconographic maps, confuses matters by stating that Eden is situated, not in the off-center location, but "in the navel of this our world, and, as Melanchthon says, *in parte terrae meliore*, in the best part thereof, that from thence, as from a centre, the universal might be filled with people and planted" (Sec. IV, 85).

Here the medieval "spiritual geography" of interpreted biblical iconography obscures the new literal positioning of Eden, just as that spiritual geography similarly obscures the literal positioning of the events, peoples and nations of the world devolving from the Sons of Noah after the Flood.

Ralegh largely penned the second and most memorable of his major late works, *The History of the World*, while in the Tower under a temporarily suspended sentence of death. In earlier years "before any wound" had been "received, either from Fortune or Time," as Ralegh states in the preface, he had planned a three-volume history; but he writes of later experiencing a somber premonition of "the darknesse of Age and Death" which "covered over both It and Mee, long before the performance" [Pref., sig. A1]. He was then consumed by thoughts about human mortality and about the mystery of God's relation to humanity as recounted in scriptures.

In this most eloquent of Early Modern revisionist universal histories, Ralegh interpreted the flow of human events in a double-focus, seemingly confused way that has left generations of critics debating whether he was an Ancient or a Modern. He displays in *The History* a deep traditional faith, actively drawing upon the biblical and pilgrimage traditions to assert the ways of a mysterious divine providence that, although frequently inscrutable to humankind, is presumed to give a higher purpose to the wildly discursive events of history.

For Ralegh a divinity shapes human history; there is an implicit belief in a divine reason for all that occurs, although the direction of this reason is sometimes unfathomable. Ralegh's narrative, however, continues to intertwine the new cosmography with the old. As an historian of empirical disposition, Ralegh earnestly endeavors to lay bare—through original critical analysis of scriptural, secular and classical sources—the human causes of events.

Ralegh's profound belief in the providence of God provided him with a transcendent medieval theological-thematic perspective from which to view what he regarded as "true," historical, secular and biblical events in this changing earthly world. Combining the moralism of medieval political-religious tracts, such as John of Salisbury's *Polycraticus*, with the empirical analysis of a Modern, Ralegh regularly assumes the voice of an Ancient in frequently pausing to reflect on the morality of individual monarchs and nations in the light of the span of history. Like an early religious writer seeking *exempla* of good and evil, Ralegh openly acknowledges his aim of imparting "How Kings and Kingdomes have flourished and fallen, and for what vertue and piety God made prosperous; and for what vice and deformity he made wretched, both the one and the other." It is this passionate moral vision of history—history seen in effect from on high in varied moral colorings and great perspectives—that gives such sweep and power to many of Ralegh's prose passages even as it distances this author from the flat, descriptive writing of many contemporaneous revisionist historians.

> wee may gather out of History a policy no lesse wise than eternall; by the comparison and application of other mens fore-passed miseries with our owne like errours & ill deservings. But it is neither of Examples the most lively instruction, nor the words of the wisest men, nor the terrour of future torments, that hath yet so wrought in our blind and stupified mindes, as to make us remember, That the infinite eye and wisdome of God doth pierce through all our pretences; as to make us remember, That the justice of God doth require none other accuser, than our owne consciences: which neither the false beauty of our apparent actions, nor all the formality which (to pacifie the opinions of men) we put on; can in any, or the least kind, cover from his knowledge. (2)

In a visual interpretation of this approach to history, the frontispiece engraving to the work—one created by Renold Elstracke after a design by Ralegh—shows at the top-center the all-seeing eye of providence directly over a flat, gnomic map delineating more than one half of a spherical earth. Figures of Good and Evil Fame blowing trumpets stand respectively on either side of the map. In the lower half of the frontispiece, allegorical figures personifying Experience and Truth flank History, who holds the map over her head while standing upon recumbent figures of Death and Oblivion.[7]

The circular map itself is marked with lines delineating many of the coasts and seas discovered or reconfigured by the new cosmography: outlines of parts of the Arctic and Antarctic, parts of North and all of South America; all of Europe, the Near East; and Africa; and parts of India. Most unusual is a small drawing in the upper center, on a theme of deep personal interest to Ralegh as a raider of Spanish shipping, showing wooden boats in a sea fight in the North Atlantic. The drawing of the sea battle is inserted just below the place where the earthly paradise traditionally appeared on medieval maps. In the only other drawing on the frontispiece map, the earthly paradise, with Adam and Eve depicted at the moment of the Fall, is shown pushed over to an upper-right, off-center position in a blank area that would be ancient Babylonia, that is, a locale comprising parts of modern Iraq and Iran.

Ralegh's frontispiece leads readers to expect a work merging historical content, Renaissance world geographic knowledge, and commentary on divine omniscience. The preface as noted confirms the author had such a plan generally in mind. Yet in Ralegh's single completed volume, the new cosmographical configurations of the world are largely blurred because of the author's stress on religious and moral themes. Ralegh in his quest for the meaning of biblical texts, together with his interest in classical civilization, throws the locus of his history, except for the Preface stressing the English monarchy, back to the southern Mediterranean where spiritual events are found to have the weightiest historical values. The traditional biblical and pilgrimage themes concerned with Eden, Jerusalem, and the Holy Land tend to take precedence over the cosmography of the Moderns.

In structuring his providential work Ralegh as a sixteenth-century author faced the daunting challenge of both retaining and yet moving beyond medieval epochal time-frames. These medieval historicist frames cast light upon Ralegh's own practices, for even in the Middle Ages organizing and writing a universal history of humankind had been a struggle in literary resolve and ingenuity. Authors picked out epochs for coverage from among those seemingly appearing in the Bible as interpreted in the tracts by Church Fathers. Most renowned were the six ages of man that followed the Creation as outlined in St. Augustine's *City of God*: namely, the epochs from Adam to Noah, Noah to Abraham, Abraham to David, David to the Babylonian Captivity, the Captivity to the birth of Christ, the birth of Christ to the Last Judgment and the eternal Sabbath. Selected epochs were "filled in" with episodes, drawn from both biblical and secular sources, according to the energy and knowledge of the author. But the will of some flagging writers on occasion failed far short of even the Incarnation, and only the authors of "epitomies" appeared able to reach the Last Judgment.[8]

In the Renaissance epochal histories that started as individual works frequently ended as joint ventures when, after the death of the original author, other writers took over to move the coverage forward. Thomas Lanquet in *An Epitome of Chronicles*, for example, began with the Creation but died before he could cover all the epochs up to and including the Incarnation. Upon Lanquet's death it was left to Bishop Thomas Cooper to expand the work following the epochal design and to publish the *Epitome* in 1549. Then Robert Crowley in a later edition of 1559 added a largely chronicle account of events related finally to the reign of Elizabeth I.[9]

The most ambitious joint project was the attempted "vniuersall Cosmographie of the whole world" organized by the Queen's printer Reginald Wolfe and involving several writers, each with an assigned subject. Abandoned after Wolfe's death, only one part of the project was completed: that written by Raphael Holinshed who produced the famed *The Chronicles of England, Scotland, and Ireland* (1577) which is well known as a primary source for Shakespeare's histories.[10]

Ralegh's massive, single-volume, unfinished *History* separated into five parts or "books," together covering the history of humanity from the Creation up to the time of the Roman empire's conquest of Macedon in 168 B.C., is a primary exemplar in historiography of the curious cultural mingling of the Ancient and the Modern. In his opening two books of epochal Hebrew history, the author is unabashedly indebted to medieval typal biblical and pilgrimage patterns. Ralegh skips from one epochal event to the next, avoiding linking narratives, concentrating in book 1, on the Creation, the First Parents in Paradise, the Fall, the Sons of Noah, Nimrod, Zoroaster, and Ninus; and in book 2, on episodes from the birth of Abraham to the destruction of Solomon's Temple. Even in these books Ralegh can to some degree be called a Modern because along with conveying traditional religious values he advances rational, literalist cause-and-effect explanations for what occurs.

In these first two books Ralegh the Ancient ultimately focuses upon Jerusalem, the cynosure of his spiritual concerns. The wanderings of Abraham and the twelve tribes are seen to culminate in the establishment of the Jerusalem Temple and the Kingdom of David. Actual medieval pilgrimage sites, so-called "stations," leading to the Holy City are discussed in book 2. In describing the journeys of Abraham and of the Twelve Tribes, Ralegh mentions by name and number many among the forty-two "stations" of the Exodus on the Sinai pilgrimage route over which actual pilgrims had traveled beginning in the fourth century on their way to Jerusalem. Of the five maps appearing as illustrations in the 1614 and 1634 edition, the third shows all forty-two Exodus pilgrimage stations, with a double line wavering from Egypt across the Sinai and then on to its termination in the Holy Land (insert between pages 218 and 219). Ralegh in his account of the biblical Exodus calls special attention in the 1634 edition to the "third Station" at Etham (222); the "sixth Mansion" of "*Elim*," the "seventh Mansion" on the "banks of the *Red Sea*," and the "Twentieth mansion" of "Sapher or Sipher," and then the "thirtieth Mansion" of "Ietaba" (300).

Yet even at the beginning of his work, Ralegh unexpectedly intrudes secular elements by juxtaposing many literal facts from British political history with epochal scriptural materials. A rhetorical preface contains a brief, highly critical, narrative of the kings of England. Past British monarchs are roundly censured for deceitful politics and fratricidal warfare, with only Ralegh's occasional patron James Ist conveniently emerging as a figure of harmony and virtue.[11] In following book 1, Ralegh then departs from secular themes in accentuating what can be called "scriptural politics." He discusses the divisive sons of Noah, the "planting" of different nations by the sons, and the "beginning of Government." Next, a very low point in human political and spiritual history is reached when the giant Nimrod separates and corrupts nations, but longed-for regeneration at last takes place stimulated by the virtuous magic of Zoroaster and the epic building activities of Ninus.

Amid this montage of British monarchical history and biblical stories, a shift toward a factual approach is most pronounced beginning with book 3 when Ralegh writes dominantly of Greek and Roman events using authoritative classical sources. He now employs sequential secular narratives of considerable length. Book 3 covers the period from the destruction of the Jerusalem Temple to the exploits of Philip of Macedon; book 4, from the Reign of Philip of Macedon to the "establishing of that Kingdome, in the Race of Antigonus"; and Book 5, from Alexander to the Roman conquest of Asia and Macedonia. The writing using established secular materials, is generally lucid and detailed, although freighted with moral judgments and quoted biblical injunctions. This first and only completed volume of the history ends, in the manner of many medieval scriptural commentaries, with a "Chronology" of dates from the Creation through the various biblical and classical epochs up to 168 B. C. (777).

By the early 1600s with writings on new lands and peoples circulating, innovative Renaissance "theorists" speculated upon and worked toward the production of a new kind of global historiography. Giovanni Botero, for example, in his very popular *Relations of the most famovs kingdomes and Common-wealths thorowout the world: Didscoursing of their Situation, Religions, Languages, Manners, Customes, Strengths, Greatnesse and*

Policies (1630), published a comprehensive world description emphasizing "situation"—that is the supposed influence of climate on the character of peoples in different regions—with an analysis of the nature of resulting political systems.[12] This novel work, which is a distant precursor of contemporary writings on the impact of "environment" on cultures, peremptorily imposed definite and limiting character traits on the peoples respectively of Europe, Asia, Africa, and the New World.

Peter Heylyn, impressed by the "diuersity" of the world's nations and cultures, ruminated in his *Microcosmvs, or A Little Description of the Great world* (1621) on how different peoples might hold different epochal points of view as the result of religion, culture, and geographical location.[13] Heylyn's small pocket-size book in one volume, however limited its source materials and assessments, exemplifies how by the 1620s historiography had moved beyond Ralegh in the theoretical direction of comparative cultural analysis. Defining "an Era or Epoche" as "the terminus a quo, from which euery reckoning of times taketh its beginning," Heylyn recognizes that, in looking beyond Christianity, the epochs of "diuerse nations" have been "diuersly different":

> The Christians make their Epoche the birth of Christ. The Mohammedans beginne their Hegira from the returne of their Prophet to Mecha. The Greekes use to reckon by Olympiads. The Romans from the building of the Citty, afterward from the raigne of Augustus. (18)

He claims, however, that the "Jewes" divide universal history into eight biblical "Epoches" dating

> 1. from the Creation. 2. from the Deluge. 3. from the confusion of tongues. 4. from Abraham's iourney out of Chaldea into Canaan. 5. from the departure out of Egypt. 6. from the yeares of Iubile. 7. from the

building of the Temple.   8. from the captiuity of Babylon. (18)

Heylyn then brashly announces the reduction of Christian epochs in his work to just two: "Reiecting the rest wee will in our historicall computation of time use only...Epoches of the world's creation, & Christ's appearance in the flesh." His study is in fact leveraged on the single epochal event of "Christ's appearance in the flesh," with all of history then neatly divided employing a "before-and-after" pattern. In adopting this simplified biblical form, Heylyn then rested his commentary on a region-by-region consideration of different societies. His work begins with Europe, then focuses in turn on the Near East, the British Isles, Africa, and the Orient, and ends with brief remarks on America and Mexico. Throughout, Heylyn displays some medieval leanings and a generally Eurocentric and British outlook, but his comparative analyses, global factual materials, and attempts to be fair tend to transcend his own British predilections. He has "entermingled," in his own words, "Geography and History (which are my chiefe scope)" together with other "diuerse studies" (18).

Heylyn remains of some note, not only for his cultural speculations, but also for his aggressive championing of historiography as a special "craft" demanding moral integrity, critical independence, and a concern above all for "truth." A genuine historian, Heylyn writes, should have

> a generous and resolute spirit, 2. An vpright and sincere
> conuerfation [conuersation], that so hee may neither be
> daunted by a tyrannicall Prince, nor transported with
> partiality, that he might dare to deliuer all the truth
> without feare, and yet not dare to relate any thing which
> is false through fauour." (19)

While Heylyn definitely strikes sparks of intellectual thoughtfulness and independence, he is still far from revolutionary.

With Heylyn one encounters an intelligent compiler and cultural commentator who ponders what it means to be a historian, but who drastically overstates his case in claiming to have invented an entirely new methodology. "The matter I deriue from others," he observes; "the wordes for the most part are mine owne, the method totallie" (no pagination). Still, in exhibiting a need to be totally original, Heylyn, the revisionary biblical typologist and moralist, takes a step into the individualistic modern world. Historiography was to be flooded in later centuries by very different non-religious but equally simplified "before-and-after" historicist productions, many of them unduly or "totalie" colored by an exclusionary overemphasis on the cultural influence of some single person or event.

Walter Ralegh, in the last three books of his *The History of the World* on mainly classical events, had to some degree turned away from the pilgrimage and biblical tradition, and had moved, if slightly, in the direction of the new, attempted empirical analysis of secular sources.

The popular epitome of Ralegh's work produced by Alexander Ross under the title *The Marrow of Historie: Or, an Epitome Of all Historical Passages from the Creation, to the end of the last Macedonian War* (1662) was in organization and content something of a throwback to medieval typological form. Ross introduced epochal events and divisions in all periods in stronger outline than in Ralegh's original work, while unfortunately deleting many of Ralegh's eloquent passages on providence, mortality, and the human condition.

"To Epitomise," Ross insists defensively, "is not an easie Work, nor needless, as some suppose" [verso A3]; and in an address to the Reader, he first advances strained "metaphysical" arguments in support of his project:

God was the first that taught us to Epitomy; for he abridged the Macrocosm into the Microcosm of Man's body: and Nature imitate's him daily; for the Eye doth

Epitomize the largest visible objects in the narrow
compass of the Chrystalline humour. So Art imitates
Nature. (verso A 3)

But Ross soon turns to core practical explanations of why his
little publication, measuring 2 1/2 by 5 inches, has a supposed
"three-fold advantage" over Ralegh's one-volume "great Book":

it is more portable, more legible, and more vendible,
then the great Book: this may bee a Pocket companion,
and it is soon read over; for every one will not take
pains to read great Volumes, and many cannot, for want
of leisure. There are also divers that have three or four
shillings to bestow on this, which have not twenty or
thirty to expend upon the great Book. (A 3)

Ross's "Epitome" retains interest primarily as an early
forerunner along with Peter Heylyn's work of what will be seen as
a virtual "genre" in seventeenth-century educational publication:
the relatively inexpensive, reductionist, pocketbook-size note or
study guide for an ever-growing number of hurried readers. Ross's
book, one of many epitomies he published in the seventeenth
century, has about it a very contemporary commercial flavor
implying a growing audience of new "consumers" probably
consisting largely of Latin school students, guildsmen and their
families.

Although Ross in his address to the Reader takes on a seeming
posture of humility toward Ralegh, his conventional metaphors of
praise for his mentor lack both grace and conviction. "He was a
Giant in knowledge," Ross writes, "and saw far, yet a Pigmie set on
his shoulders may see a little further." (4A)

Ralegh did not live to receive this dubious acclaim. In 1617
while incarcerated under a suspended sentence of death, he
convinced King James of the fanciful notion that, if released, he
would find his way to the fabled El Dorado gold mine on the upper

Orinoco River and return with great wealth. Ralegh also implausibly promised that, in carrying out his plan, he would avoid any disturbance of New World Spanish settlers, including those at Fort S. Thome on his direct route up the Orinoco. Released from prison, Ralegh broke off his writing of *The History of the World* with its spiritual themes, to follow unreliable rumors passed on by an unstable subordinate, Laurence Keymis, in a search for the longed-for source of the gold of El Dorado. In the jungles of Brazil Ralegh encountered hardships, disappointment, and Spanish who, in a brief engagement at Fort S. Thome at which he was not present, killed his son. Laurence Keymis, on reporting back to Ralegh, committed suicide. Ralegh, disconsolate, sailed back to England. His geographic illusions and resulting practical failures left him without realistic hope of receiving a final reprieve from execution.

Matthew Arnold considered Ralegh, not just as Ancient, but as "obsolete" because he accepted the Bible as an absolute authority and organized his early books in terms of biblical epochs.[14] On the other hand, Christopher Hill has argued that

> Ralegh's importance is that he employed a secular and critical approach to the study of world history which was in part a study of Biblical history; and that he did this in English, in a work which is a best-seller. So he contributed, perhaps more than has been recognized, to that segregation of the spiritual from the secular which was the achievement of the seventeenth century.[15]

Arnold and Hill are both too categorical. Ralegh's representation of history rested on a deep faith in the scriptures— reflected in *The History*'s structure and literally-interpreted scriptural content, and also in its commitment to providential design—merged and intermingled with a "secular and critical approach" as reflected in a stringent cause-and-effect rational analysis of events accepted variously on faith, on secular evidentiary grounds, and occasionally on mythic tradition. Far from

27

segregating the secular from the spiritual or of giving complete authority to one or the other, Ralegh like Richard Hakluyt, Alexander Ross, Thomas Fuller, Giovanni Botero, Samuel Purchas and so many other Renaissance writers, when confronted with troubling confusions in scriptural, empirical, and mythological fact and viewpoint, blurred or worked out relations, which appear to have functioned acceptably for them in experience but which today often seem contradictory and in need of separation. But such separation distorts both their own experience, as well as their cultural horizons. Ralegh's *The History of the World* owes much to classical historians, Church Fathers, classical and Renaissance literature, medieval and modernist cartography, new empirical analysis, medieval pilgrimage tracts, the literature of world exploration, and the author's theological speculations; and as such, *The History* emerges as a remarkable literary as well as historical work with the sweep and encompassing universality of other great, structured literary compendiums of Renaissance sensibility and learning: Edmund Spenser's *The Faerie Queene* and John Milton's *Paradise Lost*.

Unlike the monastic recluses isolated in their alpine monastery in Mathew Arnold's poem, *Stanzas from the Grand Chartreuse*, Ralegh was not exactly "between two worlds," the "one dead" and the other "powerless to be born." He was a soldier, buccaneer, explorer, seaman, colonizer, courtier, and adventurer, who was very much in and of the world at a time when Ancient and Modern outlooks, in curious juxtapositions, both carried conviction and so were very much alive. His writings and actions reflect oddly conjoined outlooks. He engaged in erratic adventures and rapacious colonial schemes, and he forged in his extraordinary and highly influential *The History of the World* that curious early Renaissance association of religious experience and empirical knowledge showing deep sensitivity to the condition of humanity.

"HIGH AND RARE DELIGHT"

Spiritual Geographic History and the Dislocation of the East

A. Conflicted World Visions

In the dedication to the first edition of *The Principall Navigations, voyages and discoveries of the English Nation... within the compass of these 1500 years*, published in 1589, Richard Hakluyt, then in his late thirties, movingly tells how his life was changed by a single meeting with a relative.

> I do remember that being...one of her Maiesties scholars at Westminster that fruitfull nurserie, it was my happe to visit the chamber of M. Richard Hakluyt my cosin, a Gentlemen of the Middle Temple, at a time when I found lying open upon his boord certeine bookes of Cosmographie, with an universall Mappe.[1]

Hakluyt explains that these items at first seemed of only casual interest. Yet his cousin, seeing him "somewhat curious," began to "instruct" him, pointing to the map with a "wand" to show "the diuision of the earth into three parts after the olde account."

What Hakluyt saw would have been some version of a traditional circular or elliptical tripartite world as it had then been rendered on so-called T-O maps for over eight-hundred years. Asia with its icons of monstrous races and mythical beasts traditionally occupied the top or Eastern half of the circle or ellipse; Africa showing the River Nile and mysterious creatures such as the Phoenix bird, the lower northwestern quarter; and Europe with its familiar cities and ports, the lower southwestern quarter. On such maps Jerusalem appeared at the very center, as has been noted, just above the intersecting bars of the T-shaped Mare Interum or Mediterranean Sea. The vertical bar of the T bisected the lower half of the earth's circular or elliptical land-mass, separating Africa from Europe and extending downward to the Pillars of Hercules, modern Gibraltar, at the outlet to the great Ocean Sea. This great, outer sea was regularly depicted as a wide, dark line surrounding the circumference of the 0-shaped earth.

Hakluyt tells how his cousin next turned to a new and different map showing a "better distribution" of the world "into more." The cousin is described pointing "with his wand to all the knowen Seas, Gulfs, Bayes, Straights, Capes, Riuers, Empires, Kingdomes, Dukedomes, and Territories of each part, with declaration also of their speciall commodities, & particular wants, which by the benefit of traffike, & entercourse of merchants, are plentifully supplied." Then the cousin, in Hakluyt's words,

> brought me to the Bible, and turning to the 107 Psalme, directed mee to the 23 & 24 verses: "they which go downe to the sea in ships, and occupy 'by the great waters, they see the works of the Lord' and his wonders in the deepe." (2)

So surprising was this instruction in discordant renderings of the earth that young Hakluyt experienced a sharp, intellectual illumination. Excitedly he explains how the "words of the Prophet together with" his cousin's "discourse" stirred strong emotions of "high and rare delight." The "doores" of a new "knowledge and kind of literature," he proclaims, "opened before me." The "impression" received, he insists, was "so deep" that it changed the course of his life:

> I resolued, if euer I were preferred to the University, where better time, and more convenient place might be

ministred for these studies, I would by Gods assistance
prosecute this knowledge and kind of literature. (2)

Like Abraham Ortelius, Samuel Purchas, John Milton, and
other prominent persons of his time, Hakluyt was strongly moved
by the Ancient Book of God's Words and the seemingly changing
Modernist Book of God's Works and Creatures, both of which
presumably pointed to "true" historical events. In Hakluyt's case the
confusions arising from the intermingling of old and new world
visions—the hierarchically ordered medieval world of iconographic
forms and earthly-heavenly spiritual correspondences, and the
unfolding expansive Renaissance naturalistic world of contorted
configuration and miscellaneous new peoples—impelled him to
assemble over his lifetime a strange assortment of medieval
pilgrimage texts and Renaissance "navigations, voyages, traffiques,
and discoveries," the collective oddity of which has been widely
overlooked.

Before examining Hakluyt's publications in the next chapter,
needed perspective can first be gained by briefly looking at the
origins of the "old" pilgrimage world iconography and considering
this iconography's disconcerting impact upon Renaissance
voyagers, historiographers, and writers—most notably upon the
prophetic pilgrimage millenarianism of Christopher Columbus.

"Geography is...The eye of History," Abraham Ortelius
announced in the preface to a seventeenth-century edition of his
famed historical-cosmographical work *Theatrum Orbis Terrarum*
(1606).[2] "The globe of the earth," Ortelius observed,

was not then further knowen, (a wonderfull strange
thing) untill in the daies of our fathers, in the yeare
1492, Christopher Columbus a Genoway, by the
commandement of the king of Castile, first discouered
that part of the West, which unto this day had lien hid &
vnknown.[3]

31

Yet in arguing for the importance of geography to all of world history, Ortelius later referred to a map unexpectedly showing the route, not of Columbus's voyages, but of the biblical Exodus:

> The reading of Histories doeth both seeme to be much more pleasant, and in deed so it is, when the Mappe being layed before our eyes, we may behold things done, or places where they were done, as if they were at this time present and in doing. For how much we are holpen, when as in the Holy Scripture, we read of the iourney of the Israelites, which they made from Egypt, through the Red Sea, and that same huge Wildernesse, into the Land of promise, when as looking upon the Mappe of Palestina, we doe almost as well see it as if we were there, I thinke any student in Diuinitie, or that History hath oft made triall. Which things being so, how much those which are students and louers of Histories.[4]

Ortelius speaks of Columbus's discovery of a new world in "the West." Columbus, until his death, insisted that he had reached, not the West, but the "end of the East," that is, the supposed Asiatic mainland that for this explorer included the site of Jerusalem. Columbus also claimed in a letter describing his third voyage that this "end of the East" was near the upraised earthly paradise.

Conflicted cosmographic traditions account for such imagined identifications, for early medieval maps of a kind sometimes consulted by Columbus, were in their overall form outgrowths of literal interpretations of biblical passages. The world's landmass was depicted in three parts because Genesis 9:19 implied a tripartite division of the earth's peoples: "The sons of Noah who went forth from the ark were Shem, Ham, and Japheth...These three were the sons of Noah; and from these the whole earth was peopled." Jerusalem was at the center because the Gospel of Matthew appeared to place the Holy City in the "midst" or middle of the earth. Passages from Exodus were thought to point to that "center," and so were illustrated on virtually all large maps from the eighth century forward with icons showing Egypt, the Red Sea, Mt. Sinai, the River Jordan, and Jerusalem. A line marking the Exodus pathway appears on the Hereford world map (ca. 1285) and was included, A. C. Cronin convincingly argues, to guide pilgrims to the Holy City. Forty-two pilgrimage "stations" of the Exodus were then marked on the pathway in maps and in illustrated bibles of the early fifteenth century and later.[5]

The eighth-century Greek commentator Cosmos Indicopleustes established a pattern for medieval maps and related tracts by placing Eden at the end of the East at the circumference of the earth's circular landmass, and Jerusalem in the middle of that landmass. The great Ocean Sea in Cosmos's representation covered the southern hemisphere and also equatorial regions supposedly too hot to be passable. Some commentators citing St. Augustine, however, claimed that both land and upside-down humanoid Antipodians existed somewhere on the underside of the earth. Over the centuries, medieval cosmographers such as the Spanish monk Beatus, who in the eighth century penned a commentary on Revelation, along with Sallust, Macrobius, Gervaise of Tilsbury, and Brunetto Latini "filled in" the globe's northern hemisphere with accounts of major cities and realms, holy places, strange beasts, monstrous races, and pilgrimage stations.[6]

So pervasive was the early belief that the holiest regions of the earth's northern hemisphere and its creatures were created by God in an essentially harmonious order, shadowing the heavenly, that for seven hundred years—from the eighth century until the rediscovery of Ptolomaic world maps in the fifteenth—the peoples of the West showed themselves often disinclined to draw even a familiar town street in realistic configuration, let alone the town itself, or the region, or the wider world. As the evidence of early philosophic conceptions and cartographic representations shows, the geographic world and its places, supposedly ordered by underlying spiritual essences, were generally conceived of and rendered in basically symmetrical iconographic hierarchical arrangement rather than in seemingly disordered "free form"

33

design. The earth was the imperfect shadow of a perfect heaven; and the earth's holiest cities beneath their veils of matter were earthly iconographic reflections of the heavenly city.

Under the hand of the local guildsman or the learned cartographer, the twisting earthly street was thus straightened and, very likely, depicted as an arm of a cross. A town might then be given the shape of a perfect circle or, if the guildsman wished to suggest some material imperfection, an ellipse. The representation of an especially long journey across Europe, such as that recorded in the thirteenth-century Itinerary of Matthew Paris, would be marked on a long, narrow parchment as a straight line, with distances recorded above the line and with cities indicated by drawings.[7]

It was left largely to sea captains and merchants to require, as a practical necessity, reasonably accurate charts, so-called "portaline" maps, with lines delineating the actual contours of shorelines and islands, and with "rum lines" designating prevailing, seasonal wind directions. On the majority of maps, however, geographic form was registered by circles, crosses, ellipses, and other iconographic markings intended to show the relative inner virtue of the immaterial essence of each site.

The world became a metaphoric Book of God's Works, seemingly scored by the Almighty with iconographic "words" in the form of holy sites or "stations" leading in "chains" of ever-increasing virtue to the earth's spiritual and geographic "navel" of Jerusalem. At each station pilgrims stopped, looked, prayed, sometimes sang, and then listened as appropriate biblical texts were read. They sought to fulfill in their own lives in figura through their ritualistic pilgrimage actions, the spiritual promise of past events signified both by the Bible and by the stations in God's Worldly Book. In A.D. 382, St. Silvia, also known as Etheria, described just such ritualistic peregrinations over a "ring" of Exodus stations on Mt. Sinai. Halting with her pilgrimage group on a narrow ledge near "the cave where holy Elijah hid" and "the church which is there," Silvia tells how an oblation and an earnest prayer were offered, and a passage from the book of Kings was read, "for we always especially desired that when we came to any place the corresponding passage from the book should be read." At a sacred site close to the summit where Moses was said to have received the Law, St. Silvia declares that "the book of Moses was read, and one psalm said which was appropriate to the place."[8] And so the group progressed station by station, following the same general ritual, over the entire ring.

By the twelfth century both Fetellus and Anonymous Pilgrim VI confirm in their tracts that a chain of forty-two Stations of the Exodus extended across the Sinai and the Holy Land to Jerusalem. "Through them the true Hebrew who hastens to pass from earth to heaven must run his race," Fetellus remarks using words also employed by Anonymous Pilgrim VI, "and, leaving the Egypt of the world, must enter the land of promise, the heavenly fatherland."[9]

After passing over the Exodus stations, pilgrims arriving in Jerusalem ritualistically acted out a series of redemptive events on another "ring," later known throughout Europe in its figured form as the Stations of the Cross. During a pilgrimage to the Holy Land in A.D. 342, the Byzantine Empress Helena, the mother of Constantine, had seemingly discovered the site and pieces of the Cross, and she displayed unique ability in finding many other sacred places in and around the Holy City. Later in A.D. 333 a Bordeaux pilgrim had also identified a series of Jerusalem stations.[10] In later centuries the number of sacred sites multiplied at an alarming rate, with nested rings of stations established in particular within the Holy Sepulcher itself.

The most sacred and longest of pilgrimages—one recorded in pilgrim tracts that served as sources for icons on T-O world maps—was the famed six-month to two-year Exodus journey beyond the sea to worldly Egypt; then across dangerous desert stations on the Sinai and over the ring on Mt. Sinai, and finally on to rings of stations in Jerusalem, ending with the ring within the Holy Sepulcher. This long pilgrimage was often climaxed, particularly after the first Roman Jubilee Pilgrimage of 1300, by a journey back across the sea to a chain of stations in the eternal city of Rome, a chain terminating at old St. Peter's Basilica.

The famed long pilgrimage "beyond the sea" to Jerusalem and back is well exemplified in the general itinerary of Bernard the Wise (ca. 870). While in Rome, Bernard and his fellow pilgrims, during an audience with Pope Nicholas, "gained the desired permission to set forth, and his blessing." Then after obtaining ship passage on the Italian coast, they "were conveyed to the port of Alexandria, the voyage lasting thirty days." The pilgrims, upon reaching the River Nile, "sailed southward six days and came to the city of Babylonia in Egypt, where one King Pharaoh ruled, under whom Joseph built seven granaries [the pyramids] which yet remain." Traveling from Babylon [Old Cairo] to the city of "Damiate" on the Egyptian coast and then to the edge of the Sinai deserts, Bernard and his group secured "camels...for the desert passage." Unlike many other pilgrims, they did not journey south and east into the desert wastes to very isolated holy sites, the ancient "ring" of stations on Mt. Sinai and within St. Catherine's monastery at the mountain's base. They proceeded instead over the coastal path to Gaza and then inland to Jerusalem. Going next from station to station on the Holy City's ring, Bernard at last ascended slanting streets to the New Jerusalem of Constantine, a complex of "four churches," including the Church of the Holy Sepulcher and Golgotha, "joined to each by partition walls which they have in common." While ardently venerating sites and relics at the New Jerusalem stations, Bernard observed "between the four churches...an unroofed court, the walls of which blaze with gold." In the middle of the court was a "space marked out by four chains" which Bernard identified, in the manner of pilgrims through the centuries who saw a stone urn at the same site, as the supposed "center of the world." Bernard and his companions, finally leaving Jerusalem and holy sites nearby, "came to the sea." And embarking, they "sailed for sixty days...to Mount Aureus," their long pilgrimage nearing its end. "Coming from Mount Aureus we arrived in Rome," Bernard writes. "In this city on the eastern side, in the place called the Lateran, is a well-built church in honor of St. John the Baptist, where is the proper seat of the successors of the Apostles. There every night are the keys of the whole city brought to the successor of the Apostles. On the western side is the church of blessed Peter, the chief of the Apostles, where his body rests. Bernard then declares that "in size there is no church like it on the whole earth."[11]

The long pilgrimage to Jerusalem and to other holy sites was so profoundly ingrained in European consciousness that it gave both theme and structure to major literary works by Dante, Geoffrey Chaucer, and Edmund Spenser. In Dante's *Commedia* the poet's journey beyond life, set in the Easter season of the Roman Jubilee pilgrimage year of 1300, accordingly has been read as an other worldly fulfillment of a foreshadowing earthly Egypt-Jerusalem-Rome pilgrimage to the gates of St. Peter's Basilica in the eternal city of the papacy. Dante has been seen to act out in figura events associated with the Sinai Exodus on the slopes of Mt. Purgatory, with the Redemption in Jerusalem on Mt. Purgatory's summit in Eden, and the Transfiguration in the poem's eternal city in Paradise.[12]

The Prologue to Chaucer's *The Canterbury Tales* depicts the beginning of a short English pilgrimage in the thirteenth century from London to Canterbury, a journey that would have been recognized in the author's time as the initial stage in the long pilgrimage to Jerusalem. Chaucer observes that one among the English pilgrims, the irrepressible Wife of Bath, has in the past made three journeys to that distant Holy City. Probably she would have followed, had she been an historical person, Matthew of Paris's thirteenth-century *Itinerary* which included Canterbury on the list of cities leading to Jerusalem.

The later partial fragmentation of medieval world iconography is evident in the heavy reliance of Edmund Spenser on imaginative faeryland action and ideological structure in his late sixteenth-century Protestant epic *The Faerie Queene*. Gloriana, the ruler of

Faeryland, has her seat in a tower of glass found to mirror the ancient stone tower on the terraced, pyramidal hill or Tor of ancient "Glassenbury," modern Glastonbury, the oldest pilgrimage center in England where, in the poem, Joseph of Arimathea is said to have brought relics of the Crucifixion. Discursive Exodus pilgrimage themes involve a crusading Red Cross Knight in Book I, a Palmer in Book II. And certain faeryland sites have been seen to shadow Glastonbury stations which in turn are sometimes types of those on the Sinai Exodus pathway.[13]

While the Prologue to *The Canterbury Tales* is stylized and brilliantly realistic, Dante's *Commedia* as well as Spenser's *The Faerie Queene* are clearly allegories but with roots in differing medieval conceptions.

Over the centuries Dante's *Commedia* has often been read, especially by Romantic critics, as basically a lurid or beautiful fiction. Yet when considered in the light of medieval tradition and culture, it has been authoritatively and repeatedly interpreted as an "allegory of the theologians" with a literal sense that is "true" because resting on the "true" words of the Bible—an interpretation apparently asserted by the poet himself in his Epistle X to his patron Can Grande della Scala.

This kind of "theological allegory," as "codified" with fourfold meanings by Thomas Aquinas in the *Summa Theologica* (1.1.10.1-3), held that the "true" literal words of the Bible necessarily pointed to absolutely "true" persons and historical events, with three spiritual meanings arising from this literal historical sense. These spiritual senses were the allegorical, here signifying the "typological" with one historical person or event, the type, pointing to another, the anti-type; next, the moral or "tropological" sense signifying some ethical value or idea; and finally the mystic or "anagogical" sense pertaining to eternity in paradise.

Dante in his letter to Can Grande, a document generally believed to have been written by the poet or by someone expressing his views, states that the *Commedia* should be treated as would biblical Exodus *Psalm* 114 (113 in the *Vulgate*): the literal sense of the Exodus signifying the historical journey of the Israelites; the allegorical, the historical Redemption of man by Christ; the moral, the conversion of the soul from sin to grace; and the anagogical, the departure of the soul from mortal corruption to eternal glory.

Because Dante in the *Commedia* engages in figural reenactments in the world-beyond of a succession of "true" prefiguring earthly biblical episodes beginning with the Exodus, his own peregrination has been seen, in accord with the pilgrimage tradition, as a "true" figural fulfillment of those scriptural events. And because actual pilgrims in the Middle Ages and Renaissance "read" from the iconography of successive rings of holy stations in God's worldly book as well as from the Bible—rings of supposedly ever-increasing virtue on Mt. Sinai and in Jerusalem and Rome— they too fulfilled in their lives the promise of those past worldly and biblical events. They became typological actors in the "present" of universal history.

The alternate medieval "allegory of the poets," as made famous by Prudentius and Martianus Capella and employed by Spenser in *The Faerie Queene*, was based upon an imaginative literal sense construed in medieval terms as a "beautiful lie," with the other three senses or meanings arising from this "lie." Under the allegory of the poets, the second sense, again called allegorical, usually signified an abstract idea *or* value rather than an historical "type" and "anti-type." The other senses of poetic allegory, the moral and mystical, were interpreted as in scriptural exegesis. Such was the fourfold theory for poetic and scriptural allegory; but in fact the four senses were almost never applied consistently by early patristic or other commentators to long passages in biblical or other works.

The text of *The Faerie Queene* at times alludes, as noted, to Exodus pilgrimage and to pilgrimage sites in English Glastonbury, thus giving Spenser's "beautiful lie" an historical cast. But the two parts of John Bunyan's later seventeenth-century prose work *Pilgrim's Progress* comprise a relatively "pure" allegory of the poets. The work's symbolic and allegorical nuances subtly reveal inner spiritual states, but the allegory in its literal sense points to no actual geographic reality or pilgrimage chain. *Pilgrim's Progress* is in its literal sense unmistakably a fiction, and is best and generally seen—with its on-the-road theme, roller-coaster spiritual ups and downs, and complex suggestiveness—in a literary tradition leading, not toward empirical historicist works, but toward the eighteenth-century fictional picaresque novel.

Renaissance historicist empirical writing about the world and its peoples, on the other hand, developed in part out of worldly and biblical-type claims to a "true" historical literal sense. Such claims underscored a belief in the external world's presumably undeniable reality as a type for the world beyond, a reality sustained by the immaterial essences of beings. But after the Protestant Reformation, when belief in essences, relics, and holy iconographic stations wavered or waned, and when long pilgrimages were gradually supplanted by voyages of discovery, this new empiricist writing, with an ever decreasing figural content, was increasingly influenced by discoverers' eyewitness testimony and seamen's plain journals.

In the early Renaissance, knowledge of the medieval iconographic world could hardly have been avoided by authors of histories, poems, and tracts. Short pilgrimage pathways featuring types of world-famous iconographic stations, replicating those in the Holy Land, were then in place in cities and towns throughout Europe and England. The Holy Sepulcher "ring" was possibly the most famed, imitated as it was in full or in part in Franciscan and other churches and cathedrals in Spain, Italy, and in other Western countries. Types or derivative forms of Holy Land "chains" could be found at Mt. La Verna in Italy, Compostella in Spain, and at Glastonbury in England. So strong was the conception of the world as a hierarchically ordered arrangement of iconographic holy places that it became a commonplace of medieval and early Renaissance historiography.

B. Columbus, the East, and Millennial Jerusalem

In the much discussed instance of Columbus in the fifteenth century, there are the strongest reasons to believe that the admiral in announcing his directional and iconographic views in his last years was neither essentially delusional, deceptive, nor suffering from senility, as some biographers have maintained. Admittedly, Columbus in his writings often stretched and colored facts to his own advantage or to match his strong ideas, and he clung with stubborn tenacity to his views. Yet like legions of writers and travelers from the Middle Ages through the early seventeenth century, he also gave great religious and literal weight to the Bible and to the then thousand-year-old pilgrimage tradition—sometimes insistently demanding agreement from his ships' crews—when trying to understand conflicting cosmographical information and genuinely enigmatic new shorelines and landscapes.

While Columbus has traditionally been treated by biographers as a practical but extremely ambitious and sometimes deceptive seaman breaking with medieval superstitions and creating a new global outlook, commentators only in the last twenty years have shown interest in the Renaissance Columbus who sought possessions, wealth, and fame; and also in the medieval Columbus who sought to make religious and practical sense out of a confounding iconographic Book of the World.[14] Yet to grasp Columbus's underlying aims and beliefs, it is essential also to see his writings in the light of the Jerusalem pilgrimage and biblical tradition that shaped both his vision and the vision of so many historiographers and cosmographers who were to follow.

Columbus's knowledge of the Jerusalem pilgrimage tradition would have rested in large measure on a source overlooked by critics. In Columbus's period members of the Franciscan order were the Church's official "guardians" of Jerusalem's Mt. Sion. They staffed hospices, as they continue to do today, on the pilgrimage chain near and within the Holy City. In the thirteenth

41

century by dispensation of Egypt's Sultan who had disrupted Exodus pilgrimages, St. Francis, the founder of the order, had journeyed from Egypt to the Land of Promise and so given the Franciscan's their special Holy Land mission as protectors of pilgrims. Francis had afterward returned to Italy where on Mount La Verna he received the stigmata, founded a monastic center that later attracted pilgrims from all over Europe, and there established a chain of pilgrimage stations replicating those on the Exodus route. It was in a cell near the pilgrimage steps up Mt. La Verna that the Franciscan, St. Bonaventure, composed his *Itinerarim mentis in Deum* (ca. 1259), a meditative study of spiritual ascent reflecting the *Scala Paradisi*, a Latin translation of Sinai Bishop John Climacus's seventh-century Greek work *The Heavenly Ladder*.

In Columbus's period, one strong strain of Franciscan teaching, as recent critics have noted, concentrated on Apocalyptic commentaries—beginning with Beatus and including Eulogius, bishop of Toledo, and the Franciscan Spiritual Abbot Joachim of Fiore (1132-1202)—on the end of world history in a millennial earthly kingdom, an event associated with the "liberation" in battle of Jerusalem and the conversion of humankind to Christianity.[15]

The prophetic Franciscan focus on the world's pilgrimage center of holy Jerusalem, on Exodus pilgrimages from sin to grace, and on a future millennial kingdom established in the East in the Holy City is etched boldly in Columbus's writings, merged in erratic ways with empirical values and new cosmological convictions. Columbus had been advised and assisted, and formally or informally educated, for many years of his life by Franciscan monks, especially those at the monastery of Palos near the port where he first set out for the distant end of the East. He was buried in Franciscan habit, having very possibly been inducted into the order as a Franciscan tertiary.[16] And following the biblical interpretative practice of positing foreshadowing and fulfilled typal holy events, Columbus in his letters, journals, and Prophetic Books audaciously "wrote himself" into Franciscan pilgrimage conceptions of world universal typal history as a central prophetic actor voyaging West to reach the end of the East. The admiral's typal world utopian dreams, including an epochal historical end to his role through an imagined conquest of Jerusalem, foreshadow typal patterns in later centuries of projected religious or secular world revolutions leading to an end of history.[17]

On his initial voyage over the Ocean Sea, Columbus on Sunday, 23 September 1492 invoked the pilgrimage type of the Exodus in speaking of his confrontation with a mutinous crew.

> As the sea was calm and smooth, the people murmured, saying that, as there was no great sea, it would never blow so as to carry them back to Spain. But afterwards the sea, without wind, rose greatly, and this amazed them, for which reason the admiral here says: "So that high sea was very necessary for me, because such a thing had not been seen save in the time of the Jews, against Moses who brought them out of captivity."[18]

The commander here presents himself, not as the customary pilgrim type of a wandering Israelite, but rather as the type of Moses himself. He turns his crew into types of unfaithful followers murmuring against their prophetic leader.

On the fourth and final voyage, Columbus, who by now had been appointed Admiral of the Ocean Sea and Viceroy in perpetuity over all the new lands discovered, writes of falling asleep and of being addressed by name by a "compassionate voice." Columbus at this time was signing documents as "Christoferens," the Christ bearer. The words spoken by the "compassionate voice," according to the admiral, indeed imply that he is a blessed but irresolute prophetic emissary and leader, a fulfilled if faltering type not only of Moses but also of King David of Jerusalem.

> "O fool and slow to believe and to serve thy God, the God of all! What more did He for Moses or for His servant David?...When He saw thee of an age with

which He was content, He caused thy name to sound marvellously in the land...Of the barriers of the Ocean Sea, which were closed with such mighty chains. He gave thee the keys; and thou wast obeyed in many lands and among Christians thou hast gained an honourable fame. What did He more for the people of Israel when He brought them out of Egypt? Or for David, whom from a shepherd He made to be king in Judea?"[19]

This emissary on the intermediate third voyage claimed to have found a holy "protuberance," a great sloping land mass rising high into the sky that was traditionally said to be located beyond Jerusalem at the "end of the East." While sailing close to the mouth of the Orinoco River off modern-day Brazil, and after noting irregular quadrant readings of the changing positions of the Pole star, Columbus came to a surprising and analogically erotic conclusion about the possible form of the earth:

that it is not round as they describe it, but that it is the shape of a pear which is everywhere very round except where the stalk is, for there it is very prominent, or that it is like a very round ball, and on one part of it is placed something like a woman's nipple, and that this part, where this protuberance is found, is the highest and nearest to the sky, and it is beneath the equinoctial line and in this Ocean Sea at the end of the East. I call that 'the end of the East,' where end all the land and islands.[20]

Medieval *mappaemundi* illustrating pilgrim tracts regularly showed that beyond Jerusalem, in a region discussed in the largely fictive pilgrimage Book of Sir John Mandeville, lay the up-raised farthest point east. Accordingly, Columbus believed that he had arrived at the "end of the East" now transposed to a position not far from the equator. And because on circular pilgrimage *mappaemundi* the Earthly Paradise was regularly depicted uplifted at the ultimate East, it can be understood why Columbus, under the pressure of the pilgrimage tradition, and thinking the fresh waters of the Orinoco River flowed downward into the sea from Eden, became convinced that Eden was situated at the top of the world in the interior of modern Brazil:

> For I believe that the earthly Paradise is there and to it save by the will of God, no man can come...I do not hold that the earthly Paradise is in the form of a rugged mountain, as its description declares to us, but that it is at the summit, there where I have said that the shape of the stalk of a pear is, and that, going towards it from a distance, there is a gradual ascent to it.[21]

In the log of his fourth voyage, Columbus proposed that biblical Ophir, famed for gold mines that supplied King Solomon, was situated somewhere in the region that is now the Isthmus of Panama. The mines, Columbus wrote, are in a warm climate "at the same distance from the pole and the equator" and so rich beyond measure (104).

Even while giving new iconographic alignment to the supposed marvels at the "end of the East," Columbus in the letters of his fourth voyage and in his Prophetic Books kept the cynosure of his possible prophetic role upon Jerusalem in the East. He had gained political and financial support for his journeys to the East in part by his announced expectation that he would there obtain plentiful gold for the Spanish monarchs, an expectation that had remained unfulfilled. As he grew older, his concentration upon Eastern gold and its uses merged with his dreams about the Holy City and his seemingly ordained prophetic part as Christoferens. For Columbus, Jerusalem, as he noted in his *Prophetic Books*, had great literal and spiritual significance:

> In a historical sense, it is the earthly city to which pilgrims travel. Allegorically, it indicates the Church in the world. Tropologically, Jerusalem is the soul of every believer. Anagogically, the word means the

45

Heavenly Jerusalem, the celestial fatherland and kingdom.[22]

Stirred by the millenarian prophesies of Joachim of Fiore and other commentators on Revelation, Columbus proposed to Ferdinand and Isabella that gold soon to be found in the Indies be used to fulfill his millennial dream of raising a crusading army of militant pilgrims in arms, liberating Jerusalem from the "infidels," rebuilding the Temple, and converting non-believers to Christianity.

Columbus observes that

David in his will left three thousand quintals of gold of the Indies to Solomon to aid in building the Temple, and according to Josephus, it was from these same lands.[23]

"Gold," Columbus continues, "constitutes treasure, and he who possesses it may do what he will in the world, and may so attain as to bring souls to Paradise" (104).

Even in his first letter to Ferdinand and Isabella, Columbus had introduced a foreshadowing type of the future liberation of Jerusalem: the Moorish surrender of the Alhambra to the Spanish monarchs:

I saw the royal banners of your highnesses placed by force of arms on the towers of the Alhambra, which is the citadel of the city, and I saw the Moorish king come out of the gates of the city, and kiss the royal hands of your highnesses and of the prince.[24]

Columbus in the log of the fourth journey cites supposed prophesies by the Franciscan Joachim and others that implicitly point to himself, Christoferons, and to his mission:

Jerusalem and Mount Sion are to be rebuilt by the hand of a Christian; who this is to be, God declares by the mouth of His prophet in the fourteenth psalm. [*Psalm xiv. 7*] Abbot Joachim said that he was to come from Spain. St. Jerome showed the way of it to the holy lady. The emperor of Cathay, some time since, sent for wise men to instruct him in the faith of Christ. Who will offer himself for this work? If Our Lord bring me back to Spain, I pledge myself.[25]

Columbus's prophetic and passionate concern for Jerusalem was clearly fostered by his conviction that he had been permitted by God to reach "the end of the East," a conviction that contributed to later perplexities in cosmographical historicism. In his journal of the first voyage, Columbus notes on 24 October 1492, that he has consulted both cosmographers' constructed "spheres" of the earth, presumably of Renaissance origin, as well as the very different flat, usually circular or elliptical, medieval pilgrimage mappaemundi. He was thus led to believe that he had crossed the Ocean Sea and had reached the far East. In writing of what he then thought was Cipangu or modern Japan (actually Cuba), he remarks that the native inhabitants

give me to understand by signs, for I do not know their language, it is the island of Cipangu, of which marvelous things are recounted, and in the spheres which I have seen and in the drawing of *mappemondes*, it is this region.[26]

The numerous islands shown at the "end of the East," at the top of circular *mappaemundi*, further misled Columbus about his position. Under Columbus's 14 November entry describing islands to the northeast of supposed Cipangu, Bartolomé de Las Casas, who had access to the original journal or a copy and made a digest of it, placed a notation explaining that

he believes that these islands are those without number which in the mappemondes are placed at the end of the east. And he says that he believes that in them there were very great riches and precious stones and spices, and that they extend very far to the south, spread out in every direction.[27]

The wrenching cartographic problem faced by Columbus was in including a medieval iconography oriented to the East on medieval circular or elliptical mappaemundi, within the configurations of very different Ptolomaic maps or spheres orientated to the North. On the flat mappaemundi projections, Eden at the farthest eastern point appeared at the outer edge, often as an island, of the northern hemisphere's circular land mass, with Jerusalem at its center. But what was the location in the new cartography of Eden, Jerusalem, the goldmines of Ophir, and other iconographic biblical sites? To make medieval projections fit Ptolomaic outlines oriented to the north in volumes such as Pierre d'Ailly's *Imago Mundi*, the work Columbus annotated more than any other he owned,[28] it was necessary to "turn" mappaemundi forty-five degrees to the right or left, so that Eden in the east was now presumably someplace toward the equator possibly on a line with the Ophir goldmines. Jerusalem, which had been previously sited at the center of the northern hemisphere's landmass, would now be someplace on the upper side of the globe. The stream of the Ocean Sea would then seemingly flow entirely around the globe at the middle in eastern and western directions; and the Ocean Sea would extend over the underside of the globe unless, as Augustine and some Church Fathers argued, there was an unknown continent, an Antipodes inhabited by Antipodians, at the bottom.

While on the first voyage, Columbus, in trying to determine his whereabouts, changed his mind and concluded that another island (modern Haiti) was the true Cipangu, and that the land he first thought to be Cipangu (modern Cuba) was in fact Cathay on mainland China. However unusual these convictions may seem in retrospect, Columbus can again be seen as engaged in trying to match strange but seemingly recognizable shorelines and geographic features in entirely reasonable ways with very vague medieval, Ptolomaic, and contemporaneous drawings of the coasts and islands of Asia. He was the first of what would be many lost voyagers who, in trying to make spiritual and empirical sense out of what they saw, insisted that they knew where they were.

Prior to his first voyage during arguments with savants and divines of the Talavera Commission before Spanish King Ferdinand and Queen Isabella, Columbus was not found delusionary, but was thought by some to be arrogant and proud. He was not challenged before his first voyage on his largely traditional medieval views, then shared by many, on the general configuration of the globe with Europe and Asia supposedly separated by a single Ocean Sea; but rather on his relatively small numerical estimate of the breadth of the Ocean Sea and of his estimate on the relative nearness of the Asian landmass.[29] The great majority of the savants and divines contended that the Ocean Sea was too wide and dangerous to be crossed from East to West, and so initially rejected Columbus's plans.[30]

As it turned out, both Columbus and the majority of savants were wrong: between Europe and the Far East lay the American continent, and beyond the American continent a second Ocean Sea.

* * *

"Columbus did not find America by chance," writes the Oxford librarian Robert Burton in the 1609 edition of his *Anatomy of Melancholy*, "but God directed him of that time to discover it." Burton, like Walter Ralegh and Columbus before him, held to the religious conviction that a divine providence shapes both individual ends and human history in ways often mysterious to human understanding. "God in his providence," Burton remarks, "to check our presumptuous inquisition, wraps up all things in uncertainty, bars us from long antiquity, and bounds our search within the compass of some few ages."[31]

Burton was distressed by the uncertainties of cosmological history. He and other seventeenth-century authors such as Thomas

Fuller, John Donne, and numerous historicists had continued to cite, often without explanation, conflicting passages from ancient and modern cosmographers and from the Bible on regions and contours of the earth. Key features of the new cosmology had by then gained general if not complete acceptance: namely, the existence of the polar caps, the new continent of the Americas, the new ocean separating the Americas from Asia, and the separation of Asia from what was now seen as the continent of Africa. Yet deep cosmological doubts remained, and Burton irritably registers what was then a common sense of confusion.

Burton, having never left England, announces that he wants to wander "round about the world" to resolve impossible geographical conflicts, and to find and "examine the true seat of that terrestrial paradise, and where Ophir was, whence Solomon did fetch his gold." Burton states that he would then "censure" cosmographies, old and new, and bring light to the darkness of global geography and history. He would attack "all Pliny's, Solinus', Strabo's, Sir John Mandeville's, Olaus Magnus', Marco Polo's lies, correct those errors in navigation, reform Cosmographical Charts, and rectify longitudes." Yet he adds significantly, "if it were possible" (412).

Protestant divine Thomas Fuller, reminding his readers that he is no "Columbus" who discovered "another world," modestly asks that he "not be condemned" for inadequacies in his historical and cartographic representations in *A Pisgah-sight of Palestine and the Confines Thereof, with The History of the Old and New Testament Acted Thereon* (1650).[32] Fuller was torn by "truths" in the new World Book seemingly different from those in the Bible.

Although he opposed Jerusalem pilgrimages, urging English Protestants to remain at home and to read the Bible, Fuller discusses the Holy Land using a reprinted map of the forty-two pilgrimage stations of the Exodus, and reprinted maps with line drawings showing the supposed pilgrimages of each of the Twelve Tribes of Israel. The reader in effect is asked to "look down" from a height upon unfolding pilgrimage events.

The problem is that Fuller was in a quandary about the geographical positioning of practically every event and site. As he admitted in his earlier book *The Historie of the Holy Warre* (1639), he had examined "thirty mapps and Descriptions of the Holy Land," without having found "two in all considerables alike." He thus placed his ultimate faith in the Bible as a geographic as well as spiritual guide. "In those differences," he writes, "wee have followed the Scriptures as an unpartiall umpire."[33] The result in both of his works is a baffling blurring of Holy Land locales. Fuller's comments on Jerusalem in *The Pisgah Sight*, for example, are typical of the quandary of other authors who consulted both scripture and the new cosmography:

> Concerning the generall situation of *Jerusalem*, three things herein are remarkable: first it was placed, as *Josephus* reports, in the very middle of *Judea*. But herein criticall exactness is not to be observed, (the heart it self is not so unpartially in the midst of the body, but that if not in position, yet in motion it propends to the left side) .... As *Jerusalem* was the navell of *Judea*, so the Fathers made *Judea* the middest of the world, whereunto ... Scripture, *Thou hast wrought salvation in the midst of the earth*. Indeed seeing the whole world is a round Table, and the Gospell the food for mens souls, it was fitting that this great dish should be set in the midst of the Board that all the guests round about might equally reach unto it; and *Jerusalem* was the Center whence the lines of salvation went out into all lands. Yea Ptolomy dividing the (then-known) world into seven Climats, placed *Jerusalem* as the Sun, in the fourth Climat, proportionably to what is said in the Prophet, *I have set it in the midst of the Nations, and the Countreys that are round about her*. (Book 3, 315, section 2)

Of all the writers who alluded to the historicist-cosmological problems of the early seventeenth-century, the metaphysical poet John Donne is possibly the most renowned for his poetic rendering in *The First Anniversary: An Anatomie of the World*, of the ugly, corrupt irregularities of the newly-discovered globe, irregularities resulting from a depicted breakdown in the spiritual correspondence between heaven and earth. The newly-discovered earth contains grotesque hills which are "warts, and pock-holes," and the entire "worlds proportion disfigured is."[34] "What Artist now dares boast that he can bring/ Heaven hither, or constellate any thing," the poet wonders, "The art is lost, and correspondence too" (ll. 391, 396). "The new Philosophy," Donne writes in a famed passage on the physical world "cals all in doubt" (l. 205).

Yet Donne, who used both the old and new learning for his poetic effects, is at his most witty and revealing in his shorter verse in lightly capturing the tipsy nature of the new cosmological history. In "Goodfriday, 1613, Riding Westward," Donne echoes Columbus in playing upon the paradox of traveling west to get east. On this holy day of Christ's passion when pilgrims moved over "stations" on the Via della Rosa to Golgotha in Jerusalem, the narrator is whirled in the wrong pilgrimage direction. "I am carried towards the West/ this day, when my Soules forme bends toward the East" (ll. 9-10).

The narrator confesses his longing to "behold those hands which span the Poles,/ And tune all spheares at once peirc'd with those holes," thus invoking the image of flat, medieval T-O maps showing the outstretched hands of Christ projecting outside the circumference of the drawn circular world. The speaker, however, has turned his back on Christ "but to receive/ Corrections" (ll. 37-38). When "corrected"—at least in part—the body of the spiritually "bent" narrator will still unfortunately be whirled to the West. But, quips this real or pseudo-pilgrim remembering the East, "I'll turn my face" (l. 42).

In "The Annunciation and Passion," Donne again focuses the old and new cartography on themes of paradoxical spiritual direction, observing that the "Abridgement of Christ's story" as announced by an angel to the Virgin Mary is so mystical that it "makes one (As in plaine Maps, the furthest West is East) (ll. 19-21) In short, the "oneness" of the joining of East and West, on a flat or "plaine" world map pressed around a globular form, is a metaphor for the abridgment of the story of the "oneness" of the human-divine Son to be born of Mary.

The lover-narrator of "The Good Morrow," awaking in bed with his mistress, ingeniously dismisses the discoveries of "sea explorers" whose flat Mercator maps of a globular earth are cut in unseemly forms having a "sharp north and declining west." The waking soul of the lover is illumined instead by the "perfect hemispheres" of his mistress's eyes, hemispheres recalling the perfect circles of medieval T-O maps with Jerusalem, in the position of the pupil of each eye, at the center (ll. 11-18). In "The Sunne Rising" the lover lying with his mistress commands her to "Look" with her eyes at "both the' India's of spice and Myne," and to tell him if the Indias are where she "lefst them" or are "here"— thus delightfully claiming possession of both eyes, and asking whether the "Myne," undoubtedly imagined glittering with gold or precious gems, remains in the Old and New Worlds or is now beside him in bed (ll. 17-8).

In "Go and Catch a Falling Star" the narrator mocks Holy Land tradition by demanding an impossible pilgrimage feat, one that implicitly derides pious pilgrim accounts of how the star of the Nativity fell to earth at the very place in Bethlehem where Christ was born.[35] Even more startling in "Elegie: Going to Bed," the narrator, an anti-type of Columbus, ostensibly makes the greatest of new world discoveries as his mistress disrobes:

> Licence my roving hands, and let them go,
> Behind, before, above, between, below.
> O my America! my new-found-land,
> My kingdome, safeliest when with one man
> man'd,
> My Myne of precious stones: My Emperie,
> How blest am I in this discovering thee!
>
> (ll.25-30)

Columbus might well have been astonished at Donne's libidinous metaphor. Yet the admiral, like the voyagers and cosmographical-historicists who came immediately after him, left a confusing legacy. Columbus had set the tone for much of what was to follow by being neither entirely ancient nor entirely modern. He believed in the spiritual "truths" and many of the literal "truths" of the old iconographic Books of God's Words and Works, while at the same time trying to adjust them to the realities of a new world which he still partly viewed with the eyes and imagination of an Ancient. He was an early example of an intelligent if stern revisionist.

In attempting to reorder the seemingly scrambled iconography in the transformed global book, Columbus clung to the Ancient medieval belief, as his *Prophetic Books* demonstrate, in the underlying spiritual significance of certain literal sites; and he did his best to replace dislocated "holy sites" in positions appropriate to their spiritual value.

Columbus, moreover, gave new credence to medieval tales of Eastern marvels and riches. His sometimes extravagant accounts, amplified by others, served to lure to the Indies in the East generations of explorers and plunderers from Juan Ponce de Leon to Walter Ralegh. In the imagination of the voyagers, the desired marvelous goal might be either a golden city, or a fountain of youth, or a gold and silver mine, or the earthly paradise itself; but it was assumed that the longed-for site rested hidden in the unknown mountains or forests of what for Columbus was the "end of the East."

In structuring his writings, Columbus gradually interposed on essentially "Modern" sequential factual voyage narratives, especially by citing and interpreting biblical passages in his *Prophetic Books*, the ancient biblical historicist pattern of foreshadowed and fulfilled prophetic typal events. And he concluded his typal representations with a projected prophetic end involving a Franciscan millennial-like conversion of souls to a paradisal state, presumably to take place on earth. This eclectic "framing" of typal events leading to a spiritually utopian end, a "framing" rendered through revisionist readings of the Bible, was to reverberate through the centuries in religious and even in secular historical designs.

Fig. 1. Henry More, etching by W. Faithorne, n.d. Courtesy of the Syndics of Cambridge University Library.

Fig. 2. Americus Vespuccius with astrolabe. Engraving by Johannes Collaert, n.d. Courtesy of the New York Public Library.

Fig. 3. Walter Ralegh, supposedly after his release from the Tower. Artist unknown, n.d.

Fig. 4. Mythic El Dorado, from Hulsius's German edition of Ralegh's *Discoverie*. Courtesy of the Henry E. Huntington Library and Art Gallery.

Fig. 5. The monstrous Ewaiepanenema race, from Hulsius's edition of Ralegh's *Discoverie*. Courtesy of the Henry E. Huntington Library and Art Gallery.

Fig. 6. Amazons slaughtering male invaders in Guiana, from Hulsius's edition of Ralegh's *Discoverie*. Courtesy of the Henry E. Huntington Library and Art Gallery.

Fig. 7. Providential eye of God surveying globular earth. Frontispiece for Ralegh's *History of the World* (1614). Courtesy of the Henry E. Huntington Library.

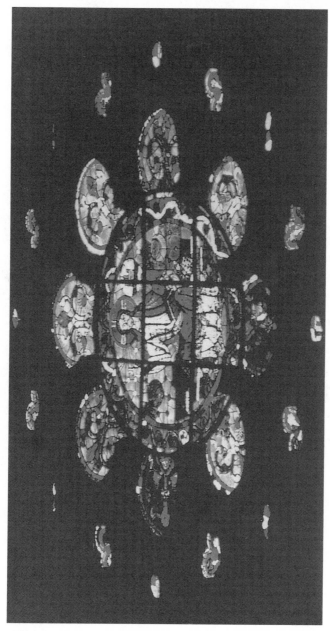

Fig. 8. Pilgrimage iconographic world, Christ as the Logos, Chartres Cathedral. Photograph: Painton Cowen.

Fig. 9. *Mappaemundi* (ca. 1285) in Hereford Cathedral, attributed to Richard of Haldingham, used as pilgrim guide to Jerusalem. Courtesy of the Dean and Chapter of Hereford Cathedral.

Fig. 10. Stone urn marking medieval geographic "center" of the world, in Constantine's Church of the Holy Sepulcher, Jerusalem. Photograph: author.

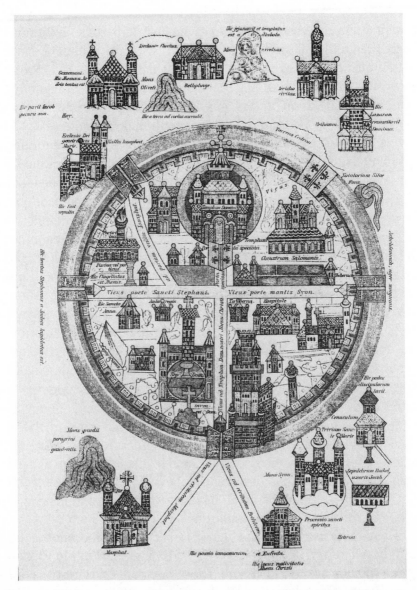

Fig. 11. Jerusalem map from Itinera Hierosolymitana Crue-signatorum (ca. 1180) depicting some of the medieval Stations of the Redemption. From *Zeitschrift des Deutschen Palästina-Vereins*, BD XV, fo. 5 (Leipzig, 1892).

Fig. 12. Exodus icon from Cosmos Indicoplenstes's ninth-century *Topographia Christiana* showing Moses (right) in the Sinai, Aaron (center), hand of God (upper right). Courtesy of Bibliotèca Medicea Laurenziana.

Fig. 13. Icon of Mt. Sinai "ring" of stations, from eleventh-century ms of Bishop John Climacus's *Scala Paradisi* in monastery at Patmos, Cod. 122, fo. Av-Br.

Fig. 14. Monastery of St. Catherine, 12th Station of the Exodus at foot of Mt. Sinai, is starting point for travelers ascending on the pathway "ring," seen veering behind the rear wall. Photograph: author.

Fig. 15. Mt. Sinai from pilgrimage pathway of Gebel St. Catherine pathway. Photograph: author.

Fig. 16. Stone stairs and Gate of Confession, Mt. Sinai. A second stone gate of St. Stephen also spans this section of the pilgrimage ring. Photograph: O. F. A. Meinardus.

Fig. 17. The Gebel Musa "ring" of stations in Jacobo di Verona's *Liber Peregrinationis* (1335). Pictured from bottom: Church of St. Catherine, checkered Church of St. Mary of the Apparition, plain, and Church of Elijah (with crosses on roof), pathway of purgation (dotted lines), summit buildings where Moses received the Laws, and repentance garden between Gabel Musa and Gebel St. Catherine at right.

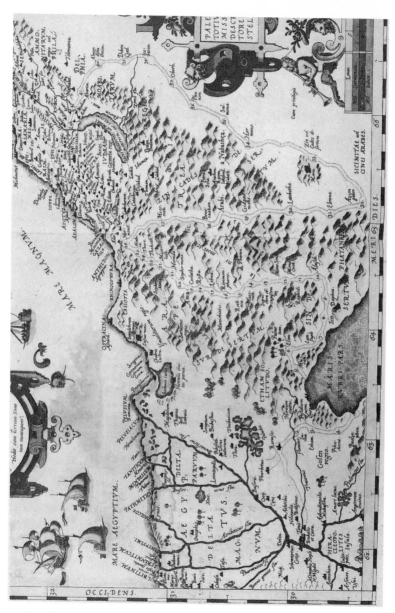

Fig. 18. The 42 pilgrimage stations of the Exodus, rendered in Ortelius's *Theatrum Orbis Terrarum* (1606). Courtesy of the Henry. E. Huntington Library.

3

RICHARD HAKLUYT AND
THE CONFUSION OF SOURCES

And cheerfully at sea,
  Success you still entice,
To get the pearl and gold,
And ours to hold,
  Virginia,
Earth's only paradise.

Thy voyages attend,
  Industrious Hakluyt,
Whose reading shall enflame
  Men to seek fame,
  And much commend
  To after times thy wit.
                                  ll. 19-24, 67-72

Michael Drayton, "To the Virginian Voyage"
Poems Lyrick and Pastorall (1606)

In publishing the revelatory book *Divers Voyages* in 1582, and then the two large editions of *Principal Navigations* in the years from 1589 through 1600, Richard Hakluyt spanned differing historical outlooks and provided key materials for a revisionist Renaissance cosmography and history. In *Principal Navigations* he followed pilgrimage compilation conventions in placing "layered" account upon account, one after the other, each one focused on the same region or site; and he allowed the pilgrim observations to be included along with those of contemporaneous travelers. Taking his inspiration from the intrepid traveler and historian Herodotus, he gave precedence to Renaissance eyewitness travelers who explored little-known regions of the world and who, asking questions of local persons, set down unique, critical geographic and historical observations usually in a matter-of-fact, literal fashion.

In a period when major European powers were competing for a foothold in the New World, Hakluyt as a British advocate was in the midst of the fray. At Christ Church, Oxford, from 1570 to 1586, he argued, in dedicating to Philip Sidney *Divers Voyages touching the discouerie of America, and the Island adiacent unto the same* (1582), for the enlargement of English colonies in North America, a view he held throughout his life.[1] Later while serving as secretary to the British ambassador in Paris, he collected information on French journeys to Canada and Florida and made suggestions on how the British might counter French moves.[2] Political and commercial interests clearly spurred his work, but so too did his deep and genuine fascination with the contours and history of the world.[3]

Hakluyt was a less than pellucid proponent of historical-cosmographical "modernism." There can be no doubt about his enthusiasm for the new cosmographical empiricism of Mercator and Ortelius; but commentators stressing his role as a cosmographical reformer regularly neglect his citations of medieval pilgrimage materials and his at times wavering viewpoints.

The famed 1589 edition of *Principal Navigations,* well known as the first extended compilation of English voyages and early travels, is a strange mix of medieval and modernist political, geographic, and historical materials.[4] The volume contains excerpts from medieval pilgrimage tracts, passages from partially mythic chronicles, extracts from letters and embassy reports, and selected fictitious narratives on supposed figures such as the Empress Helena, John Maundeville, and King Arthur. But the work takes fire from the rich printings of actual Renaissance journals on sea explorations to the New World and around the world. The documents are separated into categories by the direction of the land journeys and voyages, arranged in chronological sequence, and published usually without editorial comment except for brief prefaces and introductions.

In this first edition of 1589 in one volume, most of the travelers described or quoted in the first third of the work are medieval pilgrims to Jerusalem or to other holy centers, pilgrims recounting journeys over the ordered "geographic-iconographic" stations believed to have been scored in a World Book. Such travelers had no understanding whatever of either medieval or contemporaneous navigation. Still, tracts by pilgrims going to the south and southeast are initially featured Hakluyt explains in a preface "to the fauorable Reader," because "the oldest trauels...of the ancient Britaines, as the English, were ordinarie to Judea which is in Asia, termed by them the Holy land, principally for deuotions sake" (4).

The last two-thirds of the 1589 edition contain the eye-witness testimony of fifteenth-and sixteenth-century voyagers who wrote of an irregular, free-form geographic earth far larger and more varied than anything suggested in the "old" ordered, iconographic geography. This latter segment contains, first, journeys to the "North, and Northeastern" regions because, Hakluyt maintains, British "access to those quarters of the world is later and not so ancient as the former" (4). The work ends dramatically with memorable narrations of "westerne Nauigations" (4), including voyages to the Americas and around the world.

In his first-edition preface "to the fauorable Reader," Hakluyt calls his work a "historie" (Reader, 4), claiming it is a "*Peregrinationis historia,*" of a kind mentioned by Ptolemy. In this type of work, Hakluyt writes, "every man might answere for himselfe" and "stand accountable for his owne doings" (Reader, 4). Hakluyt implied that both travelers and readers can draw their own insights and conclusions, thus producing a more reliable kind of history. This historical method, Hakluyt insists, is superior to that of past authors who had penned "wearie volumes" as their owne, while "in deed most untruly and unprofitablie" copying from others unacknowledged writings that were then "hurled together" (Reader, 4).

Ptolemy had long before commented upon the *Peregrinationis historia* genre, having especially in mind the 5th century B.C. *Herodoti Historiae* of the wandering Herodotus who was particularly famed for his observations on Egypt.[5] Herodotus personally toured the lower and upper realms of that ancient land, but he had no knowledge of hieroglyphics and so depended heavily upon the often unreliable remarks about the past made by local priests and guides. Although Herodotus recorded many second-hand fictional tales and exaggerations, he also wrote down his own experiences and reflections on Egyptian religion, art, manners, customs, architecture, social organization, and history. His historiography stands as an early example of cultural commentary combining unique but frequently dubious accounts by others with incisive personal observations.

Hakluyt in his publications, however, provides very little commentary or narrative. This geographical reformer also surprisingly takes a medieval literalist stance toward scripture in accord with that of many early Church Fathers; namely, that only the words of the Bible, not those written by secular historians such as Herodotus, point to true historical events. "Nay," Hakluyt states in the second-edition preface "to the Reader," "there is not any history in the world (the most Holy writ excepted) whereof we are precisely bound to beleeue ech word and syllable" (Reader, unpaginated). Accepting only the Bible as a true historical document, Hakluyt then insists upon the fallibility of writings by even the most eminent of past and present historians. "Herodotus, Strabo, Plutarch, Plinie, Solinus," he remarks, "yea & a great many of our new principall writers, whose names you may see about the end of this Preface" should as mortal humans "be pardoned" for any "incredible relations" and "particulars hardly to be credited" (Reader, unpaginated). Writing of British reports on Northern voyages to Moscovia he similarly asks "pardon" for any inaccuracies, though he chauvinistically urges that the British reports may indeed be accurate.[6]

In the introductions and commentary to all his publications, Hakluyt does not in general explain what is to be believed or disbelieved in the numerous works he cites by Ancients and Moderns, or in what way the true words and syllables of the Bible are to be given historical precedence over the writings of secular historians and cosmographers. Concerning himself mainly with methods of organization, he left it to others to produce, from this scramble of old and new sources, a detailed and coherent world cosmography and history.

Examples of the mélange of Hakluyt's British pilgrimage selections and accounts are worth noting if only because they have been critically neglected. In the first edition of 1589, the contentious pilgrim-theologian Pelagius (400-418 A.D), who denied Original Sin and preached related unorthodox views, is described journeying to "Egypt, Syria, & other Countries of the East" and then returning to England (3-4). Other excerpts record how the orthodox Christian John Erigena was spiritually illumined after traveling as far as the holy city of Constantinople (4); and how another English orthodox pilgrim, Andrewe Whiteman in about 1020 A.D., went further to "Jerusalem," becoming "a witnesse of the miracles" before coming back "into his country" (5). Subsequently the monk Athelard is seen to have gone to "Egypt, and Arabia" in 1130 prior to making the usual return trip to England (5). Then the peregrinations of British William of Tyre to the Holy Land are outlined. He is said to have been a "Regular in the Church of Jerusalem, called the Lords Sepulchre." Shortly thereafter, Robert Ketenensis, an English king, is described going in 1143 A.D. "to the partes beyond the sea" to Greece and Asia, where he lived in danger among the Saracens and died far from home (6). The Holy Land exploits of England's King Richard I come next, before an excerpt on Holy Land fictive wonders by the author known as John Mandeville, a seeming pilgrim of uncertain identity who emphasized Jerusalem's spiritually preeminent location at the summit and middle of the globular earth (9-11, 25).

The pilgrimage accounts beginning with the 1589 edition, along with revealing medieval spiritual attitudes and iconographic cosmography, also present by implication a political outlook resting upon pilgrimage religious traditions espoused by Hakluyt. They suggest that the Tudor right derived by supposed succession from the Roman Emperor Constantine to political-religious authority over church and state. Constantine, who was crowned Emperor of the West in York before later assuming full control over the Roman Empire, is identified as the first Christian "Emperour and King of Britaine." Hakluyt describes how Constantine upon becoming the emperor turned the empire from paganism to Christianity. The alleged mother of Constantine, "British" Helena, is described in traditional fashion as having gone on pilgrimage to Jerusalem where she is said to have "visited all the places there, which Christ had frequented." The associated account of Constantine, "Emperor and King of Britain," underwrites the idea of a chain of rulers leading to Queen Elizabeth by way of that first "Imperiall Diademe, or Crowne to the Kings of Britain" (1-2). Authority by implication devolves upon Constantine, as it did upon the Apostles, from Christ who was crucified at Jerusalem, the Holy City that Constantine as well as his mother were traditionally said to have visited as pilgrims (2).

When Hakluyt some years later brought out his second edition of 1598-1600 printed in two and then three folio volumes, he transferred what originally had been his opening section—the Near and Far Eastern travel materials including pilgrimages to Jerusalem—to the second volume. But his work hardly gained in verisimilitude For in the first volume of 1598 (given a 1599 title page in later printings), he now wrote of journeys to the north and northeast beginning with those of mythic King Arthur, the supposed ancestor of the Tudors including Queen Elizabeth. The journeys were seen as supporting English imperial claims to northern lands and islands. King Arthur's "kingdome was too litle for him, & his minde was not concented with it," the printed narrative reads; therefore, he "subdued all Scantia, which is now called Norway, and all the Islands beyond Norway, to wit, Iceland and Greenland, which are apperteining unto Norway" (vol. 1, 2). Hakluyt the nationalist offers supposedly clear English claims to this conquered land, noting that "king Arthur obteined also in those dayes of the Popes court of Rome, that Norway should be for euer annexed to the crowne of Britaine for the inlargement of this kingdome, and he called it the chamber of Britaine" (vol.1, 2). Real and mythic figures and events crowd Hakluyt's following pages as he uncritically compiles excerpts on the northern and western movements of English Malgo, Bertus, Octher, King Edgar, Edmund and Edward, and Friar William de Rubriecis, to mention a few.

In the second volume of 1599, second edition, now containing the Near and Far Eastern travels originally placed in the first volume, Hakluyt actually intensifies interest in the importance of Jerusalem by adding a section on journeys to the Holy City "since the Conquest by the Crusaders." The politically and religiously significant pilgrimage to Jerusalem of "British" Helena, the mother of the Roman Emperor Constantine, again opens the book, with accounts of Constantine immediately following (vol. 2, 1-3). The medieval pilgrimage and Holy Land travel section now contains ten listings by Hakluyt covering journeys allegedly from 337 A.D. through 1064 A.D. After 1099 A.D., the date of the establishment of the Holy Land Kingdom of Jerusalem, Hakluyt writes of trips of notable "armed" as well as unarmed pilgrims to Jerusalem, namely, William the Conquerour, the English Lady Gutuere married to Baldwine (sic); Edgar and Rupert, Godericus, William of Tyre, John Lucy, and so on in a list that records some 64 journeys to or near the Holy City (vol.2, 1-33). The inclusions imply a continuing interest in a Christian kingdom in the Holy Land, an interest that had also motivated Columbus, with Jerusalem remaining a central theme in cosmography as in religion.

Hakluyt then moves without critical commentary to Renaissance voyages. The two editions both end with journeys to the "two" sides of America and then around the world. Readers pressing on though the massive materials gain a refreshing sense of an open and still largely unknown world.

Having great seminal value, Hakluyt's publications made accessible hundreds of Renaissance travel accounts, along with many new regional and world maps. By 1587 Hakluyt had in letters and publications called attention to maps such the "modern" world projection in Petri Martyris Anglerii's *De Orbe Novo* which left the areas of the poles blank beyond the Arctic and Antarctic circles, but which contained distorted outlines of North, South, and Central American coastlines on both the Eastern and Western shores from the Straits of Magellen in the South to Iceland in the North.[7] On the projection in *De Orbe Novo*, the Southern and Northern Pacific Oceans appear as less well known, with New Guinea and a number of islands misplaced, and the area below the tropic of Capricorn left largely empty except for the crude, extended outline of South America.

There is nonetheless a deadening weight about Hakluyt's editions, a massiveness highlighted by the author's flat, non-interpretive approach. These are editions to be consulted, read in bits and pieces, and then considered together in retrospect. They give a sprawling jig-saw-puzzle impression of parts of the world, for they lack a clear organization and a clear explanation of cosmographical content. The accounts are chauvinistically limited to "the Navigations onely of our owne nation" and of "some strangers." The fact that the different editions of the work each remained divided into three parts, with each of the parts in this tripartite arrangement centered on a different region of the world, possibly reflects the archaic influence of the tripartite division of mappaemundi. Without significant narrative or interpretive interventions by the author, readers are left to provide their own perspectives on the varied ways of viewing the earth and its history.

As "history" Hakluyt's work, in presenting a textured plethora of accounts by the "layered" statements of a great number of travelers or voyagers in given places, can be seen as a distant and admittedly vague precursor of the twentieth-century French *Annales* historical research of Fernand Braudel and his followers. The sheer density and diversity of Hakluyt's compilation, like the work of Braudel and the *Annales* historians, avoids concentration upon a single narrative chain of selected events. But Hakluyt in citing the Bible and including pilgrim texts differs from most Annales authors in offering an obscure religious context, never really developed or integrated with voyage literature, for the new naturalist world being revealed. Yet, with all their limitations, Hakluyt's editions of *Principal Navigations* were immensely important in disclosing, as truly "there" as an existing reality, a new cosmographical world that in turn required a new kind of historiography.

4

WORLD HISTORY REVISED

Francis Bacon and Abraham Ortelius

From these and all long Errors of the way,
In which our wandring Praedecessors went,
And like th' old Hebrews many years did stray
    In Desarts but of small extent,
Bacon, like Moses, led us forth at last,
    The barren Wilderness he past,
    Did on the very Border stand
    Of the blesst promis'd Land,

And from the Mountains Top of his Exalted Wit,
    Saw it himself, and shew'd us it.

        Abraham Cowley, "To the Royal Society,"
Thomas Sprat's *The History of the Royal Society* (1606)

Only a few years after the publication of *Principal Navigations*, Francis Bacon argued in *Of the proficience and aduancement of Learning, diuine and humane* (1605) for the superior empirical objectivity and great future potential of the new kind of "mixed" cultural-cosmographical history made possible by Renaissance navigational discoveries. Bacon's abstract arguments favoring the new history were by this time buttressed by the availability of splendid examples of the new form: the handsome, late sixteenth and early-seventeenth-century editions of cosmographer Abraham Ortelius's *Theatrum Orbis Terrarum*.

In 1606 Bacon was compared in Abraham Cowley's poem "To the Royal Society" to a new Moses guiding the philosophers of the

Royal Society over the route of the Exodus to the new promised land. Bacon had in effect received the mantle of Columbus as the foremost leader of the new philosophical discoverers—and with good reason.

Bacon was decisive. At a stroke by conspicuous omission, he banished from *The two Books of Francis Bacon of the Proficience and Advancement of Learning Divine and Human* (1605) the pilgrimage iconography, traditions, and medieval T-O maps that had so influenced the transitional writings of Hakluyt, Ralegh, and their contemporaries. With equal decisiveness, he unhesitatingly attacked Aristotelian natural history and deductive reasoning, while authoritatively proclaiming the Moderns superior to the Ancients in cosmographical-historical learning and in inductive philosophical analysis. As lord high chancellor of England under James I, he called the new history to the attention of his king and of the educated of his own and later generations, using his notoriety especially to advance, not only "mixed" cosmographic-cultural world historiography, but also the more focused "life histories" of important individuals, the precursor of modern biography.

Although Bacon never wrote in the "mixed" history form that so absorbed his thoughts, he did draw upon his political knowledge and experience to produce an early example of an individual biography, a short *Life of Henry VII* (1622) which put on display the author's professional astuteness in judging character, policy, and statecraft. In his theoretical writings, however, Bacon continued to give dominant weight to reflections on the new "mixed" history. He thus launched an empirical revolution in historiographical and related work, insisting that a high level of "objectivity" could be attained as the result of the new philosophy's proscription of distorting individual and collective biases. But the proper means to this history was left open, with useful aphorisms and incomplete general theories suggesting an empirical approach that others necessarily had to work out.

Before critically examining the cartographic-historical editions of Ortelius with their huge, hand-painted pages, rich designs and copious commentary, it will be useful to reconsider anew both the importance and limitations of Bacon's theoretical contributions to seventeenth-century historiography and empiricism.

Demonstrating abilities learned as an administrator and judge, Bacon in the *Advancement* defined, subdivided, and categorized Early Modern historiographical movements previously clouded in the writings of Ralegh, Hakluyt, and their contemporaries. Readers are accordingly forewarned that the lord chancellor's penchant for organizing his critiques of history and other knowledge into "parts"—a penchant Bacon himself fought against by urging the employment of aphorisms in place of methodology—is reflected in the categorical discussion of subjects in this chapter. In the course of seeking to organize knowledge, Bacon also sought theoretically to lessen or overcome conflicts between the new cosmographical-history and the old medieval and literalist biblical history by arguing for varied forms of interrelated knowledge. In his layered system, empirical studies of cosmographical-history and the new philosophy represented factual, verifiable knowledge compatible with but of a kind different from the largely theological and symbolic conceptions of the divine order of creation derived from scriptures and religious faith. Bacon's philosophical position thus markedly contrasts with that of Thomas Brown in *Religio Medici* (1643) or John Donne in the *Anniversary* poems (1611-12), writers who regularly treated empirical findings and literally-interpreted biblical passages as co-equal forms of knowledge, which, in Donne's case, were often depicted in radical conflict. Bacon, in making distinctions, deftly avoided the science-religion controversy that was to remain somewhat dormant through part of the eighteenth-century, only to break out in full force in the nineteenth.[1] In his unfinished but well-known utopian fiction *The New Atlantis* (1627), Bacon depicted an ideal island society in which religion and the new science existed harmoniously together as complementary forms of knowledge and belief. His own

"Confession of Faith" as an Anglican with Calvinist tendencies was first printed as an essay in 1641.

In his role as an advocate of the new philosophy, Bacon gave a name to innovative cultural historiography; and he offered an attempted explanation of the "science" upon which it was founded. In Book Two *Of the Proficience and Advancement of Learning*, he first identifies and discusses four traditional kinds of history: "*Naturall, Civile, Eclesiasticall & Literary.*" "*Civile*" and "*Eclesiasticall*" histories include, as Bacon explains, narrations of political events and organized religious activities.[2] But he reserves for last and with great enthusiasm emphasizes yet "another kinde of History manifoldly mixt" which extends to subjects beyond just politics and organized religion. This is a history which is compounded "of Naturall History in respect of the Regions themselues, of History ciuill, in respect of the habitations, governments, and manners of the people; and of *Mathematiques* in respect of the climates, and configurations of the heavens." This new kind of descriptive history of "Habitations, Regiments, and Manners" is designed to show differences in the peoples and cultures of the world, and can be seen to contain the seeds of what was to become anthropological investigation. And with its stress upon the location of different peoples on the globe, as determined by mathematical computation, as well as upon "Climats" influencing forms of culture, the new history embraces as well geographical-cosmographical study. This "mixed" history, Bacon maintains, is that "part of learning of all others in this latter time hath obtained most Proficience" (2.15).

It is here that Bacon makes the declaration that serves as a fulcrum for his views on the superior knowledge of the Moderns over that of Aristotle and the Ancients. "For it may be truly affirmed to the honour of these times, and in a virtuous emulation with Antiquity, that this great Building of the world, had neuer *through-lights* made in it, till the age of vs and our fathers" (2.15). Thus in a sentence the Ancients, revered for a thousand years as having unequaled knowledge and wisdom, are now placed in a subsidiary position as compared to the Moderns. Bacon recognizes that the Ancients "had knowledge of the *Antipodes*," now identified as the south-pole, but he observes in pejorative tones "that nought be by demonstration, and not in fact, and if by trauile, it requireth the voiage but of halfe the Globe." He then rises to a central pronouncement: "But to circle the Earth, as the heauenly Bodies doe, was not done, nor enterprised, till these later times." [3]

Analogically associating movements over the earth with those through the heavens, Bacon here strikes upon an incipient idea of progress. The Ancients journeyed over only "halfe the Globe." The Moderns have progressed by circling the entire earth. The next progressive step, seemingly implied either consciously or on impulse by Bacon's analogy, is one which occupied the thoughts of new philosophers such as Johannes Kepler and Tycho Brahe, and writers such as Ben Jonson in his masque *News from the New World Discovered in the Moon* (1620) and Shakespeare in *The Tempest (1613)*: the future circling of the earth from above "as the heauenly Bodies doe." Journeys to the circling moon and into space by Moderns were indeed speculated upon and imagined by these authors well known to Bacon, and were later popularized by John Wilkins in *Discovery of a New World* (1638) and Francis Godwin in *Man in the Moon* (1638). Whatever Bacon's conscious intent, the fact is that his implicit if fledgling idea of progress in cosmological discovery, fully acceded to by following generations, gave impetus in later centuries to geographical exploration of this globe; and then in this century, to the exploration of the heavens by Moderns who, in the course of their journeys, repeatedly circled the earth in space vehicles. And just as ships in Bacon's period fanned out to chart seas and lands previously unknown to Europeans, so today, in an extension of the same desire for knowledge, space vehicles arc outward to electronically "map" and explore the solar system before soaring on toward the stars.

In another key pronouncement, Bacon dramatically insists as a matter of seeming prophecy that "this Proficience in Nauigation, and discoueries, may plant also an expectation of the further proficience, and augmentation of all Scyences, because it may seeme they are ordained by God to be *Coevalls*, that is, to meete in one Age. For so the Prophet *Daniel*, speaking of the latter times, foretelleth" (2.16).

The lord chancellor admittedly is "reaching." His proof of the sweeping future "augmentation of the sciences" rests, not on any revelatory "hard science" experiment that can be repeated and verified by others under rigidly controlled test conditions, but rather on simple "proficiency" in the fragile art and empirical techniques of practical navigation, an activity then dependent upon disputed cosmological theory. For all his theorizing, Bacon may have been unable to think of a detailed and exacting hard-science experiment that could be repeated and confirmed by others, that could serve as a model for future scientific experimentation. Still, his recourse to navigation gave him a stunning example of a practical, empirical skill that had indeed led to amazing and "verifiable" geographical discoveries.

However confusing or doubtful navigational and related cosmological theory might be, the proof of that theory resided in its practical results. The predicted discovery of new seas, lands, and peoples, especially as directly experienced by mariners, was the ultimate Renaissance "reality check," more forceful even than Dr. Samuel Johnson's kicking a stone a century later to refute skepticism about the existence of the external world. Seamen sailing into the unknown in Bacon's period risked their lives on delicate navigational calculations and questionable cosmographic theories. When those who were fortunate, often after great physical hardship and torments of doubt, actually saw the strange shores of a New World appear over the rim of the great Ocean Sea, they recorded their experiences with deep emotion. Their writings left no doubt that the calculations and theories that had carried them so far indeed had reference, even when subject to some error, to an existing but previously unknown reality.

In mounting his theoretical revolution for the "augmentation" of cosmological-historiography along with all the "Scyences,"

Bacon, drawing relations among the sciences and arts, uncovers three fundamental empirical views still influencing contemporary historiographical, scientific, and critical thought. The first from *The Advancement of Learning* is his overstated but famed insistence, already mentioned, upon the necessity of inductive analysis in empirical work. The second from the *Novum Organum* is his foresighted awareness of the transparency of language and the necessity of establishing in the future more disciplined forms of empirical linguistic or other signification of a kind suggested by mathematics. And the third also from the *Novum Organum,* is Bacon's self-conscious, seminal reflection on prejudices and their elimination. In retrospect, these early Baconian views are surely open to qualification and criticism, but they were revelatory in their time and remain provocative, core pronouncements that have had great impact on the development of the new historiography.

Directly challenging the centuries-old hold of deductive logic upon Western academic philosophy, Bacon in the *Novum Organum* overstates a most valuable case by declaring without reservation that

There are and can exist only two ways of searching into and discovering truth. The one flies from the senses and particulars to the most general axioms, and from these principles, the truth of which it takes for settled and immoveable, proceeds to judgment and to the discovery of middle axioms. And this way is now in fashion. The other derives its axioms from the senses and particulars, rising by gradual and unbroken ascent, so that it arrives at the most general axioms last of all. That is the true way, but as yet untried.[4]

Bacon's espousal of analysis "rising by gradual and unbroken ascent" from particulars to general axioms is very well taken, but it should be noted that the hurried analytical leap without intermediary steps, to which Bacon objects, from the "senses and particulars" immediately to the "most general" is frequently

71

essential to the intellectual-imaginative formulation, if not of "axioms" of "truth," then of revelatory hypotheses and tentative theories. Such hypotheses and tentative theories are necessary to the invention of original experiments, which in turn could possibly validate tentative speculative views and so produce, in Bacon's terminology, a proved "general axiom."[5] Bacon's dismissal of the "hurried leap" leaves him foundering when confronted with the need to present examples of his own originally conceived experiments. What *precisely* are the new experimental philosophers in Bacon's writings supposed to be doing?

In taking up a second issue—the need for a linguistic revolution in support of the new philosophy—Bacon in the *Novum Organum* (1620) warned against "fantastical" and "contentious learning," driven by pretentious erudition couched in overly complex webs of words, learning of a type still familiar in certain contemporary academic and professional circles. In *The Advancement of Learning* he attacked too, in a passage later echoed by John Milton in *Areopagitica*, the confounding verbal disputes of neo-Aristotelian philosophers, whom he likened to spiders spinning empty webs of words. According to Bacon,

> This kinde of degenerate learning did chiefely raigne amongst the Schoole-men, who hauing sharpe and stronge wits, and aboundance of leasure, and smal varietie of reading; but their wits being shut up in the Cels of a few Authors (chiefely Aristotle their Dictator) as their persons were shut vp in the Cels of Monasteries and Colleges, and knowing little Historie, either of Nature or time, did out of no great quantitie of matter, and infinite agitation of wit, spin out vnto vs those laborious webbes of Learning which are extant in their Bookes. (1. 19; 1605 ed.)

Bacon's admonition remains unsettling. Symbolic statements with multiple and sometimes "open" meanings are, of course, an essential feature of literary and artistic expression and criticism. But currents in contemporary theoretical criticism particularly in the humanities, induced by groups each writing to those of their own persuasion, today often display a kind of corrupted, unnecessarily abstruse and often deliberately ambiguous "metalanguage." Such a language is often "privileged" and defended over expression dedicated, in so far as possible, to the clarification of linguistic meaning. In the hard sciences, although flexibility and imagination are regularly evident in the formulation of hypotheses, inductive logic and specific linguistic usage based on evidence remain essential.

Beyond "fantastical" and "contentious language," Bacon takes aim principally at the imprecision of the language of common speech. As *The Advancement of Learning* (3, 296; 4., chap. 3.) makes clear, Bacon shares with his contemporaries the conviction that before the Fall language could "grasp" the immaterial essences of beings that the prelapsarian Adam using his rational intuition, as the lord chancellor points out, gave the animals names that corresponded to their immaterial substantial forms. In the *Novum Organum,* however, Bacon, discussing the corrupted language of fallen humanity in the past and his own era, urges reform resting on empirical norms. Bacon deplores the hazy definitions of "things by those broad lines which are most obvious to the vulgar mind." Words in common usage, he insists, "oppose" and cloud those definitions made even by persons of "diligent observation" and "acute understanding," with the result that "the great and solemn disputes of learned men often terminate in controversies about words and names." These controversies proliferate, Bacon maintains in the manner of a modern linguist, because "they consist themselves of words, and these words produce others." As a way of breaking fully or partially out of this self-perpetuating verbal web, Bacon in *The Novum Organum* advises "(imitating the caution of mathematicians)" (115). He argues for the invention of new empirical verbal definitions that, with a specificity as close to mathematical signification as possible, relate words to things, events, and immediate contexts giving attention to precise identification, categorization, and ordering. "We must necessarily have recourse," he writes, "to particular instances, and their regular series and arrangement." These foresighted if limited suggestions, however open to epistemological and philosophical critique, have served and still serve as a basic general guideline to the disciplined use of language as a referent to external things, in cultural historical studies and empirical investigation.[6]

Finally, taking a stand on what is still a major issue, Bacon in *The Novum Organum* focuses on the repression or elimination of bias in critical and empirical-intellectual work, an issue crucial to the body of his publications on the reform of neo-Aristotelian learning. As a man of his period, Bacon understandably does not directly address what today, in contemporary republics and democracies, would be very familiar "social science" questions about attitudes related to politics, finance, church-state relations, gender, class, or social and ethnic groups. He was a monarchist, a British nationalist, and an Anglican. In a pre-social science period, Bacon's seventeenth-century support for the new international "mixed" historiography can nonetheless be seen as a distant, early foreshadowing step toward later comparative cultural history. But even given his seventeenth-century viewpoint, Bacon makes points about the overcoming of bias that still have resonance. He argues that dogmatic ideologies and distorting personal and collective inclinations need to be either eliminated or transcended, but certainly not used as a basis for partisan arguments or theorizing in historiography or other disciplines.

Against a background of seventeenth-century political and religious conflict underscored by opposed "leveler" and "gradational" philosophical outlooks, Bacon puts forward four now-famed axioms designed to make new philosophers conscious of prejudicial attitudes so that they may be overcome. Bacon exposes a looseness in terminology that reveals him far from having mastered the controlled scientific language he advocates. It is the thrust of Bacon's statements against prejudicial "idols" that retains argumentative force even today.

Of the four false idols named in the *Novum Organum*, that of dogmatic ideology will be considered first because of its central importance and metaphoric significance to Bacon. The author observes that

> Lastly there are Idols which have immigrated into men's minds from the various dogmas of philosophies, and also from the wrong laws of demonstration. These I call the Idols of the Theatre; because in my judgment all the received systems are but so many stage-plays, representing worlds of their own creation after an unreal scenic fashion. Nor is it only of the systems now in vogue, or only of the ancient sects and philosophies that I speak; for many more plays of the same kind may be composed and in like artificial manner set forth. Philosophy received or invented is like a Play brought out and acted, creating each its own fictitious and scenic world. (78, xliv)

Readers are in effect invited to insert a deceptive dogmatic ideology of choice—not a difficult task in any age—although Bacon names seventeenth-century neo-Aristotelianism as the supposed "dogma" he especially has in mind. In asserting that each philosophic system theatrically creates its own "fictitious and scenic world," Bacon would appear to have used the word "Play" to include the "inventions" of elaborately-staged court masques of a kind mounted by Chief Architect Inigo Jones. In masque after masque, Jones created hierarchical settings of the moving cosmos designed through their iconography both to delight the eye and, in Jones's view, to teach neoclassical philosophy. But stage illusions were employed; and Bacon in his essay "Of Masques and Triumphs" writes of how he was attracted to two visual deceptions. First, he is delighted by disconcerting perspective alterations involving the motion of scenic devices carrying main masquers, motion that "draws the eye strangely, and makes it with great pleasure to desire to see that it cannot perfectly discern." Equally deceptive and delightful are instantaneous scene changes, which, if

75

accomplished "quietly and without noise, are things of great beauty and pleasure" (20). Bacon's ingenious analogy thus captures some sense of the absorbing aesthetic satisfaction of enclosed dogmatic systems even as it deftly warns of seemingly pleasing irregularities and hidden deceptions.

Rightly skeptical about the overly rigid methodology confining much seventeenth-century Aristotelianism, he urges using aphorisms as a means of encouraging original thought. Bacon contends that

> as young men, when they knit and shape perfectly, doe seldome grow to a further stature: so knowledge, while it is in Aphorismes and obseruations, it is in groweth; but when it once is comprehended in exact Methodes; it may perchance not be further pollished and illustrated in substance (78, lxiii)

The next of Bacon's "idols," actually the first in sequence in the *Novum Organum*, is vaguely referred to as that of the Tribe, which the lord chancellor also haphazardly labels the entire "Race of man." These idols, he maintains, "are founded in Human Nature itself, and in the very tribe or race of man...the human Intellect is like an uneven mirror catching the rays of things, which mingles its own nature with the nature of things, and distorts and corrupts it" (77-78, xlii).

Moving from the collective to the singular, Bacon next assails bias inculcated by specific upbringing and education. "The Phantoms of the Cave," he warns, "are of the individual" and must be eliminated:

> For each man has (beside the generic abberations of human nature) some individual cave or den which breaks and corrupts the light of nature; either by reason of the peculiar and singulare nature of each; or by reason of education and conversation of man with man; or by reason of reading of books, and the authority of

those whom each man studies or admires;...or by reason of differences of impressions as they occur in a mind preoccupied and predisposed, or even and sedate; or the like. (77, xlii)

A third category of bias is said to accrue from business and social activity, and is again associated with "vulgar" popular expression:

There are also phantoms arising as it were from the intercourse and society of men with one another. These we call Phantoms of the Market-Place, on account of the commerce and consort of men. For men associate by means of discourse; but words are imposed at the will of the vulgar: and so a bad and foolish imposition of words besieges the intellect in strange ways. (78, xliii)

So strong are his aphorisms in warning against bias, and in promoting critical and scientific objectivity, that they have left their impact on the practices of scientists and historians into the present century.

In basic ways that today nevertheless still retain argumentative relevance, Bacon with all his limitations was, like René Descartes, one of the great Renaissance visionaries who insisted upon a new and objective empirical-philosophic study of nature that would lead, in contrast to past static, typological, and cyclical historical outlooks, to future progress in knowledge and discovery.

Bacon held in a general, if not fully formulated way, that external reality exists and that it can be empirically understood through sense experience and measurements, and through verifiable experiments "distilling" nature's supposed hidden forms and qualities. He demanded the development of a new empirical language with exacting terms of reference, and he sought the discovery of general empirical axioms from particular, repeatable and so verifiable observations and experiments. Although deficient in conceiving original hypotheses and experiments, Bacon through his powerful, theoretical advocacy of inductive reasoning served as a stimulus to later new philosophers and historicists, such as those of the Royal Society. Early in the last century, philosophic "codifications" of Bacon's flexible aphoristic outlook by Scottish "commonsense" realists became widely accepted as a basis for academic philosophy and historical research in England and the United States.[7] Key passages in his writings remain an early attempted corrective to occasional contentions that conclusions in the sciences and humanities—including historiography—are necessarily biased and unreliable.

A revolution in cosmographical historicism was underway. The account books of Joseph Mede, a teacher of John Milton at Christ's College, Cambridge, show that Mede purchased for students general "popular" works on recent transformations in history and cosmography such as the various editions of *Blunderville's Exercises*. In one such separately published exercise, *The true order and Methode of wryting and reading Histories (1574)*, Blunderville in the manner of Bacon points out the differences between poetic fables and "true" historical accounts. And in the "eight Treatises" of his much longer *M. Blvndevile His Exercises* designed "to be read and learned by all yong Gentlemen *that haue not beene exercised in such Disciplines*" (1622), the author offers instruction in mathematics and geometry as an introduction to lessons on cosmography, astronomy and navigation.[8] The lessons go far to explain Milton's comments on maps, globes, and navigation in his academic exercises and *Of Education,* and the poet's references to latitude and longitude in his *A Brief History of Moscovia* and *Paradise Lost*.

If Bacon was the general theorist of large empirical schemes and insightful aphoristic principles, Abraham Ortelius, a friend of Richard Hakluyt, was the intelligent, practical, indefatigable draftsman-cartographer, a man immersed in the intricate details of historical-geography and yet thoughtful and insightful in his matter-of-fact commentary on contrasting Old and New Worlds. In the enlarged 1606 edition of *Theatrum Orbis Terrarum,* a copy of which was in Christ's College Library in Milton's time, Ortelius insists that the study of history demands a concomitant study of relevant geography and cartography.

> For thou shalt meet with many things in the reading of Histories, (I will not say, almost all) which, except thou haue the knowledge of the countreys and places mentioned in them, cannot onely not bee well conceiued and understood, but also of times they are cleane mistaken and otherwise understood then they ought to bee.[9]

The initial edition, some ten years in preparation, of this immensely popular work was published in 1570, and then in ever-expanding editions in 1573, 1579, 1584, 1595, 1602, 1603, 1606, 1624, and 1631. Along the way in 1577, Ortelius produced a supplementary *Thesavrus Geographicvs,* printed in Antwerp by Christophori Plantini, providing expanded comparative information with related maps on modern and ancient sites and events. "Epitomes" of the ever-developing massive tome were printed in editions of 1595, 1601, 1603, and 1610. It was one of the most successful publications of the late sixteenth and early seventeenth centuries, an indicator that issues raised by the new cosmographical-history were very widely known among educated persons. Non-readers could also have been drawn to and could have learned from the publications. They had only to look at the colored maps and illustrations on nearly every page.

Two metaphors govern the total work and are repeatedly emphasized in the long, learned expositions of history and cartography: that individual human life and collective human history are a drama, and that many of the most important events in this drama are acted out over the centuries by heroes and divines on journeys through what is now visually represented as the iconographic Theatre, rather than the Book, of this World. The general medieval sense of life as a sequential "processional" movement through ordered iconographic realms thus gives way to life, though still a journey, experienced as a series of often irregularly-ordered theatrical encounters, conflicts, and heroic actions in a "free form" world.

Throughout, Renaissance regional and world maps by Mercator, Hondius, Jansson and other moderns, disclosing the seemingly disordered contours of newly discovered distant lands, replace the balanced tripartite T-O projections of the Ancients. Yet Ortelius's cosmographic-historical accounts are still intermeshed with the older typology and traditions. In introducing his major editions, Ortelius explains how the Ancients "diuided into three parts; namely, *Africa, Asia,* and *Europe*" (unpaginated, (1606); and he reproduces, as earlier observed, in a section on "The Geography of Holy Writers," a map of the medieval 42 pilgrimage stations of the Exodus along with other maps showing Jerusalem and the Holy Land (j, ij verso). Delicately designed, hand-colored borders and framing medallions, along with insets in the maps, show biblical episodes including the Fall; the murder of Abel by Cain; Noah and the Flood; and the journey of Abraham.

Yet in the body of his editions, Ortelius, after noting the three continents known to the Ancients, strongly emphasizes that "since that discovery of *America*, the learned of our age have made...a fourth part, and the huge Continent under the South pole, a fifth" (unpaginated). Maps of the explored regions of this new world appear on many pages, maps replete with mainly naturalist but sometimes fabulous renderings, large and small, of ships, giant sea monsters, ideal landscapes, and foreign peoples in native dress. Ortelius, in a gesture of openness to anticipated future discoveries, leaves unexplored regions blank, remarking in particular that "countries which as yet do lie obscured within the frozen Zones and vnder both the Poles, are left for succeeding ages to find out" (vj).

Accompanying "historical" commentary by Ortelius and other reprinted authors sets out a mélange of conventional and conflicting views on the supposed details and locations of biblical and secular events. Where was biblical Ophir, Ortelius wonders; possibly in Peru? Solomon's Navy, he speculates, would then have crossed the great Ocean Sea centuries before Columbus. And where had the Garden of Eden been placed? Was it in Syria, or at the pole in the Antarctic; or as some new philosophers thought, somewhere near the earth's Equinoctial line? In many instances, Ortelius reaches no conclusions and so leaves the answers to specific "historical" questions to later explorers and authors.

Eventually, Ortelius came to believe that, if indeed geography were the *eye of History*, then past events of different eras are best understood, not just in terms of contemporaneous outlooks, but also in the context of the geographical and cultural knowledge of the earlier periods. Accordingly, Ortelius notes that "within the compasse of that part of the world described by the old Cosmographers, all ancient *Historiography*, both *Sacred* and *Prophane*, is comprehended: in these all famous acts of mortall men, which from the beginning of the world euen unto the dates of our fathers, haue been registered" (vj).

He divided the 1606 edition of *Theatrum Orbis Terrarum* into two parts, the first containing recent maps of continents, countries, and regions of the contemporaneous world; and he included comments on peoples, customs, and history. In the second, he used recent Renaissance projections and some imaginative colored illustrations, again along with commentary, to render past events as recorded in classical literature and in literalist biblical tradition. Maps and drawings show the travels and major acts of individual figures by means of dotted lines and occasional small drawings. Included are the journeys, among others, of Jason, Abraham, St. Paul, Ulysses, Aeneas, and the Israelites. In short, he produced a limited but very handsome epitome and visual guide to biblical and classical history and literature.

Ortelius's own brusque, critical comments place past events in supposed "Modern" perspective throughout. On the page opposite the colored map of "Lativm" containing an illustration of "Mt. Circe," for example, Ortelius remarks that, contrary to what "Ancient authorities" have said, Circe can be seen to have resided on a peninsula rather than an island. He then skeptically dismisses central features of the Circe myth. They "speake many things that are not true," Ortelius declares; "Therefore let all other men say what they will, and perswade what they can, they shall neuer make me beleeue...fables" about men being turned into beasts. "It seemeth that the fable arose," he continues, "of the nature and quality of the place" (xxj).

Ortelius had created an early student "epitome" with appended criticism, a precursor of contemporary published study notes. And it was to cosmographers such as Ortelius that the educational reformer John Amos Comenius referred in his *The Great Didactic* (1627-57) when pressing for new types of books. In a foreshadowing of later debatable mass-educational practices, Comenius for better or worse urged the publication of condensations of biblical commentary, classical literature, and history for a wide audience of gentlemen, students, and general readers.

> it is therefore to be hoped that men of learning, philosophers, theologians, and physicians will render the same service to students as has been rendered to those who study geography by geographers. For these latter make maps of the provinces, kingdoms, and divisions of the world, and thus present to the eye huge tracts of sea and land on a small scale, so that they can be taken in at a glance...Why, therefore, should not Cicero, Livy, Plato, Celsus, Augustine, Jerome, etc., be treated in the same way and epitomized? These epitomes should contain the whole author, only somewhat reduced in bulk.[10]

In "epitomizing" classical and biblical materials, Ortelius as a cosmographer had embodied within his work the "battle" between Ancient and Modern outlooks. He had accepted the Ancient voyage accounts in classical and biblical literature in many cases as historically "true" while revealing himself unmistakably on the side of the Moderns. At the beginning of the seventeenth century, his was a remarkable transitional vision of the world and its history.

5

SKEPTICISM AND FAITH

Samuel Purchas, John Donne, and the Composition of *Purchas his pilgrimage*

With the initial publication of *Purchas his pilgrimage* in 1613, Samuel Purchas began a developing experiment in practical historiography that would finally evolve in 1625 into a massive Early Modern attempt at a comprehensive history of world civilizations. In four religiously oriented editions of the history published in 1613, 1614, 1617, and 1626, each one augmented; in a separate skeptical historicist tome: *Pvrchas his pilgrim. Microcosmvs, or, The Historie Of Man of 1619;* and in the huge humanist rendering of global history of 1625 entitled *Haklvytvs posthumus or Pvrchas his pilgrimes,* Purchas subsumed the religious preoccupations of Ralegh, the pilgrimage and travel excerpts of Hakluyt, the metaphysical concerns of John Donne, and many of the scientific, methodological suggestions of Bacon. Purchas had as his aim the production of an objective modernist global history of the transformed Book of God's Works and Creatures.[1] As his history changed and grew to four folios in the special publication of 1625, becoming the longest work in English published up to that time, Purchas defined in his successive volumes, amid fanciful speculations on classical and biblical figures, an explicit empirical "Method" for the writing, organization, and documentation of global history.

When in his 1625 publication *Haklvytvs posthumus or Pvrchas his pilgrimes* Purchas discussed the nature of his work in an address "To the Reader," he asked to be compared to other historians not *"in philosophicall and learned speculation of Reason, but in euident demonstration of Sense, and herein."*[2] Ignoring the aphoristic, speculative techniques of Bacon, he proclaimed a matter-of-fact, practical historicist "Method" that rested on the cumulative testimony of a multitude of presumed eyewitness travelers who, from earliest times to the present, had observed the world and its peoples. Following Bacon, however, in employing the inductive method, Purchas attempted to assemble and compose a global history, theoretically free as far as possible from political influence, using the most reliable possible "facts" and "sources" under an outlined scholarly system of disciplined documentation. The so-called travelers, all considered by Purchas to be "pilgrims in this life," were a motley lot, some of whom had never journeyed anywhere. They included ancient fictional literary heroes, figures from the Bible, medieval pilgrims, and, most significantly, a host of Renaissance explorers, adventurers, cartographers, and authors.

One can well understand why Purchas, even in his massive 1625 publication, was still beset with problems:

> for the Method: I confesse, I could not be therein exact: first because I had such a confused Chaos of printed and written Bookes, which could not easily be ordered: partly because of this Method by way of Voyages often repeates the same Countries and (though I haue often pruned repetitions) yet, sometimes admitted for more full testimonie) the same things, by diuers of our Authors trauelling the same parts, obserued, in which my Method brings in ordinarily the Authours whole Voyage there ("To the Reader," unpaginated).

The mass of materials begins to dictate the work's form:

> First, we have diuided the World in our Method into the *Old* and *New*, alloting to each his owne *Tome*, the first Ten Books to the former, the later to the other. But the Worke growing more voluminous then was expected,

> we are forced to cut each of them asunder in the midst
> ("To the Reader," unpaginated)

In allowing reasoned conceptions to grow from sensuous experience rather than predetermined abstract ideology, Purchas associates himself with workers in trades. He will deliver the "Historie of Nature," he explains, by acquainting the reader with "diversified kinds and natures, or (if that also seeme too ambitious) as Senses by Induction of particulars yeeldeth the premisses to Reasons, Syllogisticall arguing; or if we shall be yet more homely, as Pioners are employed by Engineers, and *Labourers* serue Masons, and Bricklallyers, and these the best Surueryers and Architects" (unpaginated). He announces that he supplies the concrete materials, the factual information on regions and peoples, which later theorists will use in ideologically structuring their works.

> here *Purchas* and his Pilgrimes minister individuall and
> sensible materials (as it were with Stones, Brickes, and
> Mortar) to those vniuersall Speculators for their
> Theoricall structures. ("To the Reader," unpaginated)

However obliquely, Purchas is obviously anxious to suggest that, along with being a laborer, he also is something of a masterbuilder who gives form to materials.

> And well may the Author be ranked with such
> *Labourers* (howsoeuer here a Masterbuilder also) for
> that he hath been forced as much to the Hod, Barrow
> and Trowel, as to contemplatiue suruaying. ("To the
> Reader," unpaginated)

Purchas's work frequently goes unrecognized as an experimental cultural history because of its complexity, length, erratic changes in outlook from edition to edition and, above all, because of contemporary misinterpretations of its title: *Purchas his pilgrimage, or, Relations of the world and the religions observed in all ages and places discouered.* This title, together with its variations in the four religiously-inclined editions, the 1619 skeptical historical meditations, and the 1625 humanist history, suggests either a collection of pilgrimage texts, or a single pilgrimage narrative on comparative religion. Purchas's production is clearly something else. Its early subtitle "the world and the religions observed" anticipates the author's wide swings from edition to edition between empirical "observations" of the world on the one hand, and faith-based "observations" of religions on the other; between a dominant naturalistic exposition of the earth and its history, and forays into global religious history to find a means of cultural evaluation.

Purchas's editions are today often cursorily scanned and classified as simply an enormous collection of travel tracts edited, it is usually pointed out, with less care than Hakluyt's smaller compilations.[4] In *The Historical Revolution: English Historical Writing and Thought 1580-1640*, F. Smith Fussner, overlooking Purchas as a historian, notes only that the author is the "most famous" of early collectors of "travel books, maps, and geographical works."[5] Herschel Baker in *The Race of Time: Three Lectures on Renaissance Historiography* makes no mention of Purchas at all.[6]

Most commentary on Purchas's editions, especially that published by the Hakluyt Society, understandably concentrates upon the importance of the recorded regional "discoveries."[7] Commentators usually cite whenever possible just the expansive, handsomely-illustrated publication of 1625, to the neglect of the four other editions and the 1619 meditations. Yet to appreciate the growth of Purchas as an historian, it is necessary to consider his shifts in approach and subject matter from edition to edition. These vacillations go far toward explaining how he developed his scholarly method.

In the neglected *Pvrchas his pilgrim. Microcosmvs, or, The Historie Of Man* of 1619, the lynchpin to this development, Purchas gives unrestrained if temporary reign to a profound historical skepticism. Here he denigrates human knowledge, right reason, and assumed objectivity, and so confronts many of the ideological bogies of historiography still distressing contemporary theorists. In giving full and at times exaggerated expression in 1619 to precise historicist problems, Purchas, upon overcoming his rational dilemmas, was able later to advance specific possible pragmatic solutions to vexing issues.

In his early years, beginning with his first and second editions of 1613 and 1614, Purchas produced an attempted history of religions, societies, and geography in *Purchas his pilgrimage, or, Relations of the world and the religions observed in all ages and places discouereds...In foure partes.*[8] Under this same title in 1617, he reprinted the material in a *"3d ed., much enl. with additions through the whole worke,"* while continuing to explain in all three editions his new historical method.[9]

A suffused intellectual excitement permeates his opening announcement of 1613, in a Dedication to the archbishop of Canterbury, of "an enterprise never yet (to my knowledge) by any, in any language, attempted." Purchas calls attention to the originality, difficulty, and breadth of his staggeringly large undertaking; and he insists that his "obseruations" will include "all the rarities of the World, and especially of that soule of the world, *Religion*" (unpaginated).

Religious history, Purchas states, will normally take precedence over cosmographical and all other content. "Where I have found plentiful discourse for Religion (my chief aim) I am shorter in other relations;" he writes, "and where I haue had lesse helpes for that discouerie, I insist more on the wonders of Nature *and discoueries by Sea and Land, with other remarkable accidents" ("To the Reader," unpaginated).*

This Anglican clergyman, moreover, openly professes his belief that the Christian religion is superior in spiritual "truth" to other faiths, a theological declaration of a kind common in the seventeenth century but one that today would raise objections or theoretical questions of evaluation and approach. Purchas holds to medieval notions of hierarchy in insisting that, although the "*law of*

Nature" dictates that *"all men"* profess *"some Religion,"* there is *"no admittance of Parity"* among the different religions; there is rather "inequalitie," that is, to the "equitie of subordinate Order." Among the subordinate orders are all those *"passed out-worne rites, or present Irreligious* Religion" found on the three continents of *"Asia, Africa,* and *America"* and described in his history of religious heresy. Roman Catholicism, associated by Purchas with idolatry, is said to be the "Paganisme of *Anti Christian Popierie."* Judaism as a biblical religion is ranked below Purchas's own Anglican faith and subject to criticism (unpaginated).

Purchas's actual treatment of biblical materials and world religions is far more clouded. In structuring this hybrid work, he begins with the traditional biblical epochs of the Creation, the Fall, the Flood, and the Tower of Babel. Then in a sudden alteration of mode and structure that accentuates his mixed commitments, Purchas includes an empirical geographical exposition of the entire world as then "discovered." The form of the work, now focused on regions by way of voyages, gradually evolves from rich Renaissance materials. Interwoven with a naturalistic account of geography is a naturalistic account of major world religions: Egyptian, Near Eastern and classical pagan, together with Hindu, Moslem, and far eastern. Surprisingly, a formal history of Christianity is missing. The world for Purchas would appear to have a heretical soul. The Christian convictions of the author, however forcefully avowed, are generally sublimated to his desire to present this heretical world and its inhabitants.

After the utilization of a scriptural epochal structure in book 1, the second book takes the different form of a narrative and travel history of the Hebrews. The third book relates, in the narrative and travel form of all the later books, the history of the ancient peoples and religions of Asia Minor; while the fourth book examines the relatively "modern" societies and religions of Asia proper including China. The last four books, which incorporate stirring reports of circumnavigations of the world, are concerned respectively with the peoples, religions, and lands of the East Indies, Egypt, and North Africa, Africa proper, and finally

America. The work ends with an elaborate appended "Chronologie" listing the supposed key events of world history. Purchas follows these book divisions, despite certain enlargements in content, in his first three editions.

Sometime before 1619 Purchas suffered a deep personal blow. The "piercing Arrow" of his brother-in-law's death, followed within a few weeks by the death of his brother, unleashed an outpouring of religious fervor. Inexpertly employing bizarre conceits very much like those brilliantly used by John Donne and other metaphysical poets, Purchas pens a sequence of prose meditations on man's vanity and need for faith. He remarks in anguish, with a slight flash of attempted wit, that he was overcome by the reality of death, and nearly "executed by Executorship," having been left with the "cares of another Family," along with his brother's "manifold debts" and "foure little Fatherless and Motherlesse Orphans."[10]

In publishing his meditations under the familiar and confusing main title *Purchas his Pilgrim. Microcosmus, of The Historie of Man,* Purchas, even as he extols the light of Christian faith, caustically denounces the falseness of all written histories. In traditional meditative fashion, he broods upon the "degeneration" of the "little World" of man, a "microcosm" destined to die but subject to restoration only through Christ. To provide simply a "knowledge" of Christ and Christianity, Purchas declares, becomes the "propounded taske in this Worke, to which I haue allotted this Text, a small Garden Plot, but yeelding plentie of rarities" (9-10).

Writing of "Man a little World," and "the correspondence betwixt him and the greater World" (17), Purchas, stressing conventional themes of decay and regeneration, advances in labored, pedestrian fashion conceits of a kind ingeniously individualized in the "metaphysical" poetry of John Donne, George Herbert, Henry Vaughn, and, with lesser accomplishment, Phineas Fletcher. "Is not the Haire as Grasse?" Purchas asks, "the Flesh as Earth? the Bones as Mineralls? the Veins as Rivers? the Liuer, a Sea?" (31).

No monarch of wit, Purchas does not know when to stop: "Are not the Lungs and Heart correspondent to the ayrie and fierie Elements? the Braines, to the Clouds and Meteors...? the eyes to starres. or those two Eyes of Heauen, the *greater* Lights? (31), and the circular forme of the Head, to the globositie of the Heauens?" (31).

Purchas and Donne, who both became Anglican priests in a period of violent religious schisms, shared notable similarities in their literary religious themes if not in their literary abilities. Donne in his prose work *Pseudo Martyr* (1610) claimed to have studied "the whole body of divinity" separating the major Christian faiths, and both authors were tormented by issues of heresy.[10] Just as Purchas in his three editions of *Purchas his Pilgrim* traced the heretical "soule of the worlde" through the ages, so John Donne as a poet, in *Metempsychosis or Progresse of the Soule* of 1601, writes of the soul of heresy on earth as it moves from the Garden of Eden through time into persons of his own age. "I launch at paradise," he notes in his edged satire, "and I saile towards home."[11] According to Ben Jonson in his *Conversations with Drummond*, Donne "sought the soule of that Aple which Eva pulled and thereafter... his generall purpose was to have brought in all the bodies of the Hereticks from ye soule of Cain, & at last left it in the bodie of Calvin."[12] Donne's Stanza VII, however, mentions "the great soule which here amongst us now/ Doth dwell," a possible allusion to the soul of Queen Elizabeth whom Donne, before his conversion to Anglicanism, considered a heretic.

In *The Second Anniversary: Or the Progresse of the Soule* (1612), Donne depicts the world as a dead body with its soul removed; and introduces a narrator who flies up to discover the "soule of the worlde" in heaven.[13] By contrast, Purchas, even during his skeptical ruminations, remained fascinated with the "soul" as well as the "body" of the earthly world. In "The Historie of Man" of 1619 he reflected at length and for the first time on what he conceived to be the world's "true" soul, the Christian religion, even as he raised disquieting rational questions about all world histories, questions that he later sought to answer with his "Method."

Few skeptical attacks upon historical writing and historians could be more harshly dismissive. Stung by tormenting doubts and frustrations, Purchas declared "euery Historian" to be "*a Lyar*" (588). He bitterly complains of the deceit, bias, fictional narratives, political influence, secrecy, and faulty documentation that, he contends, compromise even the best histories. With painful directness, he identifies and enumerates many of the undeniable human failures that undermine the historicist discipline.

"But how many true Histories?" Purchas asks in his 1619 edition; and in answering he unleashes a polemic against renowned classical historians and writers, Ancients whose works were read by students in Latin grammar schools and the universities. He denounces what today would be called the "narratology" used by many historians.[14] Confronting an inexhaustible array of facts, these historians, he argues, necessarily shape their narratives through selective factual exclusion and inclusion and in many instances unintentionally "devise" or "fabricate" their historical accounts. "*Xenophon* the Poet deuiseth," Purchas insists, instead of accurately recording events. He claims that Herodotus, whose travel writings are a forerunner of Purchas's own work, is rightly "called a Father of Lies" because this famed author accepts and repeats false stories told to him (586).

Purchas also denounces authors whose style of writing or speech embellish and so distort orations and events. "*Liuie,* and others," Purchas complains, "lend you long Orations, to shew, not what was said, but what They can say" (586). The use of rhetorical devices is said to be responsible for "all sorts of Juggling and Lying; it makes Men see with others Eyes, with strange Glaes, which make things seeme bigger, or less, or double, or not at all; it is Master of Mens furious Passions" (537).

And if Purchas is dismayed by narrative "lies," fantastical reactions, and stylistic distortions, he is upset too by the manipulation of historians and their writings by outside authorities. Taking special note of political influence, Purchas offers a savage critique of how state officials control and corrupt the historian and, more ominously, sometimes even threaten him physically. In Purchas's view, any historian seeking to write on state matters is placed in a hopeless position. "If a great Prince or State entertaine an Historian," Purchas observes, "he must plead (not tell) his Masters Affaires; must please and pleasure his Friends; if they neglect him, how can he know Occurrences? How will he tell a boot-lesse Truth? Boot-lesse? nay, dangerous" (587).

Purchas was also deeply concerned about the reliability of sources. One of his major contributions to historical writing consists in his self-conscious demand, despite inaccuracies in his own volumes, for more and better documentation. In his meditations he decries the ruination of history because needed sources are cut off by pernicious, over-protective state secrecy. Almost all historical writing on politics is poor, he argues, because past state records are difficult or impossible to obtain, and contemporaneous state records are secured out of reach. "Secrets" of present times, he notes, are the most rigidly held of all; and therefore the writing of contemporaneous state events is always problematical. "All Historians" he notes, "write either of things in their owne Times, which will not suffer the Secrets (forsooth) of State, that is, the truth of things, to be related; of the former, and therefore from partiall Relations, and vncertaine." He maintains that certain past powerful states banned historians from their domains to prevent the reporting of conquests: "Hence some Nations (as the Turkes, which like *Pharaohs* leane Kine, have deuoured the Fat, the best parts of the World) will haue no Historians" (586-87).

Throughout his meditations, Purchas, while committed to religious belief, strenuously attacks all highly abstract formal philosophies dependent upon reason alone. At the same time he constantly emphasizes the importance of matter-of-fact practical knowledge gleaned from "nature" and from immediate experience. He polemically dismisses the "diversified Sects" of "Philosophers" whose theoretical systems, he contends, are nothing but "Vanities" (543). He notes, for example, that

Socrates (the Oracles Wiseman) knew nothing but this one thing, that hee knew nothing. *Anaxachus* knew not so much: the Pyrrhonists Learning, no Honestie, or Vice in manners; no true being in substances: how else could he haue met with such Phantasticalities? The Academikes weary themselues in Mazes and continuall Labyrinths, being like bad Lawyers, fed on both sides." (544-45)

In a diatribe that could well elicit a measure of contemporary sympathy, this physico-theologist is prescient in at least naming what will become major fields of disputed contemporary "theorizing." He angrily insists that the distorting abstract "Speculations" of philosophers "peruert" the study of both the natural world and of "Politikes" and "Oeconomikes" [Economics] by proposing false conjectures. And in a passage that points to his own future pragmatic but also religious approach, he decries the conflicted philosophical legacy of Ancients and Moderns: "Thus is *Nature* abused to Atheisme" by misleading theories, "although euery Creature be a Period, and the whole Whole World a Booke, to teach the invisible things of God, in his visible Works" (584).

The 1619 meditations were indeed purgative, allowing Purchas emotionally to vent his deepest rational doubts while directly and passionately affirming his religious faith. Having produced his extravagantly devised meditations on Christianity, he was able to come to terms with his theoretical uncertainties and, returning to his work as an historian, to give a new humanist dimension to his study of global history. He was driven by the view that the writing of histories in the most objective and matter-of-fact manner possible outweighed the theoretical reasons for writing no histories at all.

6

TOWARD A HUMANIST GLOBAL HISTORICISM

Purchas and World Historical Discourse

In bringing out his 1625 history, Purchas makes the great change. He removes "*Religions Observed in All Ages*" from his title and no longer includes a formal history of religion. He dedicates the work to the Prince of Wales rather than to a churchman; and his new, greatly-expanded global history appears, as earlier noted, in four massive folios. For the first time Purchas acknowledges his debt to Richard Hakluyt and incorporates his predecessor's source materials under the full title *Hakluytus Posthumus or Purchas His Pilgrimes Contayning a History of the World in Sea Voyages and Lande Travells by Englishmen and others.*[1]

Purchas in "To the Reader" explains that "*Wisedome to saluation* the proper subiect of Theologie" is "not the peculiar argument of this Worke"; but he adds that theological wisdom "by Annotations, and in some parts professedly by speciall Discourses, insinuateth...the Historie." Purchas now makes it very clear that "*Naturall things* are the more proper Object, namely the ordinary Workes of God in the Creatures, preseruing and disposing by Prouidence that which his Goodnesse and Power had created, and dispersed in the diuers parts of the World, as so many members of this great Bodie" ("To the Reader," unpaginated).

While in the 1613, 1614, and 1617 editions this author tried to give religious meaning to cultural history with opening interpretive accounts of scriptural epochs, the early assertion of biblical values failed to "carry over" effectively when applied to later naturalistic tracts. The biblical epochs of Creation, Eden, the Flood, and the Tower of Babel did not fit well with Renaissance voyage narratives. And so in the 1625 publication, instead of using the "truths" of scripture in traditional fashion to shape secular factual history, Purchas employed the patterned narratives of Renaissance voyages to shape his rendering of biblical events.

Largely abandoning the epochal approach, Purchas opened book one with the Old Testament account of a voyage to Ophir ordered by King Solomon and carried out by Israelites, descendants by implication of those Israelites who had made the presumed "exploratory" journey of the Exodus. The Ophir voyage, an event barely mentioned in the Old Testament, was transformed by Purchas into an archetypal trip of discovery demonstrating "the lawfulnesse of Nauigation to remote Regions" (4). Indeed, it became for Purchas as for Columbus an *exempla* of world exploration.[2] Columbus had maintained that the Bible gave moral sanction for such enterprises. Purchas held to the same opinion but thought "*Ophir*...to be all from *Ganges* to *Menantan* to *Samatra*, on both sides; and most properly the large Kingdome of *Pegu*, from whence it is likely in process of time, the Southerly parts, euen to *Sumatra* inclusively was peopled before *Solomon's* time" (32).

The Ophir voyage and its supposed allegorical meaning, serve Purchas "as a kind of Preface or preamble to the many Histories ensuing" (4). Accepting the voyage in its literal sense as historically "true," Purchas advances a tentative reading of just its tropological or spiritual sense: namely, that "*Solomon* seemes to signifie Christ, his Navy the Church long before liuely represented in that first of Ships, the Arc of Noah" (5).

A hierarchy of heroic "types" of the explorer is then introduced. The journeys of Ulysses and Aeneas, though coming out of sequential order in time, are loosely seen as types of the Old Testament Exodus and Solomon's voyage. Solomon's "navigation" to Ophir in turn is seen to prefigure the New Testament journeys of

Christ and the Apostles radiating outward from the "center" Jerusalem to the lands of the earth.

Like Abraham Ortelius who in later editions of *Theatrum Orbis Terrarum* included maps and commentary on the wanderings of biblical and epic pagan figures as a background to Renaissance voyages, Purchas uses such supposed classical and biblical journey literature for the same purpose. In Purchas's and Ortelius's interpretations, biblical texts are clearly being adjusted to conform to the narrative patterns of Renaissance voyages, not the other way around. The epochal divisions of scriptural history are being undermined, and the Bible is being used to justify world exploration.

In volume 1, after an opening book on the "Voyages and Peregrinations made by *ancient* Kings, *Patriarkes*, Apostles, *Philosophers*, and others" (1), the work takes on intensity of feeling in book 2 on "*Circum-Nauigations* of the *Globe*" by "Fernandys Magalianes," "Francis Drake," "Thomas Candish," "Oliver Noort," "George Spilbergen," and others (33-87). Voyages to the East Indies, Indian and Japan, and Africa are traced in books 3 through 7 of volume 1, with book 8 of volume 1 suddenly shifting to journeys to Jerusalem by crusaders and pilgrims. Book 9 concentrates on travels in Arabia, Egypt, and Persia.

In this enormous and discursive work, volume 2 in 10 books covers Africa, North Africa, and Cairo, Turkey, and India, with book 8 again devoted to Jerusalem pilgrimage texts and crusading accounts. Volume 3 in 6 books centers on Russia, China, Asia, Greenland, sections of North America, Mexico, and Peru; and volume 4 in 5 books, South America, Virginia, and English plantations in the New World.

Breaking with Hakluyt's English nationalistic proclivities, Purchas's eyewitness "Pilgrimes" are by no means all English nationals. They are travelers from many lands and nationalities, but necessarily drawn by Purchas from available English and European sources. The selections are cited, despite occasional errors, with attempted scrupulousness as to sources, and in some cases "scored" by Purchas on their reliability.

Striking is the fact that Purchas, taking exception to single-author historical narration, self-consciously stresses the Modernist notion of "discourse" in using the statements of a multitude of apparently authoritative witnesses. The "discourses" are identified as being from varying points of view with no single method or "art" or philosophy imposed on what is said.

Above all, Purchas defines the work as humanistic: "Things humane, are such as Men are, or have, or have done or suffered in the world." Thus the work covers, or more often simply touches upon, the range of human activities, past and present, from nationalism and politics, through customs and religions, through economics and languages, and including the arts.

> Here therefore the various Nations, Persons, Shapes, Colours, Habits, Rites, Religions, Complexions, Conditions, Politike and Economike Customes, Languages, Letters, Arts, Merchandises, Wares, and other remarkable Varieties of Men and humane Affaires are by Eye-witnesses related more amply and certainly than any Collector ever hath done, or perhaps without these helpes could doe. (unpaginated)

Purchas in fact remarks that he is an "Ethnic" historian. "Athens," he claimed in his earlier 1619 publication, is "the mother" of disputations where many persons from many lands professed conflicting opinions. Because Purchas presents in his work his own and so many other voices, he declares, "I also haue beene an *Athenian* with these *Athenians*, one delighting *to tell* the others to *heare some new thing.*"[3] In the 1625 work, he states that he intends to reveal "with others Eyes, the Rarities of Nature" and the "extraordinary Wonders, which Gods Prouidence hath therein effected" ("To the Reader," unpaginated).

Purchas is in effect inventing a precursor to eighteenth-century encyclopedias, with eyewitness reports of the past and present serving as a "discourse" respectively on world geographic regions, societies, and cultures. The finished product is a huge, discursive work containing accounts, which often do not directly engage one another, but do nevertheless present in their diffusiveness a new Renaissance vision of the earth and its inhabitants. How then does Purchas achieve a degree of objectivity that overcomes or diminishes the prejudices and failings of past histories?

The sheer numbers of eyewitness observers, he rightly contends, afford greater accuracy and authority:

> it exceedeth not modesty to speake thus much in behalfe of this cloud of witnesses which we bring, testifying what they haue seen, that these exceed the former in certainty (relating what they have seene) and in fulness (by aduantage of New World found in, and besides the World knowne to them) no lesse then they are exceeded in Antiquitie and learning. (I, i, 2)

He tries to counteract the distorting influence of rhetorical and stylistic devices by quoting mainly factual records and relying on excerpts by many writers. Sensitive to Bacon's concerns about linguistic meaning and the relation of words to things, Purchas himself adopts, except in his meditations of 1619, the clear, precise, factual style of the new philosophers.

He strives to eliminate in so far as feasible nationalistic bias by quoting, unlike Richard Hakluyt, voyagers from many lands, thus introducing a "world of travellers." Purchas's choices in selecting travelers, ancient and modern, seem actually to be governed in general, not by the nationality or religion or position, but by the voyager's credibility as an immediate eyewitness to the events or places being examined.

If he has no practical plan to overcome state secrecy involving the hiding away, suppression, or selective "leaking" of official documents, he at least offers and follows a procedure for the meticulous citing and evaluating of those sources that do become available, so that readers can for themselves judge historical reliability.

Annoyed with what he calls the "faltie...misnaming...of authors," and the "Marginal miss-placing" of their names in books, Purchas places a "Catalogue of the Authors" at the beginning of his four editions except the 1625 publication. This list of primary writers, together with a basic "apparatus" for discerning fragmentary and inauthentic information, serves as a kind of early bibliography. In the first edition of 1613, the list in three columns occupies six pages. The list swells to eight pages in the second edition of 1614; to nine, in the third edition of 1617; and holds at nine in the large-page fourth edition of 1626.

Purchas adds special notations in documenting his sources. The letter "F" alongside an author's name in the 1613 edition "signifies that we haue but a fragment of the said Author: and Ps. brands him for a counterfeit." Authors whose works are "borrowed at the second hand," he explains, will not be cited at all; and "Authors of Maps, Translators, and Translations"—as distinguished from writers—are duly listed.[4]

Purchas, moreover, included an elaborate subject index, in three columns, in each volume of the 1613 first edition, an index that was retained and greatly expanded, first, in the 1625 publication, and then again in the 1626 fourth edition. For in publication after publication, Purchas step-by-step increased the scope of his massive collection from some seven hundred entries in the first edition to about one thousand four hundred in his last two publications.

The unpredictable Purchas in his fourth edition of 1626 again goes against expectations. Not content simply to continue augmenting his history, he felt a need to restore "soule," that is, a stronger religious evaluative dimension. Focusing again as in 1613 through 1617 on world religions along with regional societies and geography, he once more called the work *Purchas his Pilgrimage,*

Or Relations Of the World And Religions Observed In All Ages And places discouered, from the Creation unto this Present (1626).[5] Purchas obviously still had reservations about presenting events in a generally "flat, clinical" way, as he had done in much of his previous 1625 work. He accordingly opened his 1625 publication using an epochal rather then "biblical voyage" form, writing again of the Creation, Fall, Flood, and Tower of Babel before moving on to world religions and travels. But it is noteworthy that he left the humanist slant of his major 1625 publication intact, and he did not label it an "edition." His subsequent 1626 "fourth edition," although sometimes improperly bound as a segment of the 1625 work, was rather in form and content a clear continuation of the first three editions of 1613, 1614, and 1617. As an historicist Purchas had it both ways, leaning toward an essentially humanist and naturalist approach in his handsome 1625 folios, and then leaning toward a religious approach in his four interrelated editions. Yet even in 1626 in the last year of his life, Purchas responded enthusiastically to new global discoveries. His 1626 edition included three new books of eyewitness reports on Ethiopia and African islands; on parts of North America; and on Guiana, Peru, and Chile; together with separate printed compendiums by Sir Ierome Horsey on Northwestern voyages, and by George Elmacin on early Moslem history.

In a general way, Purchas's vacillating approach to universal history is somewhat similar to that of twentieth-century historian Arnold Toynbee in its stress upon religious values, but Toynbee establishes and maintains a single authorial viewpoint. In his twelve-volume *Study of History*, Toynbee at first applies his own axiomatic formulae and functional stipulations governing cultural, political, and social achievement to an examination of the cyclical patterns of birth, maturity, and dissolution of some seventeen major and four presumably lesser civilizations.[6] In later stages of his work, Toynbee grows restive about the spiritual depth and significance of his own criteria and, in his last six volumes, introduces evaluations based on qualitative principles embodied in so-called higher traditional religions. These religions, according to Toynbee, foster the spiritual unification of all humankind and are therefore part of a loftier species of society, one standing in contrast to primitive societies. Where Purchas finds a single higher religion in Christian beliefs and practices, Toynbee finds unifying spiritual values in the traditional, higher world-spanning religions identified in his study as Mahayana Buddhism, Christianity, Islam, and Hinduism, although in later years he grew critical of what he called the "sectarian" nature of Hinduism. For Toynbee the problem of the future is whether the higher religions will in time sufficiently unite humankind in brotherhood and love; or whether their antagonisms will result in social fragmentation. The traditional religions would then, he argues, be superseded by a new world religion probably arising from any one or more of about a dozen other faiths.

Purchas also saw religious values as a basis of cultural evaluation, but his determination to be empirically objective worked against his religious concerns. With such a great number of "discourses" and reports as his sources, it was perhaps inevitable that this physico-theologian became more of a seventeenth-century historical "leveler" than an evaluative cultural historian. His voice became one among a multitude of voices. There were dimensions of experience, outlook, and factual information captured in Purchas's myriad published materials that proved a check against historical oversimplification. Purchas, for example, printed nuanced eyewitness accounts both of uninhabited regions and of colonized areas; and he is notable for publishing a tract by Las Casas, though he takes exception to Las Casas's denunciations of the Spanish for their cruel treatment of New World natives.[7] Readers were in any case placed in a position to make relatively informed evaluations of events independent of any single point of view.

The skeptical attitude of Purchas toward deductive logic and grand ideological philosophies—systems comparable to the "Idols of the Theatre" denounced by Bacon—prevented him from proposing any abstract philosophy of history such as those later advanced by Comte, Hegel, and the older Marx, systems positing the presumed known operations and "ends" of history. Dedicated as he was to inductive logic and factual observation, Purchas instead outlined and put into practice a very different historicist program. Although he continued to place his faith in biblical prophecy, he codified an early practical historicist system of empirical naturalism.

Purchas called for multiple reports, reliance on concrete data, the constant publication of accumulating evidence, inductive analysis, open diversified discourse, the citation of all sources, annotations on content and source reliability, freedom from outside political or other pressures, and the widest possible unimpaired access to information. The door had opened upon the modern. Only in the publications of Purchas, ranging from pilgrimage tracts to accounts of the circumnavigation of the earth, and nowhere else in Renaissance historical publication is there a fuller revelation of the dislocating wrench from the medieval to the Early Modern.

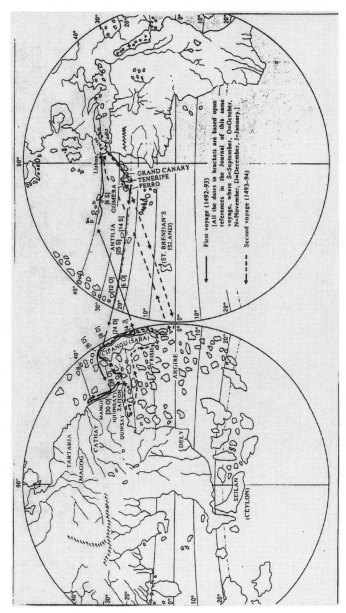

Fig. 19. Estimated route of Columbus's first two voyages west to the "end of the East" in Asia. Reconstruction by Ravenstein using the Behain globe.

Fig. 20. Pilgrimage motifs with those of global discovery on frontispiece of Purchas's *Hakluytus Posthumus* (1625). Top center: Israelite pilgrims to New Jerusalem; Elizabeth I (right) and James I (left). Circular icons depict supposed pilgrims, voyagers, and monarchs, including Noah, Abraham, Solomon, British King Edward the Navigator. Courtesy of the Henry E. Huntington Library.

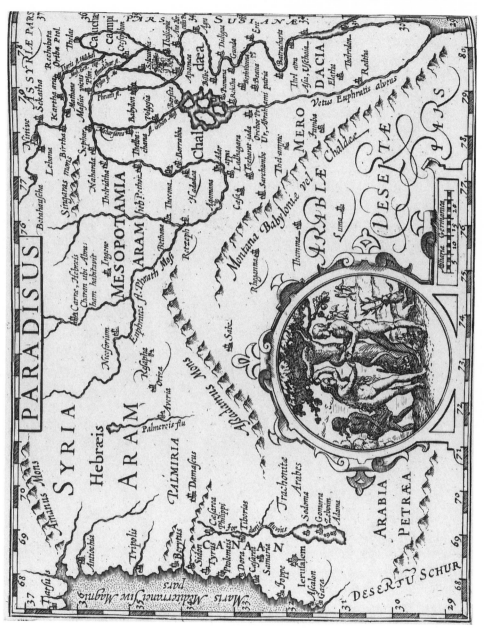

Fig. 21. Earthly Paradise on map by Mercator in *Purchas* (1625).
Courtesy of the Henry E. Huntington Library.

Fig. 22. Hondius's map of the "articke pole" depicting an imaginary sea and a land mass ("California"). From Purchas's *Hakluytus Posthumus* (1625). Courtesy of the Henry E. Huntington Library.

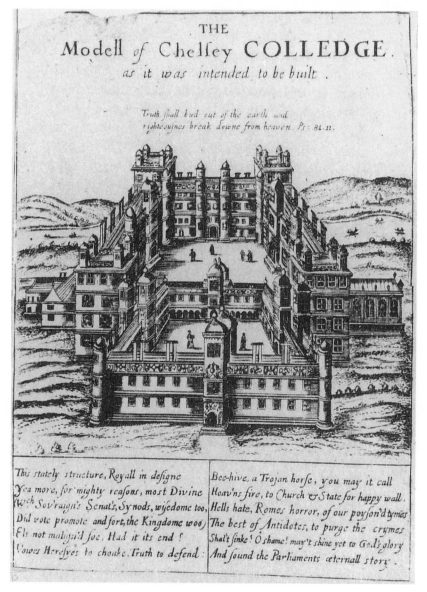

THE
Modell *of* Chelfey COLLEDGE.
as it was intended to be built.

*Truth fhall bud out of the earth and
righteoufnes break downe from heaven : Pf: 81.11.*

This ftately ftructure, Royall in defigne	Bee-hive, a Trojan horfe, you may it call
Yea more, for mighty reafons, most Divine	Heav'ns fire, to Church & State for happy wall.
Wch Sov'raign's Senat's, Synods, wifedome too,	Hells hate, Romes horror, of our poyfon'd tymes
Did vote promote and fort, the Kingdome woo,	The best of Antidotes, to purge the crymes
Els not malign'd foe, Had it its end?	Shal't finke! O fhame! may't fhine yet to God's glory
Vowes Herefyes to choake. Truth to defend :	And found the Parliaments æternall story.

Fig. 23. View of London's Chelsea College, earlier known as King's College, where Purchas wrote major parts of *Purchas His Pilgrimes*. Frontispiece of John Darley's *Glory of Chelsea College Revived* (1662). Courtesy of the British Library.

Fig. 24. Map of Europe, Africa, and Asia showing the five traditional climatic zones, with two zones near the equator long thought too warm to be habitable, published by Ortelius in 1590. Courtesy of the New York Public Library.

Fig. 25. The Angel Uriel in Milton's *Paradise Lost* watches Satan journeying from the sun to Eden. Engraving by Bromley after painting by Fuseli. Courtesy of the Henry E. Huntington Library.

Fig. 26. Frontispiece for Thomas Fuller's *Historie of the Holy War* (1636), a work that denounces crusades and Moslem jihads while confirming the traditional relationship of the Temple of the Holy Sepulcher and the European cathedral. Courtesy of the Henry E. Huntington Library.

Fig. 27. Late Greek lithograph (ca. 1778) after an early Icon of Mt. Sinai, showing the monastery and the mountain "ring" of holy stations. Photograph: George W. Allen in Heinz Skroucha's *Sinai*. Courtesy of Oxford University Press.

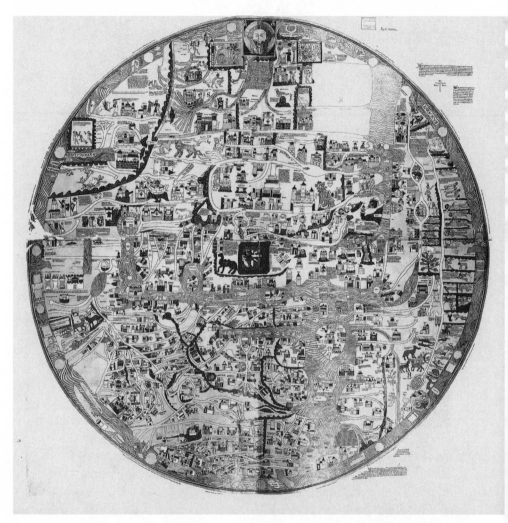

Fig. 28. Iconographic *Ebstorf mappaemundi* (ca. 1235-84) believed to have been produced to accompany Otia Imperiala (ca. 1211) by British-born Gervaise of Tilsbury. Courtesy of the New York Public Library.

7

EMPIRICAL AND PROPHETIC VISIONS

Milton and the Strands of Renaissance Historiography

In a pointed revision of the commonplace view that the deepest intellectual and emotional commitment of John Milton was to poetry, J. Milton French, considering life records of Milton and particularly his writings as a historian, arrived at a surprising conclusion, namely, that "Milton's mind...was essentially critical rather than creative." French claimed that Milton, famed as a religious poet, "was by sympathy a rationalist, a scientist, a thinker." "Intellectual problems" French continued, "offered a challenge to his mind which he could not escape." "The world," French emphatically declared, "was much with Milton."[1]

Such a claim, while compelling given the range of Milton's work, might at first seem extreme. Yet French rightly notes that "in the long years from thirty-two to fifty-two, the productive years of a poet's prime," Milton produced only a small smattering of poetry that "could have been written—and perhaps was—in about a week of running time" (476). "I doubt whether he really groaned too heavily," French observes, "under the burden of twenty years of prose servitude. If he had, he could have escaped from it—if his mind had been willing to let him!" (p. 477). Instead, as French notes, Milton penned a massive body of prose writings including an art of logic, religious, and political commentary and two distinctly different kinds of historical works: the chronicle *A History of Britain* and the experimental *A Brief History of*

Moscovia, an epitome of materials scattered in some 400 out of the approximately 5,000 pages of the 1625 edition of *Purchas his Pilgrimes*.

French thus incisively observes that Milton, following the incursion of his blindness,

> was thrown back on himself and his imagination for intellectual food. The powers of imagination were therefore released, the severe curb of his mind was loosened, and the great poems ensued. The critical and scientific tendency still remained much in evidence; and everyone knows that one stumbling-block for many readers of the poems is the aggressiveness of their theological and philosophical content. But the imaginative element had forged ahead; the simple, sensuous, and passionate had freer rein; the poet was more unhampered (476)

It was fourteen years after the restoration of the English monarchy that Milton, in the year of his death in 1674, published the twelve-book version of his heroic epic *Paradise Lost,* a work composed in the highest style of a passing Renaissance culture. Whatever Milton's other talents, his extraordinary poetic powers, for which he has been rightly most famed, had come to full blossom. *Paradise Lost* as finally completed is a twelve-book biblical epic containing classical epic devices, such as those in Virgil's twelve-book *Aeneid* and later European epics, including invocations; councils of immortals; divine and demonic interventions with humans; scenes in the netherworld; Olympian games; marvelous journeys; battles and martial maneuvers; narrations of past events; and visions and prophecies of the future. While giving his poem classical epic form and conventions, Milton adopted a biblical argument "unattempted yet in Prose or Rhime" (1.16) on the Fall of humankind and the ensuing universal history of the human race. He elucidated this argument, with great imaginative originality and power, by subsuming in his work two competing, blurred, and sometimes literally "opposed" currents of revisionist Renaissance historiography: the empirical reporting of events, and the prophetic revelation of universal historical design.[2]

The two strands are so fully and ingeniously realized in Milton's epic that they serve, although in a poem, as a uniquely informed example of those key Renaissance historicist tendencies. In later centuries, as secular historicist outlooks supplanted religious views, other historicist empirical and structural strands appeared, transformed in meaning but still reflective of Renaissance models, in the "scientific" or philosophic historicism of authors as disparate as George Frederick Hegel, Karl Marx, and Frederick Engels. In Milton's work prophetic and empirical structures, along with the patterned arrangement of cosmological references, require examination as general indicators of much in historicism that was to follow.

Because Milton's debts to the new empirical cosmological-historicism have yet to be fully explored, Milton's imaginative use of "mixed history" and "science" in his epic will first be examined. Then the poet's traditional and invented prophetic historicist structures will be taken up in the next chapter.

A number of recent critics of the later works, driven by contemporary interests, have concentrated on trying to discern Milton's mature particular positions in *Paradise Lost* on Restoration power politics, colonialism, and imperialism. Satan, for example, has been seen as reflecting in the same passages a supposedly tyrannical King Charles I, or an aging and allegedly usurping Oliver Cromwell, or possibly both figures.[3] The demonic debate in Hell has in turn been read as a parody, not only of the Roman Catholic hierarchy meeting in "secret conclave" in the Vatican, but also of the rancorous and confused Commonwealth parliament.[4] And in treating the epic as "politicized" by an assumed "genre" of cultural imperialism, the First Parents have been seen as colonialist New World "planters" in North America whose evil choices corrupt humankind. On the other hand, Adam and Eve before the Fall have been found analogous to virtuous bourgeois in a Commonwealth Eden.[5] In still another political reading, it has been maintained, without citing medieval world views against which Milton was reacting, that the poet as an English writer favors the "possession of the globe in the name of an elect nation" (55).

Such particularized political readings of Milton's late open symbolism, however suggestive, usually become by their very specificity problematic; and they are ultimately subsumed within wider meanings still in need of clarification. For in his later years Milton, deeply disappointed by the dissolution of the Protectorate, had turned from writing tracts on conflicted political issues to composing poetry on encompassing humanist and religious historicist themes.[6] The world indeed remained very much with Milton, but it was the world of universal human history seen in the light of a grand divine design.

In his middle years under the Commonwealth, as is well known, Milton had penned truculent pamphlets on the reformation of church and state in England. But the poet during this period and later refused to write directly on the civil war itself. To Royal Society President Henry Oldenburg's query of 12 December 1669 about whether or not he was "preparing something for a complete history of the English revolution," Milton acerbically replied on 20 Dec. 1659 that he had "no intention of composing a history of our troubles, as you appear to urge me to do, for it is better to pass them over in silence than to proclaim them abroad; and we do not so much need someone to write a history of them as someone able successfully to settle these troubles themselves."[7]

With the reestablishment of the monarchy, Milton was placed under house arrest, his practical political hopes for a Commonwealth government shattered. After being briefly imprisoned in the Tower where he was in danger of execution for treason, Milton upon his release more and more envisioned the kingdom of the blessed as largely an inner or otherworldly state, one gained through individual right action, obedience to divine law, and spiritual renewal through the Redemption. "Henceforth I learn that to obey is best," Adam remarks near the end of book 12 in *Paradise Lost*, "And love with fear the only God, to walk/ As in his presence, ever to observe/ His providence, and on him sole to depend."[8] The divine Providence that Ralegh had seen acting upon monarchs and nations is here largely transferred to the individual and to the spiritual quest, in the words of the angel Michael in Milton's epic, for "a paradise within" (12.586). Still, Milton, though blind beginning in the 1650s, was no quietest: "add/ Deeds, to thy knowledge answerable" (12.581-82), the angel Michael says in instructing Adam; and in the poet's late tragedy *Samson Agonistes*, the lone, blind Samson, with spiritual and physical strength restored, performs the deed that destroys the temple of Dagon and brings death to the pagan enemies of the Israelites.

The aging John Milton infused his final poetic works—the twelve-book epic *Paradise Lost*, the four-book brief epic *Paradise Regained*, and the tragedy *Samson Agonistes*—with the fullness of his lifetime experience and knowledge; and however useful the critical probing of Milton's possible last views on practical power politics, the poet's range of historical vision was far wider. In *Paradise Lost*, his most comprehensive empirical and imaginative statement on universal history, he joined the new empirical cosmographical history with prophetic biblical epochs in new generic ways.

Milton's topos, though centered on the Fall, embraces nothing less than the past spiritual history and the present and future spiritual destiny of the human race as it is acted out in a vast and only partially understood geographic world and in a confusing cosmos of immense and possibly "infinite" magnitude. The epic thus takes up what for Milton and his readers was a paramount spiritual-theological question: the degree to which all the peoples of the world, peoples known to Milton through his writing of two histories and his readings in Renaissance historiography, would be subject to the evil, manipulative, imperialist spiritual and physical control of Satan and his unholy family members Sin and Death, or would attain ever-increasing spiritual freedom and virtue through individual rational choices and through the transcendent Justice and Mercy of God the Father and Son. For in Milton's epic individuals are indeed free to make their own rational decisions. Accordingly, the power that Satan and the devils desire, in seeking revenge against God, is control by deception and fraud over the right reason of the First Parents and their descendants.

Adam and Eve and their progeny are not pressed by immortal figures to establish imperialist rule over other peoples, lands, and political establishments in the name of England. Both before and after the Fall, the First Parents—who in the epic are the only human beings in existence—and then their future descendants are designated simply as the rulers and possessors of lesser beings in the hierarchy of earthly creation. "All the Earth/ To thee and to thy Race I give; as Lords," declares the "Presence Divine" to Adam, as the First Parent avers in *Paradise Lost*, "Possess it, and all things that herein live" (8. 314; 338-40). Adam adds that the Presence, which he identifies as the "Universal Lord," further directs him to "Find pastime, and beare rule" over all lesser living things (375). With the Fall of Adam and Eve through false rational choices stirred by demonic guile, all the lesser beings or things under their rule, both in the animal kingdom and in physical and vital nature, fall with them and in this sense have been a prey to demonic ambition.

In executing the scientific historicist component of a biblical epic, Milton, in a departure from strict scriptural epochal historiography, imaginatively and uniquely employed "mixed" empirical practices. Most notably, he disclosed epic events whenever possible through the immediate "objective" or "biased" eyewitness accounts and observations of respective good and evil epic characters, observations supported by a range of navigational, geographical, and other scientific references. It needs to be recognized that these scientific allusions in *Paradise Lost* grew, not from the author's imperialist-commercial inclinations, but rather from Milton's experimental attempt in his middle years to compose a "mixed" history better and more strictly empirical than any other produced up to that time by authors such as Hakluyt, Purchas, Bishop George Abbot, and Giles Fletcher.

Milton, moreover, differs dramatically from medieval writers in his harsh dismissal of that Holy Land pilgrimage tradition, which precipitated the crusades and led to temporary western political control over the Holy Land. In book 3 of *Paradise Lost*, Milton castigates the tradition by inventing a satiric realm where "Pilgrims roam, that stray'd so far to seek/ In *Golgotha* him dead, who lives in Heav'n" (476-77). With gross and scathing ill-humor, Milton discloses pilgrims and clerics being swept "awry" over "the backside of the World far off/ Into a *Limbo* large and broad, since call'd/The Paradise of Fools" (494-960). Milton accordingly advances no arguments, such as those of Christopher Columbus in his letters, for postlapsarian Christian possession of Jerusalem.

In his middle period Milton, it should be recalled, had left his chronicle-style *The History of Britain* unfinished, contemptuously complaining that many early chronicle sources were filled with legendary "trash," that the chronicles of Malmesbury and Henry of Huntington in particular were "obscure and bloakish." "Them rather than imitate," he wrote at the time, "I shall choose to represent the truth naked, though as lean as a plain Journal."[9]

Responding to Comenius's appeals for the writing of epitomies, and to Bacon's praise of new empirical "mixed" cultural histories, Milton, with excellent focus but with occasional critical lapses in his ready acceptance of voyage accounts, produced in the mid-1650s his empirical *A Brief History of Moscovia and Of other less-known Countries lying eastward of Russia as far as Cathay*, a work with a subtitle signaling the influence of Purchas's method: "Gather'd from the Writings of several Eye-witnesses." In this reformist geographical-history replete with navigational and locational coordinates of a kind explained in Blunderville's *Exercises*, Milton "epitomized" in 109 printed pages eyewitness travel accounts scattered in a 400-page segment of Purchas's approximately 5,000 page *Purchas his Pilgrimes* (1625), and in an 800-page segment of Hakluyt's *Principal Navigations* (1598). Milton in this single work of all his writings, having decided to follow empirical dictates, listed his sources, noting on his final page some nineteen different primary accounts all of which had been previously published by either Hakluyt or Purchas, both of whom are named.

But if Milton had been harshly critical of chronicle histories, he was also critical of empirical histories. "The Writers thereof," he opined,

> though some of them exact enough in setting down Longitudes and Latitudes, yet in those other relations of Manners, Religion, Goverment and such like, accounted Geographical, have for the most part miss'd their proportions.[10]

Among these authors, Milton continues, are some who "cloy and weary out the Reader; while they tell long Stories of absurd Superstitions, Ceremonies, quaint Habits, and other petty Circumstances, little to the purpose" (A2r, 474). To correct these and other deficiencies, Milton announces his intention to compose an empirical work "which might be as a Pattern or Example, to render others more cautious hereafter" (A3r).

As Milton explains in his preface, he seeks to rectify past practices by limiting his study to "something in the description of one of two Countreys" rather then attempting an "entire Geography" of many countries or of the world (A3r). He does not anthologize his sources, as others have done, by presenting each account individually with introductory comments. Rather, "with "no cursory pains" he has "laid together" things "observ'd several times by Eye-witnesses," thus interlacing accounts and hopefully overcoming the bias of individual observation (A3v). To gain in objectivity and accuracy, he presents the accounts in the matter-of-fact language of journal composition, foregoing rhetorical eloquence of the kind used by Walter Ralegh in his *History of the World*.

Milton, moreover, seeks to exhume as noted "long Stories" on "petty matters," or on "absurd Superstitions" and "quaint Habits" of an extremist and less than credible kind. At the same time, he retains reports of strange but significant foreign customs and beliefs. But most important, Milton allows his work generally to find its own condensed "proportions" on the basis of the substantive information available on "Manners, Religion, Government and such like," including geographical features and exact locations. His is a work without a clear beginning or end, obtaining form largely from the adroit "placement" of significant observational materials rather than from a forceful imposition of political, religious, prophetic, or philosophical-ideological outlooks. Milton in fact admits to being rather pleasantly led by his materials in a given direction, and that direction is toward an evocative Far East. His epitome, he asserts, is aimed at saving "the Reader" from "the travaile of so many Desert authours; who yet with some delight drew me after them, from the Eastern bounds of Russia, to the Walls of Cathay" (A3v).

Like Columbus and most medieval and Renaissance cosmographers, Milton on the evidence of his *Brief History* is fascinated by accounts of the exotic realms of the East, realms traditionally famed as the seat of the Earthly Paradise and as a place of marvels such as those described by Marco Polo. Milton in fact rests much of his "epitome" upon the statements of English merchant adventurers who, in developing trading relations with Russia, were also seeking on the advice of Dr. John Dee a river or other route through Russia and Siberia to the Far East. The English hope of finding a Northeast passage to the end of the East—a passage comparable to the Portuguese Southeast sea route around Africa to India—accordingly underlies a number of travel passages both in *A Brief History* and in *Paradise Lost*.

From Pilgrimage to History

In the first three chapters, Milton records actual or possible river routes through Russia, with overland links between them, leading inland from Archangel on the Cronian (Arctic) Sea in the North, to "Mosco" (Moscow) somewhat near the country's center, to the Baltic states in the West, and finally to the Caspian Sea, and then northward and eastward through Siberia past the Walls of Cathay and beyond. He includes in his "mixed" cultural history descriptive, highly selective remarks on wooden villages, deer-drawn sledges, commercial practices, a corrupt and heavy-drinking Russian Orthodox clergy, a fierce and undisciplined army, and a resplendent if barbaric imperial court in Mosco.

The fourth chapter records the succession, with much internecine conflict, of a chain of Russian emperors, whose tyranny is exposed through their described cruel action, unfettered exercise of power, and excessive ceremony, descriptions presented generally without the interposed judgments of the author. Of particular note is an account of a week-long "Triumph" celebrating the coronation of the under-aged Pheodor Juanowick, a Triumph involving rituals and objects of gross splendor like those associated with the enthroned Satan in the Hell of *Paradise Lost*. The youthful Pheodor "rising from his Chair" of State receives

an upper Robe, so thick with Orient Pearls and Stones
as weigh'd 200 pounds, the Train born by 6 Dukes; his
staff imperial...beset with rich Stones; his Globe and
six Crowns carried before him by Princes of the Bloud.
(49)

And if Satan's unholy family members, Sin and Death, construct a bridge over Chaos in the epic, it should be noted that Milton describes "a kind of Bridge made three waies, 150 fathom long, three foot high, two fathom broad" over which Pheodor and his train move "above the infinite throng of People" (49). The Triumph includes a "Banquet" with nobles, "two standing on either side of his Chair with Battel-axes of Gold"; and ends with a courtly progress supposedly involving "at least 50 thousand Horse" (51).

In the last chapter Milton makes the best of what was a generally disappointing English enterprise. He writes of the English voyagers' "discovery" of Russia—not mentioning the voyagers' failure to find a water or other route to the ultimate East. And he writes too of the sometimes troublesome embassies and communications back and forth between respectively Elizabeth and James in London and the Russian emperor in Mosco.

At the very end of the geographic section of his study, Milton concludes by recording fascinating observations allegedly made in the early 1600s by Russian soldiers who, going beyond the eastward limit of English travels, apparently penetrated deep into the Orient. The soldiers, ordered eastward by Russian Emperor Michael Pheodorowick, are said to have come to a river "they durst not pass over; they saw there certain Sayles afar off, square, and therefore suppos'd to be like *Indian* or *China* Sayles, and…they report that great Guns have been heard shot off from those Vessels" (31). Milton later notes that Emperor Pheodorowick, who was obviously interested in a route to the East, sought the help of cosmographer John Dee; but Dee declined the emperor's generous offer of an honored place in the court at Mosco at a fee of two thousand pounds per year (101).

In 1618-19 in what was then the last report of its kind, Milton writes that "certain" Russians, again on orders from Emperor Pheodorowick, traveled eastward through a gateway in the Great Wall of Cathay to the imperial White City of Cathaia, a city that modern commentators locate in the ancient Empire of Peking. Milton, despite his efforts to banish superstitious tales, then repeats the claim that "in the midst of the White City stands a Castle built of Magnet" or loadstone (35)—a possible Eastern precursor of the magnetic island of the savants in the third book of Swift's *Gulliver's Travels*. Here the "King dwels," Milton writes, "in a sumptuous Palace, the top thereof is overlaid with Gold." The city, Milton continues, is but "7 daies journey from the Sea." (36). And

113

the Russians report that beyond the River Ob running through Siberia there is a sea "so warm that all kind of Sea-Fowl live thereabout as well in Winter as in Summer." Milton concludes the geographical portion of his history with the words, "Thus much briefly of the Sea and Lands between *Russia* and *Cathay*" (36).

Throughout, Milton exhibits unexpected non-judgmental reportorial discipline. He simply states in passing without evaluative political or other comment, for example, that the Russian Emperor "exerciseth absolute power" (12) and that certain Muscovite wives expect to be "beaten once a week" (19). But he admittedly cannot refrain from making occasional implied moral assessments. Speaking of the Russian Orthodox priesthood, he asserts that there are "for Whordom, Drunkenness, and Extortion none worse than the Clergy" (18).

Because founded on reports by seamen, traders, and emissaries, Milton's empirical history is filled with the language of commerce. Still, the poet's disapproval of trading ventures is more than implied. The clearest and most embracing moral judgment in Milton's work is his claim that the commercial motivations and actions of English voyagers, though seemingly heroic, were actually occasions for evil though helpful to the knowledge of geography and history.

> The discovery of *Russia* by the northern Ocean, made first, of any Nation that we know, by *English* men, might have seem'd an enterprise almost heroick; if any higher end than the excessive love of Gain and Traffick, had animated the design. Nevertheless, that in regard that many things not unprofitable to the knowledge of Nature, and other Observations are hereby come to light, as good events ofttimes arise from evil occasions. (69)

Even in the opening sentence of his work, Milton in his preface deftly denegrates motivations arising from a desire for material profit. He states rather that it is "the study of Geography" that is "profitable and delightfull." His history, Milton points out, discloses what is "useful, and onely worth observation" (A2r). What beneficially is revealed, Milton subsequently remarks, is "a knowledge of Nature, and other Observatrions." The highest profit and pleasure thus accrue, Milton suggests, from an expanding objective understanding of the regions of the world and their peoples.

Milton, exercising great stylistic and intellectual restraint, learned his new historicist lessons well. Having struggled with only some success to write an exemplary empirical historicist work better proportioned, more objective, and more selectively focused and informative than any preceding it; and having with "much travaile" and "no cursary pains" necessarily read through and excerpted materials from the massive empirical "mixed" world histories of the Renaissance reformers, he turned in his middle years from the pressure of scientific linguistic and procedural discipline, allowing his imagination and prophetic outlooks to take poetic flight while with great originality retaining many of the patterns and substantive features of his historicist experiment.

How Milton developed a paradigm for the deployment of new empirical history in his epic becomes evident, not only from a review of reformist histories and the poet's own *A Brief History*, but also from a review of the growth of Milton's "invention" out of early theatrical voyage references and related designs.[11]

In the 1640s, Milton's nephew Edward Phillips, in his *Life of Milton,* quoted a passage, later to appear as lines 4.31-42 of the epic, which Phillips stated had been composed and then read to him by Milton from his uncle's new theatrical work in progress. In the passage an anguished Satan, voyaging from the "darkness visible" (1.63) of Hell ever nearer to Eden, laments seeing the glorious brilliance of the sun. Also in the 1640s, Milton penned four outlines of a theatrical work on the First Parents' Fall finally entitled "Adam Unparadiz'd," a *sacre representazione* with a number of themes and listed patterned actions obviously foreshadowing those in the epic. The last outline opens with the descent of the angel Michael from Heaven to Eden.

Somewhat earlier in a completed and performed theatrical work of often overlooked symbolic suggestiveness, Milton had struck upon a typical sacred representational and masque pattern of movement and action that was to serve him well in structuring the empirical, eyewitness voyages and actions of immortal beings in *Paradise Lost.* In the poet's *A Mask Presented at Ludlow Castle* (1634) centered on the attempted temptation of a virtuous Lady by the enchanter Comus, action, arguments by characters, and choreographed movements unfold between two opposed chairs or thrones of vice and virtue. One chair stands in a darkened area before the palace of Comus, a figure of infernal discord associated with gods of the nether world; and the opposing chair, traditionally separated from the first by a central green-carpeted performing space, is the brightly-illumined seat of state of a noble peer who rules by way of a hierarchy of classical gods under high "*Jove*" (20). The Lady as the central main masquer, though at one point magically restrained by Comus in his chair, overcomes the arguments and temptation of the enchanter using the freedom of her mind. Upon her release, she moves together with other main masquers from Comus's darkened chair to a position before the illumined chair of the noble peer The choreographed motions of the masquers in an earthly realm between the two chairs, reaches a joyous end in a revelatory Triumph. The virtuous main performers are "presented" and symbolically unmask as known aristocrats before the chair of state; then they "*triumph in victorious dance*" before and possibly in traditional fashion around the chair (974). It should be noted too that *A Mask Presented at Ludlow Castle*, like Milton's sacred representational notations on celestial voyages, opens with the flight of an immortal figure of virtue from a "Sainted" seat in Heaven to earth (11); and concludes with the figure's flying ascent to Heavenly realms (977-92), that is, provided a levitation machine was installed at Ludlow Castle.

116

The imaginative transformation of stage chairs into the epic thrones of Satan and God, with the green space of Eden somewhere between them, would have been a quite natural step in artistic invention. Milton, after all, had long experience, beginning at the early age of seventeen in his Latin heroic poem *In Quintum Novembris* (1626), in incorporating a theatrical "disguising"—that of the disguised Satan's appearance before the Roman Pope, along with the opening flight of the Archfiend to Rome, the bacchanal anti-triumphal procession of Roman clerics into torch-lit temples, and the concluding masque-like flying descent of Fame to earth— into his heroic "epic in miniature" written under the dominating influence of Virgil's *Aeneid*.[12]

In *Paradise Lost*, demonic and divine eyewitnesses to unfolding events depart respectively from realms before or near the throne of Satan in Hell or the throne of God in Heaven, make counterbalanced wandering or direct journeys to the new world of the Earthly Paradise, and then either remain in Eden or return to Hell or Heaven.[13] Although the journeys past Ptolomaic spheres and Copernican new worlds to an irregular geographic earth derive in part from epic conventions of heroic travel, they are compared in highly innovative ways, given Milton's world and cosmic vision, to Renaissance voyages of discovery to Africa, India, South America, North America, the Arctic Ocean, Moscovia, and the Far East. The journeys are presented in theatrical contexts amid references to cartography, storms, sailing-ship calamities, navigational devices, distant oceans, and strange lands and peoples. These adventurous voyage allusions, of a kind also evident in Camoë's sixteenth-century epic *Os Lusiades* on Vasco da Gama's voyage to India around the Cape of Good Hope, replace the centuries-old tradition of medieval iconographic processional narratives ultimately figuring ordered earthly pilgrimages to the "old" geographic world-center of Jerusalem.

In the epic, in accord with new empirical as well as biblical traditions, the eyes of immortal figures in Heaven and Hell and of the two mortals in Eden, gaze upon events of the present and past.

Action begins in Hell with Satan staring with "baleful eyes" at "The dismal Situation waste and wild" (56, 60), continues in Heaven with the enthroned Father bending "down his eye" (3.58) upon Satan's movements toward Eden, and extends to the Saints in heaven who, in greeting the victorious Son after the war in heaven, are "Eye-witnesses to his Almighty Acts" (6.883). Sadly, the physically blind epic narrator, in the manner of the physically blind Milton, felt especially impelled to authenticate events, even in eternity, with many eyewitnesses.

Like the biblical eye of God that peers down upon an early revisionist representation of the entire earth in the frontispiece illustration of Ralegh's *History of the World,* so in *Paradise Lost* the eye of God the Father that looks down upon the First Parents and Satan also sees simultaneously all of the earth along with all created "works at once" (3. 59). The Father, no imperialist, immediately speaks of the free choice of Adam and Eve. And near the Father, who is paradoxically "High Thron'd above all highth," is the "Kingly Palace Gate" (505) of Heaven which is described as superior to any "Frontispiece" on earth "By Model, or by shading Pencil drawn" (506, 509). Milton, who composed and published an introduction to Ralegh's supposed work *The Cabinet Council,* here as elsewhere in *Paradise Lost,* could well have been influenced by the courtier's illustrated writings showing a new historicist world.

But to what degree is a strand of empirical new historicism evident throughout the epic?

Milton did not mock and denigrate all journeys of discovery by associating them solely with antic, confused wanderings of evil characters. He introduced also the heroic, virtuous journeys to Eden of Uriel, Raphael, Michael, and the Son, journeys also associated with the sea voyages of eyewitnesses. In each instance, it is the moral or immoral purpose and nature of the travelers, together with the symbolic significance of the pathways chosen, that dictates Milton's poetic treatment.

Divine, virtuous travelers move from point to point in the universe with such speed, assurance, and "navigational" accuracy that they serve, when visible, as navigational guides to wandering mortals on earth.

The angel Raphael, in sailing down from heaven amid planets and stars, passes easily through harsh earthly polar winds. Then in lower airy realms Raphael slows or directs his descent by fanning one or more of his wings.

> Down thither prone in flight
> He speeds, and through the vast Ethereal Skie
> Sailes between worlds and worlds, with
>   steddie wing
> Now on the polar winds, then with quick Fan
> Winnows the buxom Air
>
> (5.266-70)

But, however direct Raphael's cosmic voyage, not even the angel is certain of the nature and location of distant objects seen as possible navigational points in the unexplored universe. The obscure, far-away forms, some perhaps imagined, are said to be as mysterious as those on the moon viewed through Galileo's perspective glass, or as those appearing to a Pilot navigating in the region of the floating island Delos and of islands covered by clouds. Raphael navigates down past "worlds and worlds" without clear points of reference

> ...As when by night the Glas
> Of Galileo, less assur'd, observes
> Imagined Lands and Regions in the Moon:
> Or Pilot from amidst the *Cyclades*
> *Delos* or *Samos* first appeering kenns
> A cloudy spot
>
> (5.261-66)

Uriel, one of seven Angels "nearest" to the heavenly "throne" who serve as God's "Eyes," avoids all winds by gliding to earth on a celestial navigational beam, a ray of sunlight. As a messenger who is said to undertake "swift errands over moist and dry,/ O'er Sea and Land" (652-53), Uriel descends with the speed of a shooting star which is said to point the way, like a navigational compass beacon, to mariners sailing in vaporous and potentially windy seas.

> Thither came *Uriel*, gliding through the Even
> On a Sun beam, swift as a shooting Starr
> In *Autumn* thwarts the night, when vapors fir'd
> Impress the Air, and shews the Mariner
> From what point of his Compass to beware
> Impetuous winds
>
> $\qquad\qquad\qquad\qquad$ (4.555-60)

Just before descending to earth in book 10 to pronounce judgment on the First Parents, the Son, accompanied by an angelic band, is an eyewitness to an extraordinary "prospect" when

> ...from his radiant Seat he [the Son] rose
> Of high collateral glorie: him Thrones and Powers,
> Princedoms, and Dominations ministrant
> Accompanied to Heaven Gate, from whence
> *Eden* and all the Coast in prospect lay.
> Down he descended strait; the speed of Gods
> Time counts not, though with swiftest minutes
> $\qquad$ wing'd.
>
> $\qquad\qquad\qquad\qquad$ (10.85-91)

Recent criticism of *Paradise Lost* has been unduly concerned with allusions to supposed "colonial" ventures in Virginia and North America. Yet in adopting a global vision, Milton depicts the journeys of Satan, his demonic bride Sin, and his only Son Death as a metaphor for desperately hazardous, meandering world voyages for avaricious reasons of trade and possessions—voyages involving extraordinary navigational exploits, confusions, and errors—to supposed paradisal realms in many regions of the earth.

Satan in analogy takes the Southeast trading sea route, the low way to the Edenic East as described in *Purchas his Pilgrimes* and illustrated in Ortelius's *Theatrum Orbis Terrarum*. This is the route opened by Vasco da Gama around the Cape of Good Hope and across the Indian Ocean. The Archfiend assumes "swift wings" (2.631), and begins a careening voyage on these "Sail-broad Vans" (2.927). Like a fearful ship's captain aware of the dangers of the open sea, Satan, hugging the shoreline, first "scours the right hand coast and sometimes the left" (2.633) but at times "shaves" the "Deep" (2.634) tentatively venturing seaward. And just as seamen were often temporally barred from passage around the Cape of Good Hope at the tip of Africa by stormy seas, so the Archfiend is briefly blocked at the Gate of Hell. Near the Gate the Archfiend, filled with illusory hope, appears as do trading ships reflected mirage-like in the clouds:

> As when far off at Sea a Fleet descri'd
> Hangs in the Clouds, by *Equinnoctial* Winds
> Close sailing; from *Bengala*, or the Isles
> Of *Ternate* and *Tidore*, which Merchants bring
> The spicy Drugs: they on the Trading Flood
> Through the wide *Ethiopian* to the Cape
> (2.636-41)

Passing the Gate of Hell, Satan moves beyond all shores into the storm-tossed Chaos of "a dark/ illimitable Ocean without bound" (2.634). The Fiend's anti-epic voyage exceeds in its perils those of classical heroic travelers, for Satan is said to be "more endanger'd, than when *Argo* pass'd/ Through *Bosporus* betwixt the justling Rocks" (2.1017-18), or when "*Ulysses* on the Larboard shunn'd/ *Charybdis*, and by th' other whirlpool steer'd" (2.1017-20). When Satan finally breaks out of the tumult of Chaos "Like a weather-beaten Vessel" with "Shrouds and Tackle torn" (2.1043-

44), the Fiend at last views the distant new world "in bigness as a Star/ Of smallest Magnitude" (1052-53). But he is, if anything, even more perplexed by a vast universe lacking recognizable navigational signs.

Ascending to the lowermost stair of a ladder leading to the Gate of Heaven, the Archfiend "Looks down with wonder at the sudden view/ Of all this World at once" (3.542-43).

> At sight of all this World beheld so fair.
> Round he surveys, and well might, where he stood
> So high above the circling Canopy
> Of Night's extended shade; from Eastern Point
> Of *Libra* to the fleecy Star that bears
> *Andromeda* far off *Atlantic* Seas
> Beyond th' Horizon; then from Pole to Pole
> views in breadth, and without longer pause
> Down right into the World's first Region thows
> His flight precipitant
>
> (3.554-63)

Taking flight once more, he shows himself a poor navigator.

> ...Thither his course he bends,
> Through the calm Firmament, but up or down
> by centre, or eccentric, hard to tell,
> Of Longitude
>
> (3.573-76)

Finally upon approaching the happy isle, the new world of Eden, Satan experiences the delight of mariners who, having negotiated the Cape, enjoy the first exotic odors of the East:

> ...As when to them who sail
> Beyond the *Cape of Hope*, and now are past
> *Mozambique*, off at Sea North-East winds blow

> *Sabean* Odors from the spicy shore
> Of *Araby* the blest, with such delay
> Well pleas'd they slack thir course, and many a
>   League
> Cheer'd with the grateful smell old Ocean smiles.
> So entertain'd those odorous sweets the Fiend
> Who came thir bane
>   (4.159-68)

Sin and Death, also seeking a route to Eden, metaphorically attempt a northeast passage by water to the East as it is described in Purchas and in *A Brief History of Moscovia*, a passage from England north around the tip of Norway and east through the Cronian Sea, the Arctic Ocean, to the Russian port of Pestora. From there the seamen hoped to find a great river, which occultist and navigational writer Dr. John Dee insisted existed, flowing through Moscovia to the Indian Ocean and so on to the supposed Edenic realms of the East. This was the impassable "imagined way," the sea route through terrible Arctic ice fields to a blocking Russian land mass that led to the deaths by freezing, as Milton recounts in his history, of British seamen such as Hugh Willoby and his crew. Sin and Death are halted by conflicted forces

> As when two Polar Winds blowing adverse
> Upon the *Cronian* Sea, together drive
> Mountains of Ice, that stop th' imagin'd way
> Beyond *Pestora*, Eastward
>   (10.289-92)

They then throw "Over the foaming deep" of Chaos "high Archt, a Bridge/ of length prodigious" that eventually stretches all the way to Eden (10.301-02).

The destination of cosmic eyewitness travelers is, of course, Eden, a holy site identified by Dante in the *Commedia* as a fulfilled type of Jerusalem. Milton gives the garden as first seen by Satan a theatrical cast by making it a

> A Silvan Scene, and as the ranks ascend
> Shade above shade, a woody Theatre
> Of stateliest view
>
> (4.140-42)

Although Milton wavers on cosmology by introducing both Copernican space and Ptolomaic spheres, it needs to be stressed that the poet also wavers on whether prelapsarian Eden was in the East at the summit of the globe, in an appropriate typal position on medieval *mappaemundi*, or whether it was off somewhere on the earth's side as the new cosmology might be construed as suggesting.

Milton is precise only in placing Eden in Mesopotamia, the region on the earth's surface selected as the Garden's site by Ralegh and as so designated in the Bishop's Bible.

> ...for blisful Paradise
> Of God the Garden was, by him in the East
> Of *Eden* planted; *Eden* stretch'd her Line
> From *Auran* Eastward to the Royal Tow'rs
> Of Great *Seleucia*, built by *Grecian* Kings,
> Or where the Sons of *Eden* long before
> Dwelt in *Telassar*: in this pleasant soil
> His far more pleasant Garden God ordain'd
>
> (4.208-15)

But where was Mesopotamia before the globe was tilted by the Almighty as punishment for the Fall? Was the Garden in Mesopotamia at the top-center of the globe or was it at the side?

Before the Fall, the surface of the "Centric Globe," according to the epic narrator, had probably been ideally aligned so that the constantly-temperate Paradise was either at the top and center of the earth, as in Dante's *Commedia*, or somewhere on or near the equator. Milton, as was his custom on certain difficult issues of divine historical cosmography, obscures the point and so in effect has it both ways. In the epic, the narrator simply explains that "Some say" after the Fall the poles of the earth, poles once perfectly aligned to the axial of the sun, were tilted by about twenty-five degrees, a punishment for sin causing an elliptical orbit for the sun and troubling variations in climate. The Almighty, the narrator states,

> ...bid his Angels turn askance
> The Poles of Earth twice ten degrees and more
> From the Sun's Axle; they with labor push'd
> Oblique the Centric Globe
>
> (10.668-71)

Recent criticism has assumed that Milton, although locating Eden in Mesopotamia, associates Eden with a colonized, or soon to be colonized, North American island; for the leaves covering the Fallen First Parents are said to be like those seen by Columbus covering otherwise nearly naked native Americans.[14] But because Milton sought to introduce unusual world-wide references, the passage in fact implies a possible association with an alternative location in a more temperate clime. Adam and Eve are said to gather leaves as

> broad as *Amazonian* Targe,
> And with what skill they had, together sew'd,
> To girt thir waist, vain Covering if to hide
> Thir guilt and dreadful shame; O how unlike
> To that first naked Glory. Such of late
> *Columbus* found th' *American* so girt
> With feather'd Cincture, naked else and wild
> Among the Trees on Isles and woody Shores.
>
> (9.1111-18)

The leaves covering the fallen First Parents, like those worn by native American inhabitants, are thus in size associated with a tree growing in the lush, tropical Amazon in South America, the area Columbus on his third voyage identified as the possible site of the Earthly Paradise. In keeping with the practice of world-wide reference, Milton then adds that the Tree of Knowledge is comparable to one that grows in another region named in medieval works as a possible site of Eden; namely, the Indian subcontinent. The tree is "such as at this day to *Indians* known/ In *Malabar* or *Decan* spreads her Arms" (9.1102-03).

Earthly human history centers on Adam and Eve, and is revealed by eyewitnesses. And if Ralegh in his *History* manages to make two medieval "historical" sites on earth—Eden and Jerusalem—cynosures of attention in his unfinished universal narrative, so Milton, with heightened "new historical" immediacy and a completed universal narrative, highlights the same two places but to much greater dramatic effect. Satan initially looks down upon the world above an opening in a sphere over Eden, an opening which after the Fall moves to a position over Jerusalem on Mount Sion.

> Direct against which op'nd from beneath
> Just o're the blissful seat of Paradise
> A passage down to th' Earth, a passage wide
> (3.526-29)

This large gap contracts and changes position in accord with the sinfulness of future stages of human history. The narrator notes that the gap over Eden is "Wider by far" than the smaller opening that will someday replace it "Over the *Promised Land* to God so dear,/ By which, to visit those happy Tribes,/ On high behests." The gap is also said to be "Wider by far than that of after-times/ Over Mount Sion," the site of Jerusalem.

This opening thus provides altering perspectives not only on Eden, the site of the beginning of human history traditionally

126

illustrated and discussed in numerous cosmographical and religious books, but also on the locales of other central events in human history: the Exodus and the Redemption. In a volume already cited as influencing Milton, Thomas Fuller's *Pisgah-sight of Palestine*, these last two holy sites and events had been represented, as if seen from above, with written accounts and accompanying directional lined maps providing a supposed "history" based on the movements of the twelve tribes of Israel and of holy persons.

When a final sweeping view of the world is introduced in book 12—a view seen by Adam from the highest hill in Eden—the last place visible is the "unspoil'd" Amazonian realm, with the supposed golden city, made famous by Ralegh in *The Large and Beautiful Empire of Guiana.*

> ...yet unspoil'd
> *Guiana*, whose great City *Geryon's* Sons
> Call *El Dorado*: but to nobler sights
> *Michael* from *Adam's* eyes the Film remov'd
> Which that false Fruit that promis'd clearer sight
> Had bred;
>
> (11. 409-14)

Given Milton's focus on the entire human race and its universal history, "new world" geographical references associated with postlapsarian Eden and the First Parents by no means point just to colonial North America, and especially just to colonial Virginia. In the new mixed historical-geographical literature, Central and South American locales in or close to equinoctial zones, together with newly discovered islands off the coast of India, are by implication referred to as edenic or utopian realms. Bacon, after all, located his utopian, fictional New Atlantis off the coast of Peru. Columbus, as has been noted, believed the earthly paradise possibly to be near the Orinoco River in the Amazonian jungles; and Ralegh, the golden city of El Dorado, near the Orinoco's head in the Amazon. Milton's empirical allusions draw upon such past associations, even while fixing the site of Eden, not in the New World, but somewhere in Mesopotamia.

As even the opening lines of *Paradise Lost* make clear, the epic is hinged upon the "disobedience" of the First Adam, and the contravening future Redemption of humanity by the Son, the Second Adam. Milton in *Paradise Lost*, whatever the emphasis of his typal historicist representations in earlier works, took this underlying design for human history with deep seriousness, and he was unique in presenting special perspectives on its unfolding, through allusions to Heavenly epic history, using the now-archaic but then-emotive theatrical forms of the Triumph and Anti-Triumph.

8

THE PROPHETIC UNIVERSAL HISTORY OF *PARADISE LOST*

Paradoxical Triumphs and Transcendent Designs

...Divine
Historian, who thus largely hast allay'd
The thirst I had of knowledge, and voutsaf't
This friendly condescension to relate
Things else by me unsearchable, now heard
With wonder...

> Adam's remarks to the "Divine Historian"
> Raphael upon learning "The secrets of another
> World, perhaps/ Not lawful to reveal"
> *Paradise Lost,* 8.6-11; 5.569-70

An inward triumph doth my soul up-heave
And spread abroad through endlesse spersed air.
My nimble mind this clammie clod doth leave,
And lightly stepping on from starre to starre
Swifter then lightning, passeth wide and farre,
Measuring the unbounded Heavens and waftful skie

> Henry More, *Democritus Platonissans, or An
> Essay upon the Infinity of Worlds out of
> Platonick Principles* (1646)

To give a total, transcendent prophetic structure to his epic
by depicting divine "historical epochs" in a timeless eternity, a

paradox to begin with, Milton, while indebted to the Bible and a range of classical and other literary sources, had little choice except imaginatively to invent much of what he presented of "events" in Heaven and Hell. The poet might well have experienced something of the confoundment expressed by Raphael, the Divine angelic Historian of *Paradise Lost*. Raphael appears to be questioning himself as much as Adam in asking,

> ...how shall I relate
> To human sense th' invisible exploits
> Of warring Spirits; how without remorse
> The ruin of so many glorious once
> And perfect while they stood; how last unfould
> The secrets of another world, perhaps
> Not lawful to reveal?[1]

"What if Earth/ Be but a shaddow of Heav'n" (574-75), Raphael finally asks. Implicit in the angel's question is the disquieting thought, one that probably occurred to Milton that perhaps it is not. Milton's developed invention, the poet's prophetic historicist idea or Argument as first stated in book 1, was so grand that it also worried Andrew Marvell in his brief commendatory poem first published in the 1674 edition:

> Heav'n, Hell, Earth, Chaos, All: the Argument
> Held me misdoubting his Intent,
> That he would ruine (for I saw him strong)
> The sacred Truths to Fable and old Song
>
> (5-8)

In developing his historicist idea or invention, Milton first had to decide upon what biblical "events" in eternity, most of them beyond time and others directly intersecting with earthly episodes in time, constituted the ultimate history of Heaven and Hell. He also had to decide upon the patterned divine "frame" and "structure" for other-worldly events and for all of universal history;

and he had to determine how, in the words of Raphael, "By lik'ning spiritual to corporal forms" (574), this otherworldly history might be immediately represented. Because recent critics have often concentrated on passages seemingly pointing to specific early issues of British politics or colonialism, critical attention has been distracted from the originality and strangeness of what finally emerges as Milton's idea and representation of God's grand historical design.[2] Milton's containing form serves as a culminating imaginative example of Renaissance prophetic structures.

The paradoxical problem of a narrative history in a timeless eternity, where presumably all events coalesce into an eternal present, gave Milton the freedom to experiment with varying historical designs; but it obviously disoriented the poet. Even God the Father in book 3 is forced into evasions. "If I foreknew," the Father ambiguously remarks of the Fall of Adam and Eve which has yet to take place on earth, "Foreknowledge had no influence on their fault" (3. 117-18).

Milton finally hinged the idea or "Argument" of his epic's history of humanity, as developed from his middle-period outlines of the planned sacred representation "Adam Unparadiz'd," upon the Fall and Redemption of the First Parents in an early Eden. But he hinged the underlying meaning of the epic's divine universal history upon the Triumphant revelations of the Son united to a heavenly Father, the last depicted essentially as the representative of Justice, and a concomitant revelation of the anti-Triumphant Fall and punishment of Satan, the embodiment of evil in Hell.

While the completed version of *Paradise Lost* is clearly a biblical epic beginning *in medias res* and having a Virgilian twelve-book form and the traditional devices of classical and Renaissance heroic poetry, the divine universal history of the epic, a subject here in need of examination, gains its prophetic structure from the epochal revelations in eternity. The divine Triumphs and the infernal Anti-Triumph have been seen to feature immortal figures, who wend their way back and forth through the cosmos between an earthly Eden in a realm of time, and the thrones of God and Satan beyond time. These journeys thematically bind together the eternal history of Heaven and the temporal history of the world, with a final end of earthly human history brought about by an Apocalyptic and Millennial joining of the two realms.

With a subject as unlimited as eternity itself, Milton innovated by trying out and interjecting into his epochal structure, however experimentally, a developmental or "progressive" design, and also an implied Platonic cyclical design. Counterparts to one or more of Milton's three basic historicist patterns, which poetically coalesce in the symbolism of the Triumphs and Anti-Triumph, will be seen to reappear in later centuries in the often rigidly imposed structures of very different scientific and philosophical historicist works.

In addition, the complex total design of universal history in the epic is repeatedly explained by divine characters—the Father, the Son, and the angels Raphael and Michael—in conversation with one or more other figures. The divine plan is in turn disputed by Satan and the devils in hell who strive to impose a different model, and is constantly commented upon by the inspired epic narrator through whom all is envisioned. Given the fact that the argument of the poem, in the words of the epic narrator, is to "justifie the wayes of God to men" (1.26), the epic can be seen to contain multiple explanations, as well as eyewitness observations, of events which are introduced to allow the reader, in the spirit of reformist empiricist historicism, selectively to gain from varied outlooks what it is presumed will be an authoritative idea of the poem's universal history.

At the climax of each epochal revelation in Heaven, it is the Son—depicted in the respective fulfilled roles of Redeemer, Creative Agent, Righteous Warrior, and Judge—who is recurrently "unveiled" as the Second Person of Godhead and as the universal source of Mercy.

The Triumph of the Son's Redemption of the human race is forecast early in book 3 when the Son, directly represented in Heaven, announces his redemptive role. "O unexampl'd love," the narrator joins the angels in singing of the Son,

> Love no where to be found less then Divine!
> Hail Son of God, Saviour of Men, thy Name
> Shall be the copious matter of my Song
> (3.410-13)

In book 5 the angel Raphael tells Adam in Eden of the epochal Triumph of the Son's "begetting," an event based upon a paraphrase of Psalm ii, 6-11, and read by critics as suggesting the "exultation" and showing forth or the unmasking of a Son previously concealed in the "bosom" of the Father. Alternately, the "begetting" has been interpreted, through reference to passages in Milton's *De Doctrina Christiana*, as the actual "creation" of the Son by the Father, a view that would be considered heretical by the body of English seventeenth-century theologians.[3]

Thereafter, the angel in book 6 speaks of the Son's Triumph in Heaven following a military victory over Satan and the rebellious angels, a Triumph staged on a day foreshadowing that of the Son's future resurrection on Easter Sunday. In book 10, as Raphael explains, the Son Triumphs after the Creation, an event commanded by the Father and carried out in six days by the Son. Finally in book 12, the stern but forthright angel Michael, replacing the angel Raphael as a divine historian, tells Adam of the Son's future Triumphant Redemption, Second Coming, and role as Divine Judge, the last event leading to an "end" to human history.

The epic's central earthly event, the Fall of the First Parents in the Garden, is directly represented in the immediate "present" of book 9, but the future epochs of earthly human history are simply related to Adam in Eden by the angel Michael, with learning aids in the form of epochal visions.

In a work beginning *in medias res* and having composite historicist structural features, the epochs of eternal and also earthly prophetic history, although interwoven, can be seen to be scattered non-sequentially throughout the narrative in direct depictions, "flashbacks," and finally in the visions and prophecies of the last two books. The search by critics for an evenly spaced foreshadowed and fulfilled pattern of unfolding epochal events in the epic's central books—an epochal pattern like the sequential one underlying Dante's *Commedia*—has proved unavailing. Long stretches in Milton's middle books are empty of such references, for Milton has limited his use of epochal history, employing instead long passages on eyewitness travels and sightings, and on imagined invented action. The prophetic epochs that appear, though scattered, are given novel dimension by being interjected in unanticipated order, elaborated with original Miltonic details not found in scripture, and then related in general ways thematically to the Triumphs and the Anti-Triumph which are intended to disclose and "justifie the wayes of God to men" (1. 260).

While Milton in his sonnet "To My Friend Mr. Henry Lawes on his Airs," called attention to Dante as another poet of the realm beyond life, Milton and Dante display instructive differences in their structural and narrative practices. In the *Commedia* Dante depicts himself as a living mortal walking through, observing, and learning from a varied but essentially ordered hierarchical other-world, an effect the poet achieved by apparently inventing his composition in Scholastic fashion, as the last chapter of his *Vita Nuova* suggests, by initially conceiving of its "end" as a final heavenly vision involving Beatrice.[4] Then, Dante's "disposition" of this pilgrimage epic could proceed "backward," probably even before the composition of major passages, until the poet attained a full grasp and delineation of his work's total poetic form.

Milton by contrast, as his nephew Edward Phillips recorded in a brief biography of the poet, completed in his middle years a passage from a theatrical work then in progress on a Satanic flight to Eden. In later years in composing *Paradise Lost*, it has been noted, Milton introduced this passage on Satan's voyage to the Garden at the beginning of book 4.31-42. The poet in fact opened his epic with a different event, "worked through" structural and substantive problems; integrated theatrical, classical, and other associations; arranged or rearranged components to fit the conventions of a ten-book epic; and then adjusted all to a classical twelve-book form.

The preeminent divine event of Heavenly history in *Paradise Lost,* the "cause" of all action in eternity, is the Triumph of the Son's "begetting" in book 5. It is this Triumph which stirs an envious Satan to revolt against God and finally leads to the infernal Anti-Triumph of the Archfiend in book 10. Both events are depicted—not as imitations of the celebratory triumphant "processions" of the restored English monarchy in the 1660s—but rather as patterned reflections of the elaborate, indoor, royalist Jacobean and Caroline staged masques or Triumphs of the early seventeenth century.[5] Although these lavish court Triumphs were abandoned in the 1640s with the overthrow of the monarchy, Milton, an anti-monarchist, in seeking a celebratory form that could communicate the joy of spiritual victory, saw fit to transcend politics and to use the royalist *genre* to extol a Godhead of infinite Justice and Mercy.[6]

When in *Paradise Lost* the Son is begotten on a recurrent immortal day in a cyclical Platonic "great Year" (5.583), the heavens themselves become a theater for a transcendental Triumph involving song, dance, revels, and feasting that correspond to theatrical cyclical dance and divine revelry in the lesser theater of the physical cosmos. The epochal representation with its reference to the "great Year" implies that this event, celebrated with dances imitating what was then widely regarded as the cyclical movement of the encompassing spheres, is recurrent. This implication of recurrence, introducing a second possible historicist form coalescing with the epochal, would have been derived, not only from Plato's *Timaeus* (39D) and from biblical passages, but also from seasonally repeated biblical sacred representations and masque Triumphs.[7] The cyclical nature of such festivities places on the center stage of universal history the Son's eternal yet possibly endlessly-repeated revelation as an ultimate figure of divine Mercy; and foreshadows Satan's antithetical eternal yet possibly endlessly repeated revelation on the same stage as a figure of ultimate evil.

The angels are described wheeling with a seeming mazy irregularity considered to be consonant with divine harmony.

> That day, as other solemn dayes, they spent
> In song and dance about the sacred Hill,
> Mystical dance, which yonder starrie Spheare
> Of Planets and of fixt in all her Wheeles
> Resembles nearest, mazes intricate,
> Eccentric, intervolv'd, yet regular
> Then most, when most irregular they seem
>
> (5.618-24)

This dance in turn mirrors the seeming mazy irregularity of the circular choreographed dances that climaxed masques such as Aurelian Townshend's *Temp Restored* (1632). This presentation at Whitehall featured Queen Henrietta Maria and her ladies dancing in the roles of Stars; and the youthful Alice Egerton, the Lady in Milton's *A Mask Presented at Ludlow-Castle* (1634), in the role of an Influence of the Stars. Milton's musician friend Henry Lawes, a member of the King's Music, would by tradition have appeared in the theatrical heavens of the presentation as a Sphere.

The angels next reflect earthly performers and guests enjoying a traditional masque banquet after the revels, but the angels far surpass earthly revelers by standing in "perfect" cyclical formation: "Forthwith from dance to sweet repast they turn/ Desirous; all in Circles as they stood," (630-31). Unlike drunken earthly masquers who knocked over banqueting tables following the *Masque of Queenes*, the temperate angels "Quaff immortality and joy, secure/ Of surfeit where full measure only bounds/ Excess" (63-40).

In book 5 just before the "begetting" in eternity, the narrator describes the Father, in whom the Son is said to be "imbosom'd," as enthroned on "a flaming Mount, whose top/Brightness had made invisible" (597-99). In book 3 the angels also affirm the Father to be "thyself invisible" as well as "Thron'd inaccessible" (3.375, 377). But in the invocation to book 3, Godhead is said by the epic narrator to be manifest in an "eternal co-eternal beam" (1-2). Also in book 3, though at a point of "time" in eternity apparently after the "begetting," "the Son of God," according to the epic narrator, is said to have been "seen/ Most glorious" by the "blessed Spirits elect,"

> ...in him all his Father shon
> Substantially express'd, and in his face
> Divine compassion visibly appeer'd,
> Love without end, and without measure Grace
>   (3.139-42)

When the Son in eternity then announces his intention in the eternal future to redeem the as yet unfallen First Parents, He is greeted by angelic "Jubilee" song and ritual. The epic narrator, however, neither calls this preliminary celebration a Triumph nor does the narrator describe the features of a Triumph such as a procession, or a "revelation" or unmasking and a banquet. The angels in paradoxical "numbers without number" are said to shout sweetly,

> As from blest voices, uttering joy, Heav'n rung
> With Jubilee, and loud Hosanna's fill'd
> The eternal Regions: lowly reverent
> Towards either Throne they bow, and to the ground
> With solemn adoration down they cast
> Their Crowns inwove with Amarant and Gold
>   (3. 347-52)

"Jubilee" celebrations in Jewish history, it should be recalled, were held every fifty years in a cyclical pattern, and thus served as a model during the Renaissance for cyclically-repeated Roman Jubilee-year pilgrimages. Again Milton has included a divine structured epochal event in eternity which paradoxically could also be endlessly repeated. "Time" and unfolding action in eternity are seemingly again mysteriously coalesced.

In book 5 on that heavenly day when the "embosom'd" Son is "begotten" and, in the Father's phrase, divinely installed as one "whom ye now behold," the Son becomes visible as the anointed

137

and appointed "Head" of the angels at the Father's "right hand" (603-5). The invisible Father is then in analogy compared, through "Divine Similitude," to the shining "conspicuous count'nance" of the Son. (3.384-87). Whatever might have been the evolved theological position of Milton on Godhead in his last years—and his precise position given the complexity of the issue remains uncertain—the words of the Son's Triumph in book 5 suggest a co-eternal Godhead with the Son "embosomed" in the Father, that is, with identity concealed in the manner of a masquer; and then with the "Son" "begotten" in the sense of "shown forth" with the disguise removed.[8]

This divine "begetting" at the beginning of "Heav'ns great Year" shadows earthly court Triumphs celebrating, not the "creation" of the Christ child, but the showing forth of the Son in the form of the Christ child at the Epiphany. The feast of the Epiphany was in fact a favored date for the great "unmaskings" at court and at country estates. Of the fifty-three major court masques presented from 1603 through the year of their discontinuance in 1641, thirteen were performed on the night of the Epiphany and another twelve within five days of that feast. And if in *Paradise Lost* the triumphant "begetting" or revelation of the Son occurs at the beginning of the great Year, possibly on a cyclical basis as an anti-type to the suggested possible cyclical punishment of Satan in Hell, it should be noted that the majority of major court masques, twenty-nine in all, were performed in January, the first month of the new year. Revels at Court and at the Inns of court on specified themes continued during the holidays over two-week periods, with preliminary festive evening celebrations and nights of "misrule" serving as introductions or antitypes to major masques on other evenings. The thematic links among the extended sacred representational, masque-like episodes in the Heaven and Hell of Milton's epic—particularly, the Jubilee festivities in Heaven in book 3, the "begetting" of the Son in book 5, and the "devolution" of Satan in book 10—match on a transcendent plane those of cyclically presented mundane revels.

Antithetical to the seminal and harmonious Triumphant "begetting" of the Son is the grotesque Anti-Triumph of Satan in Hell, a theatrical revelation of monstrous misrule.[9] Satan's degrading Anti-Triumph begins when the Archfiend enters the infernal palace Pandemonium disguised as a "Plebeian Angel militant/ Of lowest order." Although invisible while taking a seat on his throne, Satan suddenly becomes visible, appearing sparkling and "Starr-bright" like a masquer in a shimmering sequined costume during a masque discovery. Satan, however, can only shine forth "With what permissive glory since his fall/ Was left him, or false glitter" (442-52). In the unfinished poem *The Passion*, the narrator exclaims "O what a Mask was there, what a disguise!" in speaking of the divine Son's seeming masque costume, a glittering "starry front low-roofted beneath the skies" (18-19). In *Paradise Lost*, the antithetical false glitter of the evil Archfiend vanishes when in an "unmasking,"

> ...down he [Satan] fell
> A monstrous Serpent on his Belly prone,
> Reluctant, but in vaine, a greater power
> Now rul'd him...
>
> (513-16)

In *Paradise Lost* a multitude of devils stand outside the palace Pandemonium "Sublime with expectation when to see/ In Triumph issuing forth their glorious Chief" (536-37). When Satan finally appears bent to the ground, transformed into a monstrous serpent, the devils in turn also transmogrify into serpents, uttering, not a harmonious revels song, but "A dismal universal hiss, the sound/ Of public scorn" (508-09). They crawl and roll in a twisted anti-revel to a tree laden with seemingly delightful fruit. They then indulge in a punishing, infernal banquet which is introduced in a way conforming to the patterns of masque ritual. In tasting this fruit, they "Chew'd bitter Ashes" (566).

In contrast to the single transgression of Adam and Eve, they recurrently Fall subject to their own illusion:

> With hatefullest disrelish writh'd thir jaws
> With soot and cinders fill'd; so oft they fell
> Into the same illusion, not as Man
> Whom they triumph'd once lapst
>
> (570-73)

The linear structuring of prophetic epochal events is yet again simultaneously pressed into a possible cyclical pattern. Milton is again imaginatively playing with the paradoxes of form in eternity. Although the epic narrator takes note of "some tradition" holding that the devils "dispers'd/ Among the Heathen" (579-80), the narrator adds that the devils are

> Yearly enjoyn'd, some say, to undergo
> This annual humbling certain number'd days,
> To dash thir pride, and joy for Man seduc't.
>
> (575-77)

This Anti-Triumph of grotesque serpents, an eternal punishment depicted in seemingly both epochal and cyclical fashion, is a key structural event in prophetic universal history; for it recapitulates elements of the Son's harmonious Heavenly "begetting," and the First Parents' discordant Fall, and sets the stage for an end to human history through the final epochal intersection of the heavenly and the human.

Experimenting with another idea for a patterned end to human history through its integration with the divine, Milton in books 5 through 8 interposes a third containing historicist structure: a gradual spiritual evolution of an unfallen Adam and Eve to a condition close to that of the angels. Earth and Heaven would then conjoin in an ideal eternal kingdom of bliss.

Milton's references to the establishment of this ideal kingdom point, not to a sudden movement of beings up the hierarchical chain from one epoch of earthly history to a higher earthly epoch under the governance of Christ, but rather to an evolved realm in which matter has been by degrees gradually transformed into spirit.

This transformation goes forward until "all becomes immortal" and Earth becomes one with Heaven in an eternal Paradise.

Because discussions of this transformation take place between Adam and a partially material angelic historian who eats lunch with "concoctive heate" (5. 437), Milton may well be reacting to the materialist views of Thomas Hobbes who in the *Leviathan* argued that existing being is constituted of matter having extension and density, that matter when in motion is governed by mechanistic laws, and that material human beings in a primitive "state of nature" would war with one another unless restrained by an all-powerful monarchical ruler, a "mortal god."[10] Milton by contrast partially accepts but modifies the new materialism by apparently holding to Aristotelian metaphysical conceptions of a "first matter," "Indu'd with...forms," (3.472-3), by presenting an almost fluid gradation of being from the "corporeal" to the "incorporeal" (5.413), while retaining Aristotelian degrees, and by presenting the prelapsarian First Parents in a peaceful "state of nature" exercising the free rational choice that Milton, as a political pamphleteer, associated with citizens of a free Commonwealth. Milton in his writings makes no reference to mechanistic theories governing the motions of matter, theories of a kind held by René Descartes and Isaac Newton as well as by Hobbes.

In book 5 of *Paradise Lost* the angel Raphael, during that extraordinary prelapsarian lunch with Adam in Eden, explains how in a rising continuum that is also scaled, matter transforms into spirits which feed the rational soul:

> Mans nourishment, by gradual scale sublimed
> To vital Spirits aspire, to animal,
> To intellectual, give both life and sense,
> Fans and understanding, whence the Soul
> Reason receives, and reason is her being,
> Discursive, or Intuitive; discourse
> Is softest yours, the latter most is ours,
> Differing but in degree, of kind the same.
>
> (483-90)

Raphael's remarks are confirmed when Adam, though usually employing analytic or "discursive" rational powers, tells of his intuitive rational grasp of essences. Adam states that after his creation, as the newly-created animals approached him two by two, he with "sudden apprehension" intuitively "nam'd them as they pass'd" and without rational analysis "understood/ Thir Nature" (8. 352-54). Eve similarly knows and names the flowers.

Raphael, out of respect for Adam's basically analytic way of knowing, next explains discursively how the corporal "bodies" of human beings may someday further transform from matter into spirit.

> ...time may come when men
> With Angels may participate, and find
> No inconvenient Diet, nor too light Fare:
> And from these corporal nutriments perhaps
> Your bodies may at last turn all to Spirit,
> Improv'd by tract of time...
>
> (493-8)

On the assumption that the First Parents will remain faithful to God, Raphael then comments on the "end" of human history, but with obvious uncertainty over whether that "end" will be on earth or in heaven. Raphael suggests that the First Parents, eventually taking on an ever more spiritual form, might in the future "wingd ascend/ Ethereal, as wee, or may at choice/ Here or in Heav'nly Paradises dwell" (498-99).

In book 7 Raphael again refers to a final, paradisal kingdom. Quoting words spoken by God the Father in announcing the Creation of the earth and its sole inhabitant, the angel recounts to Adam how the Father proclaims that He

> ...will create
> Another World, out of one man a Race
> Of men innumerable, there to dwell,
> Not here, till by degrees of merit rais'd

> They open to themselves at length the way
> Up hither, under long obedience tri'd,
> And Earth be chang'd to Heav'n, & Heav'n to Earth,
> One Kingdom, Joy and Union without end.
> (154-61)

But Adam and Eve fall. The divine historian Raphael's speculations about possible spiritual progress are replaced by a tragic disruption, leading to a different prophesied future end to human and divine history. Raphael's original progressive design had depended upon Adam and Eve gradually lifting themselves through right choices near to the level of angels and perhaps beyond. But with the Fall, Sin and Death will find the power to complete their giant bridge binding Hell and its horrors to Eden; and in counterpoint, the Garden will lose its ready access to Heaven by way of a wide "passage" through the spheres and a mysterious ladder with "stairs" leading up to Heaven's Gate. The passageway after the Fall will narrow (3.526-32) and may possibly even be tilted so that the earth is no longer aligned with the heavenly gate. Under these circumstances, the First Parents' tragic descent into sin will require the direct, multiple interventions of the Son, who at the command of the Father sets another historicist design in motion by announcing to the First Parents their expulsion from Eden.

The second divine historian, the angel Michael, then descends to the Garden to instruct Adam. In book 11 Michael takes Adam to the highest mount in Eden and shows the First Parent visionary masque-like scenes of future human spiritual decline, silent *tableau vivants* of evils resulting from the Fall. These visions of turmoil, suffering, and death are centered upon Old Testament epochs— those of Cain and Able, Noah and the Flood—interspersed with visions largely of Milton's own invention: the sick and dying in a "Lazar-house" (480), the orgiastic Anti-Triumphs of the lustful People of the Plain (11. 723), and the horror and destructiveness of a battle. The thematic and theatrical nature of the visions presented and explained by Michael, and their many non-biblical iconographic features, grow in part from a notation by Milton in the final outline of his planned sacred representation "Adam Unparadiz'd": an Angel appears to Adam and "causes to passe before his eyes, in shapes, a mask of all the evills of this life & world" (311).

At the beginning of book 12, Adam learns of a low point in future epochal history. Michael tells the First Parent, without recourse to a vision, of the tyrant Nimrod, a type of Satan, and of his vain building of the linguistically-divisive Tower of Babble. The Nimrod epoch marks the last and most degenerate of the "evils of this life and world." From this juncture on, the angel Michael instructs Adam verbally, appealing to the First Parents' intellect instead of his senses, concerning an ascending series of spiritual epochs rising "From shadowie Types to Truth, from Flesh to Spirit" (303). These biblical epochs have been found to have been thematically developed by Milton from the last two sentences of "Adam Unparadiz'd": the figure Mercy appears before Adam, "comforts him, promises the Messiah, then calls in faith, hope & charity; instructs him" (311).

In place of the figure Mercy, Michael gradually comforts and then renews the faith and hope of Adam by speaking of the sons of Abraham, the Israelites Exodus from Egypt, Moses's reception of the Old Law on Mt. Sinai, David's establishment of a Holy Land kingdom of David, the Son's Redemption, Ascension, and Second Coming, the final actions making possible a paradisal end to human history. The total historiography in *Paradise Lost*, although often considered pessimistic, is thus turned in the last book to this rising hierarchy of epochal biblical events which, as the angel Michael properly notes, concludes in spiritual Triumph and so allows the fallen Adam to meditate on the "happie end" (12.605).[11]

Recent readings of the supposed "nightmare" of history in the last books overemphasize the anti-masque-type visual representations of the "evills of this life & world" in Book 11.[12] Greater attention needs to be given to the embracing, emotively uplifting, main masque-type Jubilee and Triumph celebrations of the Son in the early books, and to their relation to the spiritually ascending biblical epochs culminating in the Son's final Triumphs in book 12. The angel Michael's explanations of future events are indeed arresting, for they can be seen progressively to change Adam's total experience of history. Early readers—motivated after a bloody religious and political civil war to consider seemingly prophetic insights into the future, and alive to the experience of celebratory masque Triumphs and public processions—could also be expected to grasp the epic's spiritually positive conclusion to universal history.

Adam sorrowfully realizes that he and Eve must leave the Garden, and he knows that he will confront terrible evils in the world. Still, the angel Michael affirms that if the First Parent adds Deeds, "Faith," virtue, "Patience, Temperance," and "Love/ ...call'd Charity" to his "knowledge answerable," he will "not be loath/ To leave this Paradise, but shalt possess/ A paradise within thee, happier far" (12.585-87). Michael states further that when the end of human history arrives, the entire corrupted earth will be spiritually restored for the virtuous to a condition consonant with a "paradise within." The angel announces that "Earth/ Shall all be Paradise, far happier place/ Then this or *Eden*, and far happier days" (12.463-65). The First Adam understands at last the role of the Son as the Second Adam; and the First Parent fervently gives expression to his release from incipient pessimism and despair:

> O goodness infinite, goodness immense!
> That all this good of evil shall produce,
> And evil turn to good, more wonderful
> Than that which by creation first brought forth
> (469-72)

Milton in his early years had in fact thought that, despite the Fall, a conflict-free, ideal earthly state was at hand. In *Animadversions upon the Remonstrant's Defence against Smectymnuus* (1641), the poet openly declared that the Son's worldly "Kingdome" is about to be established.[13] And in *Of Reformation in England* (1641) Milton announced that the "shortly-expected King," the Son, "shalt open the Clouds to judge the severall Kingdomes of the World, and distributing *National Honours* and *Rewards* to Religious and just *Common-wealths,* shall put an end to all Earthly *Tyranies*, proclaiming thy universal and milde *Monarchy* through Heaven and Earth."[14]

But in his later years Milton, as passages in *Paradise Lost* and other writings suggest, lost his belief that the Second Coming was imminent. In *De Doctrina Christiana* on the basis of citations of Matt. xxiv, 36; and Mark xiii, 32, the author traditionally and appropriately identified as Milton, observes that "Only the Father knows the day and hour of Christ's coming."[15] He adds that on that day the "kings and priests of God" will "reign with Christ a thousand years" during what is called the "first resurrection" (*CPW*, 6.625). Satan will return, Milton maintains, after the thousand-year reign, unleashing the evil forces of Gog and Magog which nevertheless will be overcome by the righteous in the battle of Armageddon (*CPW*, 6.625). After this victory, the author states citing Luke 1.33, the Son will rule and "there will be no end to his kingdom" (*CPW*, 6.627).

Of the "end and conflagration" of the world, Milton writes, "whether this end means the actual abolition of the world's substance, or only a change in its qualities, is uncertain, and does not really concern us" (*CPW*, 6. 627). He then adds that "our glorification will be accompanied by the renovation of, and our possession of, heaven and earth and all those creatures in both which may be useful or delightful to us" (*CPW*, 6.632). In the words of God the Father in *Paradise Lost,*

> The World shall burn, and from her ashes spring
> New Heav'n and Earth, wherein the just shall dwell
> And after all this tribulations long
> See golden days, fruitful of golden deeds.
> With Joy and Love triumphing, and fair Truth.
>
> (3.334-38)

The powerful though spare prophetic millenarian language in Milton's epic will later find a secular counterpart in the plain, argumentative language of nineteenth- and twentieth-century earthly utopianism. And elements of Milton's prophetic and empiricist global representations will be found to embody structures and themes complimented, with different secular meanings, in historicist writings of later centuries.

In developing his strange historicist invention partially unveiling "The secrets of another world," Milton imaginatively and originally rendered the paradoxical intersection of a timeless eternity and human history employing multiple historicist designs. First, a linear movement underlies all events, a movement unfolding by way of traditional and invented heavenly and worldly epochs, depicted out of sequential order, that are directed toward a final apocalyptic end ushering in an eternal utopian union of heaven and earth. Next, within this linear epochal movement, key events—the revelation of the fullness of Godhead with the "begetting" of the Son, and the revelation of the punishment of Satan with the Archfiend's metamorphoses into a monstrous serpent—are depicted as timeless occurrences that nevertheless possibly recur again and again in a cyclical pattern. Milton, in placing his art above his republican politics, recognized the emotive appeal and the cyclical iconography of the indoor, staged masquing Triumph and so, even though it had been a royalist form before the English revolution, introduced it at the core of his epic heaven to unveil the Son.

In the temporal earthly world before the Fall, a progressive or developmental historicist design applies. The First Parents in Eden can rise, as the angel Raphael explains, through their free rational choices in a seeming evolving continuum, but also paradoxically by "degrees," from matter into spirit all the way to the level of angels and possibly beyond. But after Adam and Eve fall downward into sin, a dizzying but traditional medieval and Renaissance "roller-coaster" historicist design prevails. Through the Redemption, the First Parents, in what will be a paradoxical Fortunate Fall, will be spiritually uplifted by the Son and joined

147

directly to Godhead, rising far higher than they had sinfully descended.

Milton's is a subsuming poetic historicist vision, for at the end of mortal time, the poet suggests that all contradictions, antipathies, and political forms will disappear as the world is joined in an ideal union with eternity. As God the Father in book 3 says to the Son, using the "All in All" term for the Christ of I Corinthians 15.28,

> Then thou thy regal Sceptre then shalt lay by,
> For regal Sceptre then no more shall need,
> God shall be All in All.
>
> (3. 339-41)

9

AN OVERVIEW: ON "THE END OF HISTORY" AND THE PATTERNED FORMS OF WORLD HISTORICISM

Hegel, Marx, Globalization, and Beyond

The empirical and prophetic strands of Renaissance cultural historicism left their mark upon a number of the designs, practices, and even the language of historicist works in later centuries. But these later approaches to global as well as regional cultural historicism were extremely varied and were carried forward, as examples drawn from major works will illustrate, under ideological assumptions about reality often quite different from those of the Renaissance historicist reformers. Some of these assumptions had their roots in Renaissance thought in the areas of philosophical logic and mathematics, and of materialist, mechanistic physics.

In a sweeping and provocative generalization by a philosopher versed in both modern mathematical theory and Platonism, Alfred North Whitehead, noting the influence upon philosophy of seventeenth-century logicians and physicists from René Descartes through Isaac Newton, observed that "the enormous success of the scientific abstractions, yielding on the one hand *matter* with its *simple location* in space and time, on the other hand *mind*, perceiving, suffering, reasoning but not interfering, has foisted onto philosophy the task of accepting them as the most concrete rendering of fact." Whitehead here takes exception to the theoretical separation by Descartes, Locke and others of the supposed immaterial and logically analytical "mind" from supposed particles of extended and corporeal "matter," the last having simple location in space and explained when in motion in terms of mechanist principles. Noting that such theories were not in accord with modern physics and philosophy, Whitehead suggests that they were the productions of mathematicians for mathematicians." The great characteristic of the mathematical mind," he writes, "is its capacity for dealing in abstractions; and for eliciting from them clear-cut demonstrative trains of reasoning, entirely satisfactory so long as it is those abstractions, which you want to think about." Whitehead concludes,

> Thereby, modern philosophy has been ruined. It has oscillated in a complex manner between three extremes. There are the dualists, who accept matter and mind as on equal basis, and the two varieties of monists, those who put mind inside matter and those who put matter inside mind.[1]

While contemporary theories of mind and matter are far removed from those of the past, it has long been evident that in the seventeenth century a general philosophic breach opened between idealist, monist currents stressing immaterial mind and universal ideas, and materialist, monist currents stressing Early Modern conceptions of corporeal matter including that of the body. The breach appeared too in seventeenth-century dualist philosophical systems such as that advanced by Christ's College, Cambridge, and Neo-Platonist Henry More. In his published tracts, poems, and letters, this Anglican theologian-philosopher, who corresponded with René Descartes, sought in original ways to relate what he believed to be the "incorporeal substance" of the soul and its faculty reason; with impenetrable, corporeal, matter which he considered subject to Cartesian "mechanic" principles.[2] The philosophic ramifications of seventeenth-century, mind-body dissociations run deep, and may well have influenced, as Whitehead and others have speculated, a later widening academic separation of science, presumably weighted toward the study of "matter," from the humanities, presumably weighted toward the study of "mind."

From the perspective of an overview, the mind-body dissociation registered clearly in later idealist and materialist currents of historicism. As religion and theology gave way to secular outlooks, the dissociation surfaced in determinist or semi-determinist monist theoretical systems claiming empirical or philosophic knowledge of the universal historical processes, structures, and even the supposed "ends" of history, systems reflective in their design, if usually not their substance, of Renaissance faith-based models. So long as the theoretical universal "scientific" and philosophic historicist systems, particularly those propounding future utopian or catastrophic ends, remained predictive and problematical, resting on the force of argument and of evidence, they afforded sometimes illuminating, if also sometimes troublesomely restrictive, outlooks on the panoply of historical possibilities. But when such theoretical systems were insisted upon in the name of science and philosophy as inevitable, then this strain of theoretical historiography took on, in ways concealed by empirical or philosophic terminology, the absolute "truth" of prophetic designs. Past openly acknowledged faith in presumably transcendent divine revelation was replaced by unacknowledged faith in supposedly "inevitable" earthly historical outcomes which neither science nor philosophy, given the anomalies of history, could possibly postulate with certitude.

As will be seen, most of the later universal historicist designs touched upon at the end of this chapter are of another kind, being generally naturalist in approach in the sense of showing an interest in events and objects for their own sakes, in recording and analyzing events up to, but not beyond the contemporaneous "present," and in avoiding statements about supposedly known historical "ends." Verifiable evidence of the sort sought by Bacon, Purchas, and others becomes the bedrock of these historicist undertakings, distinguishing them from the abstractions, summations, and absolutism of some forms of philosophical and theoretical historiography.

During the French enlightenment in the period of Voltaire, Diderot, and Montesquieu, the direction of human history was presumably charted by generally skeptical philosophers and their followers. Human reason was envisaged as raising humanity by stages to a higher socio-political plateau and then on to the harmonious unity of humankind under reason. Yet following the enlightenment, belief in the power of humans to direct historical development was somewhat supplanted by a widespread faith in inalterable economic, biological, and related materialist and evolutionary trans-human historical "forces" pressing events and helpless individuals upward or into decline, with or without the rational consent of the individuals, toward some clear and certain end. Anyone surrendering to the presumably upward surge of such forces, and acting so as to support their inevitable outcome, could be assured of a victorious result. Because theorists sometimes insisted that a utopia, though inevitable, was immediately attainable only by force, impassioned believers acting to hurry along the establishment of an ideal society frequently thought themselves justified in using the most violent means.

Among a most incongruous and yet not atypical group of end-of-history theorists, who all surprisingly mirror in their systems elements of Renaissance designs, are the idealist philosopher Georg Wilhelm Friedrich Hegel, the materialists Karl Marx and Friedrich Engels, the socialist Robert Owen, and the recent and far less well known liberal-democratic economic "Globalist" Francis Fukuyama.

Hegel was directly influenced by Protestant biblical tradition; Engels in his coauthoring of works with Karl Marx, by socialist Robert Owen's secular reinterpretation of biblical and Miltonic designs; and Fukuyama by a stated desire to supplant religious utopianism with a world-wide secular liberal economic and political society. An initial cursory examination of this largely "activist," end-of-history wing of historiography will provide perspectives and contexts for comments later in this chapter on central movements in contemporary historicism.

152

Arguably the most full-blown of the secular modernist historicist systems mirroring the prophetic, and the one most influential in its varied ideological offshoots, is Hegel's effort to found a philosophy of universal history positing an inevitable historical process with a clear "end." In Hegel's *Philosophy of History*, the rhetorical, repetitive, ponderous and sometimes poetic abstractions of mid-nineteenth-century idealist German philosophy, centered on universal Reason and its dialectical relation to the empirical particulars and a so-called rational Spirit of the World, supplant Milton's prophetic epic renderings of a personalized Infinite Godhead of Reason.

Hegel, on the basis of his historicist philosophical analysis, claimed an end or a near-end to social and political history had been reached in Germany in his own time. "The History of the World," Hegel declares of the presumed dialectical progression of the rational World Spirit in earthly peoples and civilizations, "travels from East to West, for Europe is absolutely the end of History, Asia the beginning." In Hegel's view, the developing synthesis of Consciousness evident in the European libertarian rational enlightenment, illumined by the German Protestant religion, helped to generate recognition of that human freedom that represented history's "end." Consciousness then had come to a conception of freedom in the German nations at, in Hegel's words, *"the last stage in History, our world, our own time."*[3] Among Hegel's immediate followers, there remained the question of whether in their "own time" this "Consciousness" had been synthesized without contradiction in the fulfilled Rational Being of the World. The general opinion held was that, if a determinist "end" to history had not been reached, it was imminent.

Hegel, who had been moved by the sight of Napoleon entering the university town of Jena after a victorious battle, had been impressed by the French Emperor's code promulgating the rights of man. Although Hegel was later critical of Napoleon's rule, the philosopher conceived of the code as a logical development of contested ideas influencing German rational libertarian convictions and policies. Hegel's views in this area can be seen as stemming in

153

a general way, without suggesting the influence of specific documents, from an earlier tradition of English revolutionary libertarianism in part embodied in the arguments of Milton's anti-censorship tract *Areopagitica* (1644).[4] But while Milton in this tract addressed to the English parliament places stress upon the freedom and capacity of each individual to make right rational decisions, Hegel emphasizes that freedom established by law and decree in state and religious institutional documents. He also finds that a few "heroic" leaders advance collective freedom and justice through ideas and actions that are presumed emanations of the rational World Spirit.

Hegel also held to generalities that had much in common with the Providential historicism of Ralegh and Milton. Hegel himself notes that his philosophic view of universal Reason, immanent in the self-realizing World Spirit, is comparable to a religious position, namely "the *religious truth*, that the world is not abandoned to chance and external contingent causes, but that a *Providence* controls it." He thus associates the directing force of Reason, as an existent universal in his idealistic philosophic "science," with that of the Providential Christian God. Readers are asked to observe how the religious "truth…that a Providence (that of God) presides over the events of the world—consorts with the proposition in question; for *Divine* Providence is Wisdom, endowed with an infinite Power, which realizes its aim, viz., the absolute rational design of the World" (12-13).

In *The Philosophy of History*, Hegel asserts fundamental idealist conceptions that he considers to have been "established" in German and classical idealist philosophy, and he writes assuming his readers are idealists who agree. It "has been proved in Philosophy, and is here regarded as demonstrated," Hegel states, that the "'Idea' or 'Reason' is the *True,* the *Eternal,* the absolutely *powerful* essence; that it reveals itself in the World, and that in that World nothing else is revealed…" This conception of Reason is said to be "no hypothesis." Rather, Hegel claims that it has been

proved by speculative cognition, that Reason—and this
term may here suffice us, without investigating the
relation sustained by the Universe to the Divine
Being—is *Substance*, as well as *Infinite Power*; its own
Infinite Material underlying all the natural and spiritual
life which it originates, as also the *Infinite Form*—that
which sets this Material in motion...It is *the infinite
complex of things,* their entire Essence and Truth. (9)

"Reason" or "Idea," according to Hegel, is self-sufficient; but it
interpenetrates with the dynamic rational Spirit immanent in the
world and in human Consciousness. Reason in itself, Hegel
continues,

is exclusively its own basis of existence, and absolute
final aim, it is also the energizing power realizing this
aim; developing it not only in the phenomena of the
Natural, but also of the Spiritual Universe—the History
of the World. (9)

Hegel on the grounds of his "scientific" philosophy then goes
on to make the claim, stingingly mocked in Voltaire's satiric novel
Candide with special implied reference to the philosopher
Gottfried Leibnitz, namely, that "Reason is the Sovereign of the
World, that the history of the world, therefore, presents us with a
rational process" (9-10). Hegel, however, insists that this rational
process becomes evident from a philosophical study of the
collective historical dynamic of states and people, rather than from
the often chaotic experiences of individuals.

Two other key "given" assumptions underscore Hegel's
historicism. "All will readily assent to the doctrine," Hegel asserts
of Reason's "penetralia" of the World Spirit's properties, "that
Spirit, among other properties, is also endowed with Freedom" (10,
27). He then further states that "The History of the world is none
other than the progress of consciousness of Freedom" (19).

155

If the narrator of Milton's *Paradise Lost* seeks to "justifie the wayes of God to men,"[5] so Hegel in his *Philosophy of History* writes "that the History of the World, with all the changing scenes which its annals present, is this process of development and the realization of Spirit—this is the true *Theodicea*, the justification of God in History. Only *this* insight can reconcile Spirit with the History of the World—viz., that what has happened, and is happening every day, is not only not 'without God,' but is essentially his Work" (457). Still, in studying the philosophy of history, Hegel observes that "We must proceed historically— empirically." He refuses to be "misled" by false inventions, "for example, a widely current fiction, that there was an original primeval people taught immediately by God, endowed with perfect insight and wisdom..." (9). "This ante-history"—stories or myths about Eden or the early origins of peoples—"lies out of our plan" (60).

In short, Hegel is constantly aware of the relation between elements of Protestant prophetic religion and his own conceptual historicism. On the one hand, Hegel strains to distinguish his historical philosophy from religion and to make known his debts to the partly theological speculations of the philosopher Leibnitz. But on the other hand, Hegel assiduously calls attention to parallels and seeming identities between religious prophetic historicism and his ideological historicism. In attempting to create a philosophy of history, Hegel combines idealist conceptions of a developing Reason, with an epochal conception of historical "form" having a millenarian-type "end" reflecting Renaissance prophetic design, with a modernist Renaissance empiricist concern for factual events, global geography, and regional civilizations. He claims to be scientific while at the same time asserting absolutist philosophical knowledge of universal historical structure. Accordingly, he couches his formulations in vague idealist philosophical and religious language, adding also selected facts embedded in empirical terminology, so that his rhetoric remains to this day subject to conflicting interpretation. It comes as no surprise that Hegel's philosophical followers soon after his death split into religious and non-religious factions. Passages in his work are still read with different literal, ideological, or metaphysical-religious weightings, with the readings frequently mirroring the strong philosophical divisions of the commentators.

Hegel transcends the relative geographical provincialism of later social historical theorists—notably Friedrich Engels and Karl Marx—who were concerned largely with historical developments in industrial Europe and England and also in Russia. In a section of his study entitled "The Geographical Basis of History," Hegel examines the epochal stages of universal history in terms of the supposed dialectical dynamic of the "World Spirit" in successive "*Peoples*" and "Totalities that are States" categorized into distinct cultural "Worlds," each examined with an awareness of the new Renaissance and enlightenment global geography (14). The frigid continents of the Arctic and Antarctic, along with the central African continent, are dismissed with limited comments as regions lacking in rational "Universality" (93), and no serious evaluation is given to North and South America. But in the body of his study, Hegel stresses the dynamic of the Spirit in relation to events in first the "Oriental World" of the Far and Near East, next in the ancient "Greek World," then in the imperial "Roman World," and finally in central Europe and especially in the "German World." The Far East receives relatively limited treatment apparently because of Hegel's restricted knowledge of the area. Individual nations in each cultural World are singled out and analyzed with concern for geographical region, level and stage of civilization, internal cultural dialectical contradictions, and alleged degree of collective rational self-realization.

Summarizing in passing the ancient and present World of Asia, Hegel boldly states that

The Orientals have not attained the knowledge that Spirit—Man *as such*—is free; and because they do not know this, they are not free. They only know that *one is free.* But on this very account, the freedom of that one is only caprice. (18)

The Greek and Roman Worlds are said to manifest higher stages of rational self-realization:

> The consciousness of Freedom first arose among the Greeks, and therefore they were free; but they, and the Romans likewise, knew only that *some* are free—not man as such. Even Plato and Aristotle did not know this. The Greeks, therefore, had slaves; and their whole life and the maintenance of their splendid liberty, was implicated with the institution of slavery: a fact, moreover, which made that liberty on the one hand only an accidental, transient and limited growth; on the other hand, constituted a rigorous thralldom of our common nature—of the Human. (18)

Finally, a new consciousness is attained at the last stage of the World Spirit's inmost self-realization.

> The German nations, under the influence of Christendom, were the first to attain consciousness that man, as man, is free: that it is the *freedom* of Spirit which constitutes its essence. This consciousness arose first in religion, the inmost region of Spirit. (18)

Whatever the judgment on the "totality" of his wide-ranging idealist philosophy, Hegel considered here as a philosopher of world historicism reopened a troublesome current by reemphasizing a principle of classical logic—that of contradiction—which was traditionally applicable only at the highest levels of abstraction beyond material physics. He employed this logical principle together with Platonic conceptions of ideological progression, through dialectical dialogue, to rational synthesis and sometimes to alleged absolute truth. And he imposed these logical devices in a deductive way, moving from the abstract to the particular, as the means of gaining presumed philosophical understanding of the universal form and meaning of history.

158

However morally valuable Hegel's ideological emphasis upon the development of human freedom, a vast reductionism in historicist practice occurred. Inductive reasoning resting on experimentation and direct evidence, the basis of the scientific revolution sparked by the ideas and practices of Bacon, Purchas, Newton, and others, was very moderately used by Hegel, but ultimately subordinated by him to dialectics. Hegel's empiricism, as demonstrated in his treatment of the concrete particulars of global geography and cultures, consisted mainly in dialectically impressed and readily questionable generalities and strong opinions. He and his followers attained their dominating perspectives by "clothing" the devices of dialectic logic in large and sometimes polemical historical generalizations—with oversimplified definitions of cultural "contradictions" serving for entire civilizations—and then imposing them deductively upon the extraordinarily complex phenomenology of history. Meaningful distinctions, anomalies, and nuances, the seedbed of empirical discovery and original historical insight, were lost. And while all was put forward in the name of scientific philosophical historicism, Hegel's historiography in its conclusions about civilizations and peoples all too often rested unduly on forceful, repetitious ideological assertion.

Two famed radical followers of Hegel accepted dialectical analysis and a millenarian-type end of history, but they rejected Hegelian idealism together with Hegel's stress upon ideas of freedom. Friedrich Engels, the coauthor with Karl Marx of the *Communist Manifesto* (1848) and other works, joined with Marx in dramatically altering Hegel's historicist design by declaring the imminent end of history, not in a peaceful resolution of contradictions, but in a bloody world revolution. As is well known, this conflagration was supposed to usher in a presumably inevitable utopian one-class society without political or cultural contradictions. The two revolutionists thus reintroduced into universal history an Armageddon-like event, a penultimate battle that was to pit the oppressed proletarians and their intellectual supporters against exploiting classes.

159

Engels was pointedly critical of Hegel. While making literalist use of dialectics and other features of Hegel's thought, Engels reacted strongly against what he understood to be the philosophical substance of Hegel's historicism. "Hegel was an idealist," Engels complained, "to him the thoughts within his brain were not the more or less abstract pictures of actual things and processes, but conversely, things and their evolution were only the realized pictures of the 'Idea,' existing somewhere from eternity before the world was. This way of thinking turned everything upside down, and completely reversed the actual connection of things in the world."[6]

Engels advanced the basic elements of the epochal or period pattern of universal history, but he did so as a staunch materialist who used Hegelian dialectics in a literal way to disclose alleged "contradictions" in the class and economic make-up of society. And following the tradition of epochal historiographers, Engels inserted into his epochal design, at least by powerful suggestion, a pivotal human figure.

"His name will endure through the ages, and so also will his work!" Engels intoned at the graveside of Marx on March 17, 1881 at Highgate Cemetery, London. Engels exhibits the faith of a secular apostle in claiming that Marx with his materialist dialectics had "discovered the law of development of human history." Marx is therefore said to be "a mighty spirit" whose death represents "an immeasurable loss" to "historical science."[7]

Engels' historicism in effect took on an almost full epochal structure; that is, a pattern admittedly lacking a clear beginning or "Creation," but otherwise containing a number of epochs or periods separated by implication into a major Old and New division. Marx was placed in this great mythic divide, with history continuing thereafter only to terminate in a worldly conflagration followed by a transformed society of the elect.

The shadowed epochal form of Engels's historiography, with its Hegelian and its Renaissance historicist background, owed much to the literalist epochal historical outlook of a contemporary, the famed social reformer Robert Owen. Engels was well versed in

Owen's ideological plans to create a new society through a moral and educational revolution, and he demonstrated his empathy for Owen's project by contributing in the 1882-84 period to *The New Moral World,* probably the most significant of the numerous journals in which Owen's articles appeared. In an 1880 essay "Socialism: Utopian and Scientific," Engels expressed his deep admiration for Owen, noting that "Every social movement, every real advance in England on behalf of the workers links itself on to the name of Robert Owen" (615). The very word "Socialism" in Engels's title was so closely associated with Owen that, when Engels and Marx collaborated on the Manifesto, the pair appeared obliged to call their ideology "Communism" to distinguish it from Owen's then far better known variety of collectivism. A central theme of "Socialism: Utopian and Scientific" reinforces this difference. Engels, for all of his regard for Owen, argues that the reformer was definitely wrong, that Owen was setting himself against the forces of history in saying the transition to a utopian society would be peaceful. Scientific truth, Engels asserts, proves that historical contradictions would soon produce a world battle.[8]

Although Owen was a rationalist and behaviorist who rejected all religions, his secular reinterpretation of biblical epochal patterns, to which Engels in part objected, nevertheless proved influential. Owen posited a generally steady stage-by-stage improvement of humanity without overwhelmingly irregular disruptions. He excoriated the exploitation of workers, particularly women and children, in the frequently unregulated heavy industries of nineteenth century England. But in his many speeches and printed tracts, and his *The Book of the New Moral World* (1836), he argued that a rational secular moral education in a rational secular social environment would finally result in an ideal society insuring human happiness. Owen himself made faltering efforts to establish some small model villages, but he later abandoned these limited projects in favor of working for a general regeneration of society.

Biblical and Miltonic allusions add dimension to Owen's often flat, matter-of-fact prose. But in discussing the shaping social

161

impact of science and new inventions in *The Book of the New Moral World* (1836), Owen displays his generally pedestrian style and literal, behaviorist thought in making the doubtful claim that "Milton, Bacon, Locke, Newton, etc., among moderns, would in all probability, if they had lived before the invention of letters, have been ordinary men."[9] Flashes of missionary zeal, however, illumine his rhetorical announcements of an impending ideal society.

"The time approaches," he declares of a new, ascending "spirit" immanent in nature and the world, "when in the course of nature, the evil spirit of the world, engendered by ignorance and selfishness, will cease to exist, and when another spirit will arise...." This new spirit, a force of regeneration, will be found

> emanating from facts and experience, which will give a
> new direction to all the thoughts, feelings and actions of
> men and which will create a new character of wisdom
> and benevolence for the whole human race. This is the
> "NEW MORAL WORLD" in which evil, except as it
> will be recorded in the past sufferings of mankind, will
> be unknown. (xv)

For Owen this transformed world is not far away. Rational "truths," he insists, "openly and generally promulgated" in a reformed educational system will be accepted "in a short period" (11. 67). In complaining that a false and "irrational education" has spread error and made "the earth a Pandemonium," Owen metaphorically identifies earthly evil with the monstrous infernal Palace Pandemonium in book 1 of *Paradise Lost*, the "seat" of Satan and the site of illogical and willful speeches by the Archfiend and his demonic followers. But reformed education of a moral kind in a controlled environment, Owen maintains, will make "the earth a Paradise" (9.92)." The secular Owen here appears to draw indirectly upon the educational and moral reformer Milton; for the poet in his optimistic early prose tract "Of Education" (1644) seemingly ignores the doctrine of original sin in writing that the aim of education is to "repair the ruins of the first parents"

(Flannagan, p. 980). Owen, writing in a Miltonic vein, goes on to assert that in a transformation having millennial overtones, through education and proper moral development, "the whole human race, and the earth will be changed, in consequence, into a terrestrial paradise" (ix, 67).

In an 1837 debate with the Christian divine J. H. Roebuck, Owen, as noted by Ernest Lee Tuveson, gave vent to his longing for that inevitable end-of-history paradise in words echoing Isaiah's visionary description (2:4) of the New Jerusalem of the "last days," words later to appear in numerous Communist publications:

> Oh…that the time may now commence when men shall become rational, and, in consequence, turn their spears into pruning hooks, and their swords into ploughshares; when each man shall sit under any vine, or fig tree, and there shall be none to make him afraid.[10]

Engels, in his own polemical tracts and in those he coauthored with Marx, replicates Owen's shadowed millennial themes and excited missionary tone, but turns his attention from "ploughshares" and rational enlightenment to economics, class conflict, and the presumed absolute necessity for the impending, Armageddon-type world battle. In his essay "Socialism," Engels prophetically announces that the violent and inevitable revolution will propel "man from the kingdom of necessity" to a kingdom beyond all contradictions (638). "To accomplish this act of universal emancipation," Engels continues, "is the historical mission of the modern proletariat," and by means of this mission man will become "the lord over Nature" (639). But the millennial background of such declarations is now obscured by an insistence that the supposed theoretical truth of the end-of-history "mission" rests upon science. "This is the task of the theoretical expression of the proletarian movement," Engels writes, "scientific socialism" (639).

Together as coauthors of the Manifesto, Engels and Marx in their opening paragraph posit the antithetical social groups in the alleged class wars of past historical periods:

> Freeman and slave, patrician and plebeian, lord and serf, guildmaster and journeyman, in a word, oppressor and oppressed, stood in constant opposition to one another, carried on an uninterrupted, now hidden, now open fight, a fight that each time ended, either in a revolutionary reconstruction of society at large, or in the common ruin of the contending classes.[11]

In their last paragraph, the co-authors return to their Armageddon theme:

> The Communists disdain to conceal their views and aims. They openly declare that their ends can be attained only by the forcible overthrow of all existing social conditions. Let the ruling classes tremble at a Communist revolution. (362)

Marx in an earlier tract, *The Poverty of Philosophy* (ca. 1847, first edition), revised by the author in 1876 and corrected by Engels in 1885 and 1892, saw history ending when "there are no more classes and class antagonisms." "Till then," Marx added in a final passage citing a quotation in French, "on the eve of every reshuffling of society, the last word of social science will always be: 'Le combat ou la mort; la lutte sanguinaire ou le néant. C'est ansi que la question est invinciblemen posée. [Combat or death; bloody struggle or extinction. It is thus that the question is inexorably put.']"[12]

Marx, suffering in later years from pleurisy, attacks of bronchitis and other ailments, hardly passed his last years on the barricades. He took frequent trips to the Continent, and one to Algiers; but his was basically a sedentary existence of meetings, speeches, leaflets, heady revolutionary talk and days spent in reading *The Economist* at the British Library, by tradition, at his favorite end-of-the aisle location, row AA, seat G-7. He died peacefully in his London flat on the afternoon of 13 March 1882 after taking wine, milk, and soup.[13]

The bloody battle that was to engulf Europe and the world clearly did not take place as prophesied. With the demise of Communism as a major political force in Europe and as a governing institution in Russia, and with the expansion of a rapidly changing international global economy in the later twentieth century, prophesying the form of universal history and of future events has generally lost credibility in the West. Exotic modern varieties of historical universalism, however, still occasionally appear. Recently, for example, Francis Fukuyama has given an ironic twist to German idealist and Marxist anti-capitalist theory by choosing to build again upon Hegelianism while placing faith in free enterprise economics.

Fukuyama is one of the most recent and novel in that line of commentators who, under whatever discipline, claim to know much about the end of history and conveniently adjust their analysis to that end. In *The End of History and the Last Man,* Fukuyama adopts in a measured, practical way a Hegelian "directional" dialectic design for universal history, but with an "end" in liberal, democratic, controlled free-enterprise societies of equality and freedom.[14] Invoking an often-discussed issue, Fukuyama argues that the "globalization" by democracies of economics and culture and, indirectly, of liberal politics is the means to that "end." Whereas, Hegel conceived of the historical end as having been nearly or actually reached in 1806 in the rational world spirit of a supposed German liberal state and the Protestant religion, Fukuyama argues that the true "end" is on the verge of being reached—since it has not yet been entirely realized—in the consciousness manifest in the liberal political and social establishments of major democratic Western industrial countries. Such states are said to have generally resolved their central dialectical historical oppositions, although Fukuyama, as a flexible and practical theorist rather than a formal philosophical idealist, allows that held-over oppositions of race and class are still being worked out. In liberal democracies with regulated free enterprise economies, he argues, structures have been created for stimulating individual choice, for generating wealth in varied social sectors, and for solving those conflicts of "equality" and equity that remain.

Authoritarian governments that have attempted rigid and almost total control of complex economies, like those of the former Soviet Union and Maoist China, are seen as failures. They either collapse as in the case of the Soviet Union and its satellites, Fukuyama argues, or begin to adapt to free enterprise systems as in the case of authoritarian China. Eventually, he maintains, even the most authoritarian nations of the third world will adapt to free enterprise systems and be parties to the "end" of human historical development.[15]

Fukuyama's metaphor for the present historical situation rests on the equation of peoples and states to wagon trains on a trail leading to a town. Some of the wagons will break down, become lost, or wander down byways before returning to the trail. But in the end, all of the wagons will make it to the town.

Given his deep interests in technology and economics, Fukuyama is best described as a non-philosophical materialist. The idealist and semi-religious abstractions of Hegel are gone from his work, and in their place are occasional expressions, reminiscent of Marx, of antipathy to all religions. The God of Fukuyama, that is, the author's conception of the underlying force of history, appears to be economic and technological.

In place of the weighty philosophical somberness and absolute pronouncements of Hegel, and the harsh polemical dogmatism of Marx and Engels, Fukuyama, writing in a far lighter intellectual vein, exhibits a kind of heady Wall Street exuberance. All will eventually be well, even in most parts of the economically crumbling third world, if economic globalization is pursued and liberal democracy fostered. Fukuyama's optimism about the course of future world history is problematic at best, and his semi-dogmatic, prescriptive outlook suffers from the human author's supposed "knowing" in advance what the end of history will be. Events can then be fitted into this secular millenarian-type design so that everything turns out right in the end.

Despite Fukuyama's optimistic assertions, many underdeveloped countries grow poorer in relation to the wealth of developed nations, and significant human rights abuses continue throughout the world. Funds provided by Western governments and multi-national corporations to the totalitarian leaders of third-world nations often impede rather than advance liberal reforms. And in a manner unanticipated by Fukuyama, the growing globalization of cultures and markets has provided impetus to the globalization of previously-localized religious, economic and nationalist conflicts. Resulting outbursts of international terrorism have in turn given rise to recent Near Eastern wars, with violence and social and political dislocations continuing even after major-force combat has ceased. While globalization under present conditions and under loose systems of regulation apparently increases general wealth, debates persist about its overall benefits. The world-wide globalization of freedom, equality, and economic stability proclaimed by Fukuyama has yet to appear.

While regional and global outbreaks of violence have had multifarious causes, it is notable that in the Near East, where disputes over the control of many supposed holy places have flared since the crusades, resurgent outlooks drawn from archaic pilgrimage iconography continue to clash and strangely commingle with empirical and naturalist views. Arguments still rage over the physical "possession" of specific stones, caves, hillsides, and other pilgrimage stations that, although long venerated by religious peoples, in fact have no historical authenticity as the actual sites of religious events. Yet in even recent historicist writings, unexpected assumptions about the literal locations of such alleged holy places, assumptions resting exclusively upon imaginative pilgrimage spiritual geography, continue to reappear amid essentially empirical analysis, thus adding an emotive and in many cases a critically unexamined dimension to analytical discourse. The ghosts of medieval pilgrimage iconography still haunt contemporary historicism.

What an examination of determinist "end-of-history" structures makes especially plain is that acknowledged or unacknowledged belief in the inevitable future establishment of a terminal ideal or utopian world society on earth, whether the product of human action or inalterable historical "forces," is a belief that, however much desired, cannot be supported by philosophic or scientific historicist studies. This fact becomes all too apparent when immediate "dates" or time frames are set for the great transformational event—and then pass by. If belief is to be maintained, the "inevitable" is "rethought" and on occasion becomes the supposedly "predictable"; but with the passage of time, the "predictable" without analysis is sometimes assumed once again to be the "inevitable."

Insistence upon absolutist rational knowledge of history's future "end" as an element in historicist thinking has almost invariably led to disillusionment. Whether it is the theorist who posits a termination of history in a given time-span, or the dedicated reformer who promotes revolution expecting the imminent formation of a utopian society, or the economic "globalist" who proclaims history's terminus in a liberal, free-enterprise, international society—all exceed human historicist knowledge and so are vulnerable to the extraordinary surprises, dull repetitions, linear developments, and random accidents that unfold in the mysterious and irreversible flow of time.

* * *

The varied structures of Renaissance world historicist works, those without absolutist end-of-history pronouncements, have in themselves had an unexpected pattern of recurrence in historicist cultural works of later centuries. The "approach" and usually the substance of these subsequent historicist studies have, nevertheless, changed significantly with the development of scholarly and scientific disciplines.

At present the few attempted universal cultural histories tend to be humanist in outlook, relying upon the natural sciences and other disciplines to supply methods, perspectives, and phenomenological data. Such non-deterministic works eschew absolutist postulations, especially those on the "end" of history as unknowable, and concentrate instead on uncovering naturalist and philosophical values underlying the development and decline of civilizations.

Shorter works on cultural history, usually focused on a region or limited topic, tend to take individualized form from available source materials, with authors working out thematic and structural relations depending on the content of texts and documents. Milton so ordered his empirical *A Brief History of Moscovia*, simply stopping when his sources were exhausted and giving the impression to some that his completed work was unfinished. Authors of global histories, confronted with a seemingly limitless ocean of materials, necessarily tend to superimpose some overall ideological design which by its very configuration suggests or implies a direction or meaning to history.

The most substantive and authoritative cultural and attempted world histories have avoided pronouncements on inexorable historical processes and have structures ranging from an epochal or limited period form, to a repetitive or cyclical return form, to evolutionary or "progressive development" form—many with subtle and overlapping structural variations.[16] In seeking to move beyond factual comparative statements to evaluative judgments embracing the full range of human and social concerns, authors on occasion can be found, openly or by indirection, resting some portion of their evaluative analysis on faith-based secular or religious views not open to empirical verification. Technically, these histories then take on the qualities of theodicies, though the complete works remain essentially naturalist in content.

In the eighteenth century, structural categorization by period, the organizational method that dominated subsequent historical writing, was used in the rationalist productions of Voltaire, Diderot, Montesquieu and other French encyclopedists. Voltaire,

169

too, followed epochal period patterns in his seminal cultural history *Essai sur les moeurs et l'esprit des nations* (1745–53), covering the thousand-year span from the Carolingians to Louis XIV.[17]

In the nineteenth century, progressive developmental or evolutionary historicist designs appeared, with Auguste Comte coming close to a kind of secular prophecy in his *Cours de philosophie positive* (1830–42) which depicted humanity, in a kind of reversal of religiously oriented historicism, as moving from primitive theological cultures, to philosophical, to superior scientific or positivist outlooks.[18] Under the influence of later philosophic reflections such as those by Herbert Spencer on historical, biological, and cosmological evolution in *Synthetic Philosophy* (1884–87).[19] H. G. Wells popularized evolutionary historicism in his often republished *Outline of History* (1931). Wells in this work penned an occasionally speculative general account, beginning in prehistoric times, of progressive human development in the matrix of the evolution of the universe.[20]

Cyclical patterns of recurrence, suggested centuries ago by Plato and Aristotle, and employed by, among others, Livy and Machiavelli in their histories of classical Rome, were adopted in new ways by Giambattista Vico in his *Scienza nuova* (1720–21).[21] For Vico, changes in ancient Roman law served as an important index to presumed structured cyclical, political, and social alterations in a number of societies and civilizations. Versions of cyclical structure—based on the notion that certain patterns can be detected in the rise, decline, and fall of one or more civilizations— underlie a host of other works. These include Edward Gibbon's four-volume *The Decline and Fall of the Roman Empire* (1776– 88), a political and cultural analysis with a skeptically ironic treatment of religion. Oswald Spengler's largely determinist *The Decline of the West* (1918–22) examines a supposedly failing Western civilization as an organism having parallels to biological entities.[22]

In relatively recent times, Arnold Toynbee in his *A Study of History* (1934–61) spans a misty divide between the essentially empirical and the partly theological, while at the same time

170

rejecting dogmatic dialectical and end-of-history theories. After recording parallel elements in the growth and decay of major and minor civilizations in his study's initial six volumes, Toynbee saw fit in his last six volumes gradually to merge his basically cyclical analysis with conceptions of a possible spiritual process of linear development reflective of biblical patterns. Accordingly, he included in later segments—together with his continued and sometimes strident criticisms of nationalism and past religious failures—what he called the religious meta-history of key civilizations, a meta-history of those religious values which he had come to believe tended to unify humankind.[23]

Toynbee's simultaneous acceptance of seemingly conflicted designs, one with religious overtones, has been roundly and sharply criticized, yet it mirrors the sometimes inclusive practices of pre-Cartesian Renaissance historicists and, in its embrace of multiple historicist concerns, has evoked from reviewers glancing association with works by Milton and Hegel.[24]

More recently still, Felipe Fernández-Armesto has returned to a Renaissance historicist preoccupation in *Civilizations* (London, 2000) by adopting a regional approach to world cultures, but with contemporary stress upon the shaping role of environment. "Civilization is seen here," he writes, "as a kind of relationship between human society and the natural world."[25] Fernández-Armesto shows himself firmly in the naturalist historical tradition in exploring cultures arising in differing areas such as the tropics, arctic wastes, highlands, seaboards, and deserts. His work in theme is suggestive of seventeenth-century historicist Giovanni Botero's concern with "situation" and "climate," but without any of Botero's preemptory cultural judgments. For Fernández-Armesto, who avoids comparisons of civilizations while calling considerable attention to the achievements of some small and remote societies, "the degree to which a particular society is civilized is measurable on a scale of its own making" (xii).

In retrospect, it is clear that the turbulent marriage of Renaissance historiography to Renaissance cosmography, at first a cause of great confusion and a subject of satires by John Donne and others, fostered by the middle of the seventeenth-century cultural atmosphere engendering a powerful belief in the reality of the new external world, a belief so strong that it stands in graphic contrast to a strain of late twentieth-century skepticism resting on extreme theories of linguistic indeterminacy and extreme postulations of corrupting individual and collective bias. Samuel Purchas in 1619 overcame his rational skepticism as a historian in the face of the astonishingly rich empirical vision of a spacious new world. Renaissance voyagers had expanded the earth and its history just as in the twentieth century Voyager spacecraft—named to commemorate a tradition of continuing discovery—have together with ever more sophisticated space vehicles expanded historical and empirical knowledge of the solar system and the wider universe.

At present a general tension exists between an aggressive and cumulatively productive scientific culture dedicated to discovering verifiable processes and constituents of external being and human nature through experiments open to revision; and some currents in humanist culture dedicated to insisting, in a pendulum swing from the dogmatic structuralism of the nineteenth century to an extreme of late twentieth-century and now twenty-first-century relativism, that historiography is little more than linguistic fiction and subjective bias, and that it is best practiced in dense monographs on the smallest possible subjects. Such extreme views had not taken hold among most reformist historians of the seventeenth century. Fledgling science and historiography joined in seeking a reasonably objective, verifiable representation of a vast, new global reality.

In the Renaissance, the breakthrough discoveries inaugurated by the voyages of Columbus to the "end of the East"—together with the discoveries of the Americas, the Asiatic coastlines, the Siberian wastes, the islands of the Pacific, and the icy seas surrounding the polar caps—left deep impressions on the educated classes of Europe. The discoveries were often so unexpected, so forcefully experienced, and so richly reported in multiple accounts, that skepticism about their fundamental reality—as distinct from vexing debates over geographical location and exaggerated claims—dissipated by the end of the seventeenth century. Mariners in particular had been jolted out of doubt. Those who had come to disbelieve Columbus and had murmured against their commander on the first voyage dropped to their knees and begged forgiveness upon at last landing, against all expectation, upon the longed-for beaches of "the East." They were among the countless Renaissance seamen whose lives had been saved when, after weeks of fear and deprivation at sea, they were guided to strange shores by tenuous navigational and cosmological calculations and faith in a Providential God. They, like the educated persons of the West, came intensely to believe in the reality of an expanded earth with an expanded history. It was Bacon who instilled the notion that the discoveries by Moderns made possible by navigational science presaged the future advancement of learning in all fields, that science was but one form of learning among differentiated kinds of knowledge that would result in a new mixed history of the earth and its peoples.

The great contribution of late-Renaissance historiography, spurred by the reportorial literature of discovery, was to impress upon historical practice, which at the time remained largely prophetic in its structuring, strong primary documentation, a greater acceptance of multiple viewpoints arrived at by critical rational analysis, a rising concern about individual and collective distortion and bias, a tendency to treat religions in a comparative and factual as well as an evaluative way, a new focus on cultural and social content, and an increasing restriction of coverage to selected world regions. What emerged was a dawning consciousness that the collective history of peoples could best be understood in the light of their respective civilizations unfolding in time. Empirical methods acted as the essential base for the new works, although Baconian theories of different divisions and kinds of knowledge and values permitted the development of disciplines including theology relatively free of the conflicts inherent in the assumption that all knowledge is of the same kind. Under the growing pressures and restrictions of empiricism, universal histories, initially embracing all things from the beginning to the end, gave way to world cultural histories not ranging beyond the contemporaneous present and finally to cultural histories of particular regions and peoples.

Global histories are not impossible to produce, as numerous examples through the centuries show; but the form is impossible to produce in an authoritative way using strictly empirical norms. That is why tangential or actual prophetic approaches will not go away, why noticeably varied authorial treatments are so prevalent. Given the inexhaustible particulars of phenomenological reality, the extraordinary scope of global events over the centuries, the plethora of data in empirical reporting, the omissions and distortions in even the best of records and narratives, and the extreme difficulty in establishing any evaluative approach finding wide agreement, world histories are bound to be provisional. In their present phase, many of the works still include overt or implied faith-based evaluative assumptions, whether of a religious or secular ideological kind. In short, world histories are the most extravagant and voluminous extension on an epic scale of the encompassing critical essay, the analytical empirical report, and quite often the moral, philosophical, or theological overview—a massive "trial" of outlook and evidence—offering changing perspectives and insights on a perennial subject of importance: the family of the human race in all regions of the world in all recorded times.

NOTES

INTRODUCTION

1. In "The History of Globalization—and the Globalization of History?", *Globalization in World History* (London, 2002), editor A. C. Hopkins, referring to this collection of new essays by the Cambridge University history faculty, states that "the impulse to produce a universal history gained distinction and influence in the eighteenth century, when the philosophers promoted a new, cosmopolitan ideology." Hopkins observes that Kant in particular "advanced a speculative plan for spreading a cosmopolitan liberal order that would underpin a state of permanent peace" (12).

"Contributors to the debate on contemporary globalization," Hopkins continues, excepting the authors he has edited, "often look back through the twentieth century and a few extend their interest into the nineteenth century, but none give serious thought to the centuries between 1600 and 1800" (24). A second volume of essays by the Cambridge history faculty, *The Future of the Past; The Big Questions in History*, ed. Peter Markland (London, 2002), was accordingly published to provide long-term rather than short-term views of globalization and history. Out of the nineteen articles in the two volumes generally on specialized themes, three directly and helpfully embrace selective Renaissance issues; namely, Richard Drayton's "The Collaboration of Labour: Slaves, Empires and Globalization in the Atlantic World, c. 1600-1850" (*Globalization*, pp. 98-144); Amira K. Bennison's "Muslim Universalism and Western Globalism" on Muslim "land-of-Islam" and "land-of-war" world divisions and their decline (*Globalization*, pp. 74-97); and Jonathan Riley-Smith's "Religious Authority" (*Future of the Past*, pp. 1-15). Not one addresses the major Renaissance figures of the fifteenth through the seventeenth centuries considered in the present study, although notes and references in the essays contribute a valuable store of information on early periods and non-Western historiography. Most of the essays are weighted toward historical issues of the eighteenth century to the present, thus reflecting Hopkins's view that the recent impulse toward cosmopolitanism in the history of globalization was felt beginning in the eighteenth century.

Hopkins claims the "main weakness" of the preceeding period, which would include the Renaissance, "is its failure to take into account non-European perspectives on World globalization" ("The History of Globalization," p. 27). The present study stresses in nuanced ways, however, that Renaissance writers, while using biblical and other traditional materials, were heavily dependant as historical reformers on Renaissance regional and world voyage sources; and those sources immediately available in the West were written overwhelmingly by Europeans who at the time were the only seamen then circumnavigating the globe. As world historians, most Renaissance writers usually, but not always, displayed a decided European bias in their perspectives. But as world historiographers, they frequently devised and sought to apply empirical approaches and methods aimed at objectivity that transcended limiting European outlooks, that underlay eighteenth-century encyclopedic rationalism and that foreshadowed strains of twentieth-century empirical methodology.

2. See the international listings in Chapter II, *n*6, of pilgrim text sources, including those texts edited by Franciscans and published by the Franciscan Press in Jerusalem. It should be noted that long pilgrimages to Jerusalem, the medieval "navel" of the world, took participants through regions of the Near East beyond the sphere of Latin culture. In the Holy Land and Jerusalem, pilgrims from Africa and Asia as well as Europe regularly visited monasteries, hospices, churches, and holy sites controlled by Roman, Greek Orthodox, Coptic, and Syriac denominations. Jewish pilgrims from Egypt, Spain and other locales also journeyed to Jerusalem's holy places. And after the rise of Islam in the seventh and later centuries, pilgrims regularly passed through Muslim lands or, as crusading pilgrims-in-arms, fought against Muslim combatants. By way of the pilgrimage tradition, Byzantine, Muslim, and other Eastern influences thus filtered into Latin culture and literature.

3. See the sources for voyage accounts in chapter 3 on Richard Hakluyt, *n*1, 2; and throughout chapters 5 and 6 on Samuel Purchas.

1. RALEGH'S HISTORICIST INHERITANCE

1. Ralegh, *The Pilgrimage. Written by Sir Walter Ralegh, Knight, After his Condemnation, The Day before his Death*; London, Printed by George Larkin, 1681, unpaginated. All quotations are from this publication. When first printed in 1604 by T. C. for William Cotton along with a work entitled *Daiphantus* by "An. Sc.," the poem appeared without attribution under the title *the passionate mans Pilgrimage.* A strong textual tradition has resulted in the poem's rightly being ascribed to Ralegh; for in addition to its appearance under his name in the 1681 printing and in Bodeleian ms. Eng. Hist. c272 (a ms. assembled about 1628), the work in its setting, wit, themes, and spiritual passion reflects typical elements in this courtier's writings. Ralegh has accordingly been listed as the author in the notes and commentary of the standard edition of *The Poems of Sir Walter Ralegh,* ed. Agnes M. C. Latham (Cambridge, Mass., 1962), pp. 49-51; and in *Sir Walter Ralegh: Selected Writings,* ed. Gerald Hammond (Manchester, 1984). Raleigh Trevelyan in *Sir Walter* Raleigh (London, 2002), pp. 391-93, repeats a traditional view in surmising that Ralegh, when incarcerated for the first time in 1603, penned the verse after learning his execution for treason, later reprieved by James 1st, was scheduled for Dec. 13th of that year. However, Philip Edwards in "Who wrote 'The passionate man's pilgrimage'," *English Literary Renaissance* 4 (1974): 83-97, following Pierre Lefranc, *Sir Walter Ralegh, Ecrivain* (Paris and Québec, 1968), pp. 84-85, has raised questions about the alleged time of composition, the irregular metre, and the seeming Catholic nature of this pilgrimage verse by a presumed Protestant courtier. Although recognizing that the poem could have been composed by Ralegh late in 1603 during the poet's imprisonment under a death sentence, Edwards suggests an unknown author.

Neither Edwards nor Lefranc read *The Passion* in the light of the medieval pilgrimage tradition, nor do they take into account the force of that tradition as discussed in the next chapter, sections I and II, and in notes 6 through 14. Ralegh's verse in fact merges "old" conventional processional pilgrimage with "new" witty unconventional allusions to earthly law-court depravity, the paradox of decapitation, and providential entry into the court of heaven. Stephen Greenblatt in *Sir Walter Ralegh: The Renaissance Man and His Roles* (New Haven and London, 1973), p. 123, thus appropriately finds the mixed nature of this pilgrimage-occasional poem in irregular metre in the self-dramatizing, original mode of Ralegh. The verse is not so much somewhat Catholic, in the often partisan meaning of that term in Renaissance England, as late medieval in its traditional signification of earthly pilgrimage as an allegorical type for the journey of the soul from earth to heaven, a metaphoric identification retained in Protestant as well as Catholic writing. Yet like Ralegh's *The History of the World,* which combines references to the ancient forty-two Stations of the Exodus with original historical analysis, the poem invests the ancient pilgrimage tradition with novel, topical elements.

2. Ralegh, *The History of the World*; London, Printed for Walter Bvrre, 1614. Huntington shelf mark 289707. All quotations of *The History* are from this edition. See also *The History of the World. In Five Bookes* ; London, Walter Bvrre, Printed in 1634, but with a 1614 title page. Huntington shelf mark 21776. Ralegh's *The History* was also republished in the seventeenth century in 1617, 1621, 1628, 1652, 1666, 1671, 1677, and 1687.

3. Ross, *The Marrow of History: Or, an Epitome Of all Historical Passages from the Creation, to the end of the last Macedonian War.* First set out at large by Sir Walter Rawleigh, and now Abbreviated by A. R, 2nd ed.; London: Printed by John Place and William Place, 1662. Ross, like Thomas Blunderville who wrote academic exercises, apparently found a regular reading audience for his epitomies, publishing, for example, mixed opinions on the human body in *Arcana Microcosmi: Or, The hid Secrets of Man's Body discovered; In an Anatomical Duel between Aristotle and Galen concerning the Parts thereof:* As also, By Discovery of the strange and marveilous Diseases, Symptomes & Accidents of Man's Body. With A Refutation of Doctor Brown's *Vulgar Errors,* The Lord Bacon's *Natural History,* and Doctor Harvy's Book *De Generatione,* Comenius, and Others; London, Theo Newcomb, 1652. In this work, unlike his condensation of Ralegh, he points out his differences with others including Francis Bacon, whom he attacks for holding that the alchemical creation of gold is possible. See also Alexander Ross, *Mystagogvs Poeticus, or The Muses Interpreter: Explaining The Historical Mysteries, and mysticall Histories of the ancient Greek and Latine Poets.* Here *Apollo's* Temple is again opened, the *Muses* Treasurers the second time discovered, and the Gardens of *Parnassus* disclosed more fully whence many flowers of usefull, delightfull, and rare Observations, never touched by any other *Mythologist* are collected, 2nd ed.; London, T. W. for Thomas Whitaker, 1643. Ross published as well an epitomie of world religions entitled *A View of all Religions of the World, From the Creation, to these time together with A Discovery of all known Heresies in all Ages and Places*; London, Printed for Iohn Saywell, 1653.

4. Sir Walter Ralegh, *The Discoverie of the large and bewtiful Empire of Guiana, with a relation of the great and Golden Citie of Manoa (which the Spanyards call El Dorado) And of the Prouinces of Emeria, Arromaia. Amapaia, and other Countries, with their riuers, adioyning,* London, Robert Robinson, 1596; unpaginated title page; intro., 3. Huntington shelf mark 17919. A detailed summation of the historical background to Ralegh's Guiana expedition of 1595 appears in Raleigh Trevelyen's *Sir Walter Raleigh,* pp. 231-50. For a discussion of the roles, ventures, and activities of Ralegh, see Stephen J. Greenblatt, *Sir Walter Ralegh: The Renaissance Man and his Roles.* Greenblatt has rightly called attention to Ralegh's self dramatization, and his stylized projection of elements of his own personality into his writings.

5. See the *Book of Sir John Maundeville*, ed. Thomas Wright, *Early Travels in Palestine* (London, 1848), pp. 220, 276. The *Book* circulated in French, Latin, and English versions has long been attributed possibly to Jean de Bourgogne and Jean d'Outremeuse. It contains an account of a journey beginning in England in 1322 to the Holy Land, then to the regions of "Prester John," and finally back to the west in 1356. The arguments for various authors, and the view that one of them had actually been to the Holy Land, are presented in *The Buke of John Maundeuill,* ed. George F. Warner [British Museum, Egerton Ms. 1982 together with French text, notes, and intro., including illustrations from British Museum Ms. 24,198] Westminster: Nichols and Sons for the Rorburghe Club, 1889. See also *The Voyages and Trauailes of* Sir *John Mandeuile KNIGHT*, London, Thomas Snodham, 1625, Huntington shelf mark 62427; and *The Bodley Version of Mandeville's Travels,* ed. M. C. Seymour (London, New York, Toronto, 1963).

6. See John G. Demaray, *The Invention of Dante's Commedia*, (New Haven and London, 1974), pp. 119-26, 169-77.

7. In an accompanying introductory poem, Ralegh writes that the personified figure "grave *Historie*" raises events from "*Death* and darke *Oblivion*" to "good, or evil *Fame*." but that "High *Providence* oversees all that occurs." Cicero, to whom Ralegh is indebted, provides a famed definition of history in *De oratore,* ii, ix 36, trans. E. W. Sutton (Cambridge, Mass., 1942). The Latin text in this Loeb Classical Library edition reads: "Historia vero testis temporum lux veritatis, vita memoriae, magistra vitae, nuntia vetustatis." The translation by E. W. Sutton is rendered as "History …bears witness to the passing of the ages, sheds light upon reality, gives life to recollection and guidance to human existence, and brings tidings of ancient days."

8. See the analysis of a range of late medieval epochal histories in C. A. Patrides's *The Phoenix and the Ladder: the rise and decline of the Christian view of history* (Berkeley, 1974).

9. Thomas Lanquet and others, *An Epitome of Chronicles*, London: no listed printer, 1559.

10. Holinshed, *The First [Last] volume of the Chronicles of England, Scotland, and Irelande.* London: George Bishop, 1577. For English historical writings from the end of the fifteenth century to early in the seventeenth, see May McKisack, *Medieval History in the Tudor Age* (Oxford, 1971); F. J. Levy, *Tutor Historical Thought* (San Marino, Calif., 1967); F. Smith Fussner, *The Historical Revolution: English Historical Writing and Thought 1580-1640.* (London, 1962); Herschel Baker, *The Race of Time: Three Lectures on Renaissance Historiography* (Toronto, 1967); Charles L. Kingsford, *English Historical Literature in the Fifteenth Century* (Oxford, 1913), and J. G. A. Pocock, *The Ancient Constitution and Feudal Law: A Study of English Historical Thought in the 17th Centuries* (Cambridge, 1957).

11. Christopher Hill in *Intellectual Origins of the English Revolution* (Oxford, 1965), 195, repeats the view that Ralegh's work helped to establish "the groundwork for the English Revolution" through its strong criticisms of past British monarchs, but it should be noted that this revolutionary "groundwork" is limited to a few pages of the Preface and was probably added by Ralegh as a late afterthought. The body of Ralegh's unfinished work is the epochal and narrative history of the human race.

12. *Relations of the most famovs kingdomes and Commonwealths thorowout the world: Discoursing of their Situation, Religions, Languages, Manners, Customes, Strengths, Greatnesse and Policies*, English trans. R. I.; London: Printed by John Haviland, 1630. This work was translated from the Italian into Latin, Spanish, French, as well as English.

13. Peter Heylyn. *Microcosmvs, or A Little Description of the Great world.* A Treatise, Historicall, Geographicall, Politicall, Theologicall. Oxford: Printed by John Lichfield and Iames Short, 1621, p. 18. Dedicated to Charles, Prince of Wales.

14. Arnold, *On Classical Tradition*, ed. R. H. Super (Ann Arbor: 1960), pp. 26-28.

15. Hill, *Intellectual Origins of the English Revolution* (Oxford: 1965), pp. 183, 187-88. See also F. J. Levy, *Tutor Historical Thought* (San Marino, 1967), 294, who notes that

Ralegh embraced both the empirical and religious historical traditions of his time and so "recapticulated the entire sixteenth-century development" of English historical thought.

2. "HIGH AND RARE DELIGHT"
A. Conflicted World Visions

1. See the first edition of *The Principall Navigations, Voiages and Discoveries of the English nation, made by Sea or ouer Land, to the most remote and farthest distant Quarters of the earth at any time within the compasse of these 1500 yeeres: Diuided into three seuerall parts*, London: George Bishop and Ralph Newberie, 1589, p. 2.

2. Abraham Ortelius, *Theatrum Orbis Terrarum. The Theatre of the Whole World,* English tr.; London, John Norton, 1606; "to the courteous Reader," unnumbered page. Huntington 62823.

3. "The Geography of Holy Writers" subsection: "A draught and shadow of the ancient Geography," fol. v. j.

4. *Theatrum Orbis Terrarum,* "to the courteous Reader," unnumbered page.

5. See the monograph by G. R. Crone published with *The World Map by Richard of Haldingham in Hereford Cathedral* (London, 1954). See also reproductions of early *mappaemundi* reproduced in Leo Bagrow's *History of Cartography*, rev. and enl. R. A. Skelton, trans. D. L. Paisey, (Cambridge, Mass., 1964.); and C. Raymond Beazley's *The Dawn of Modern Geography*, 3 vols. (Oxford, 1906). See also Marcel Destombes, *Mappaemondes: A.D. 1200-1500* (Amsterdam, 1964), pp. 21-23.

6. See in particular the medieval and early Renaissance texts of Holy Land pilgrimages published by Franciscan editors in Jerusalem, namely, *Western Pilgrims*, ed. Eugene Hoade (Jerusalem, 1952) with an excellent bibliography of English pilgrim texts of the fourth through the seventeenth centuries (pp. 80-114); *Leonardo Frescobaldi, Georgio Gucci, and Simone Sigoli: Visit to the Holy Places*, trans. Fr. Theophilus Bellorini and

Fr. Eugene Hoade, preface and notes Fr. Bellarmino Baggatti (Jerusalem, 1948); and Nicollo of Poggibonsi, *A Voyage Beyond the Seas*. trans. Fr. Theophilus Bellorini and Fr. Eugene Hoade, intro. Fr. Bellarmino Bagatti (Jerusalem, 1954). See also the medieval pilgrimage writings published individually and then collectively in the late nineteenth century, by a British-controlled organization, under the title *The Palestine Pilgrims' Texts Society*, 14 vols. (London, 1887-97). These repeated accounts in texts of the same Holy Land pilgrimage rituals and iconographic stations, with limited geographic and positivist comments, belong essentially to the literature of "spiritual travel." See too Mahfouz Labib, *Pèlerins et Voyageurs au Mont Sinai*, Cairo, French Oriental Insititute, 1961; *Itinéraires à Jérusalem et Descriptions de la Terra Sainte,* ed. Henri Michelant and Gaston Raynaud (Geneve, 1882); *Itinera Hierosolymitana et Descriptiones Terrae Sanctae*, Titus Tobler and Augustus Molinier (Osnabruck, 1966), *Itinéraires Russes en Orient*, ed. Mme. B. Khitrowo (Osnabruck, 1966); and *Deutsche Pilgerreisen nach dem Heiligen Land*, ed. Reinhold Rohicht (Aalen, 1967). See also Julia Bolton Holloway's "The *Vita Nuova*: Paradigms of Pilgrimage," *Jerusalem: Essays on Pilgrimage and Literature* (New York, 1998), pp. 101-20, on the allegorical meaning of the pilgrimage Stations of the Exodus as reflected in the themes and structure of Dante's *Vita Nuova*. An account of the Exodus, Jerusalem, and Rome Stations appears in John G. Demaray, "Patterns of Earthly Pilgrimage in Dante's *Commedia:* Palmers, Romers, and the Great Circle Journey," *Romance Philology* (November, 1970), 239-58; and "Pilgrim Text Models for Dante's *Purgatorio*," *Studies in Philology* (January, 1969): 1-24. Donald R. Howard in *Writers and Pilgrims: Medieval Pilgrimage Narratives and Their Posterity* (Berkeley, Los Angeles and London, 1980) provides what he terms an "aerial view" or "capsule history" of selected pilgrimage texts with stress upon the literary values of later works (ix, 53).

7. *Grand chronique de Mathieu Paris*, trans. Huillard-Breholies (Paris, 1840-44).

8. *The Pilgrimage of St. Silvia of Aquitania to the Holy Places,* intro., notes, trans. John H. Bernard (London, 1891), pp. 15-16. For a detailed account of the long pilgrimage and its rituals, see also John G. Demaray, *The Invention of Dante's Commedia* (New Haven, 1974), chapter 1, "Pilgrimage in the Source Book of the World"; and chapter 5, "Through Shadowy Realms of the Living."

9. Fetellus, *Description of Jerusalem and the Holy Land*, trans. James Rose MacPherson (London, 1896), p. 14. *Itinerary from Anonymous Pilgrims I-VIII,* trans. Aubrey Stewart (London, 1894), p. 40. Stewart's translation is based upon the text published in *Oesterreichischer Vierteljahreschrift fur Katholische Theologie,* notes V. Newmann (Vienna, 1868, 1870).

10. *Bordeaux to Jerusalem*, trans. Aubrey Stewart, notes. C. W. Wilson (London, 1887), pp. 19-25.

11. *The Itinerary of Bernard the Wise*, trans. J. H. Bernard (London, 1893), pp. 3-10.

12. See the extended discussions of Dante's "theological" allegory, with its back-references to earthly events, in A. C. Charity, *Events and their Afterlife: The Dialectics of Christian Typology in the Bible and Dante* (Cambridge, England, 1996); and in Charles S. Singleton, "In Exitu Israel de Aegypto" *Seventy-Eighth Annual Report of the Dante Society* (Boston, 1960): 1-24; Dante *Studies I: "Commedia" Elements of Structure* (Cambridge, Mass., 1954); and *Dante Studies II: Journey to Beatrice* (Cambridge, Mass., 1958). Erich Auerbach in *Dante Poet of the Secular World,* trans. Ralph Manheim (Chicago, 1961) argues in a figural reading that the *Commedia* is a fulfilled type of earthly life. See William Anderson's tracing of earthly pilgrimage *figura* in the *Commedia* in *Dante the Maker* (London and Boston), 1980, pp. 331-332; Rodolfo Benini's association of Mt. Sinai and Dante's Mt. Purgatory in "Il grande Sion, il Sinai, e il piccolo Sion," *Rendiconti della Reale Accademia dei Lincei,* 5th ser. 23 (Roma, 1915): 1-27; and the Egypt-Jerusalem-Rome typology and the differing approaches to Dante's allegory in John G. Demaray, *The Invention of Dante's Commedia,* pp. 93-115 and throughout, and in *Dante and the Book of the Cosmos* (Independence Square,

184

Philadelphia, 1987), pp. 32-104. An analysis of the fourfold senses of medieval Biblical exegesis as it relates to Dante and other early writers, together with a bibliography, appears under the heading *In exitu Israel de Aegypto* (entry, John G, Demaray) in *The Dante Encyclopedia*, gen. ed. Richand Lansing et al. (New York and London, 2000): 506-08. See also the voluminous body of patristic allegorical and symbolic interpretations of biblical passages in *Patrologiae cursus completus, Series Graeca*, ed. Jacques Paul Migne, 161 vols. in 166 books (Paris, 1857-66) and *Series Secunda* [Latin], ed. Jacques Paul Migne, 221 vols. (Paris, 1844-55). Although Julia Reinhard Lupton's ideological study of "narrative logics," *Afterlives of the Saints: Hagiography, Typology, and Renaissance Literature* (Stanford, 1996), is not directly concerned with traditional pilgrimage texts and related medieval allegorical writings, the work does afford insight into the later Renaissance fragmentation and reconfiguration of diverse secular and religious types and icons in art and literature—particularly in Boccaccio's *Decameron*, Vasari's *Lives of the Artists,* and Shakespeare's *The Winter's Tale.* Lupton maintains, for example, that Shakespeare's play "performs" as "an *iconography of idolatry*" and accordingly "constitutes 'secular drama'" through "the reanimation of the fragments left over by the repeated breaking of idols in the history of the West" (pp. 177-78).

13. See the discussion of pilgrimage themes in the *Faerie Queene* in John G. Demaray, *Cosmos and Epic Representation*, pp. 122-75.

B. Columbus, the East, and Millennial Jerusalem

14. See Tezevtan Todorov, *The Conquest of America: The Question of the Other,* trans. Richard Howard (1982; New York, 1984), pp. 14-50. As Todorov has shrewdly remarked, Columbus was both an intense observer and an intense reader of signs. The details that Columbus notes here as elsewhere are not attempts to record the world as it presented itself to his eyes, as Todorov makes plain, but compilations of significant iconographic markers usually having biblical connotations (p. 89). See also Stephen Greenblatt, *Marvelous Possessions: The Wonder of the New World* (Chicago, 1991), for an analysis of Columbus's imaginative and mythic elaboration in reporting his discoveries.

Franciscan typal identifications of newly-discovered regions with the Holy Land and biblical events, identifications of a kind made by Columbus, are discussed in John Leddy Phelan's *The Millennial Kingdom of the Franciscans in the New World*, 2nd ed. (Berkeley, 1970). The numerous medieval and early Renaissance typal reproductions in the West of the Holy Sepulchre, located at the world's alleged center in Jerusalem, are examined in Damiano Neri's *Il S. Sepolcro riprodotto in Occidente* (Jerusalem, 1971). Norman Cohen has traced medieval millinarian notions in general as related to Jerusalem in *The Pursuit of the Millenium* (New York, 1961).

Recent assessments of Columbus as a Renaissance colonizer, exploiter, and explorer appear in Kirkpatrick Sale, *The Conquest of Paradise: Christopher Columbus and the Columbian Legacy.* (New York, 1990), and Michael Paiewonsky, *The Conquest of Eden 1493-1515.* Rome, St. Thomas, Tortola: MAPes MONDe Editore, undated.

Heroic representations of Columbus first appear in a biography by the admiral's son, Ferdinand Columbus, in *The Life of the Admiral Christopher Columbus*, tr. and intro. Benjamin Keen (New Brunswick, 1959). The standard biography of Columbus is that of Samuel Eliot Morison, *Admiral of the Ocean Sea: A Life of Christopher Columbus,* 2 vols. (Boston, 1942).

15. See *Dante and the Book of the Cosmos,* pp. 27-83.

16. A. Milhou, *Colón y su Mentalidad Mesiánica en el Ambiente Franciscanista Español* (Valladolid, 1983), pp. 42-45.

17. *The Libro de las profecias of Christopher Columbus*, a facing page edition. Trans. and notes, Delno C. West and August Kling (Gainesville, Fl, 1991). See also *Christopher Columbus's Book of Prophecies, Reproduction of the Original Manuscript with English Translation*, ed. and trans., Kay Brigham (Barcelona and

Fort Lauderdale, Fl., 1991). In Fol. 4, "Letter from the Admiral to the King and Queen": Columbus restates his "argument for the restitution of the Holy Temple [in Jerusalem] to the Holy militant Church" (Kay, p. 178), and then in later segments, refers by means of biblical quotations to the conversion of humanity to Christianity under the auspices of his own actions as authorized by the Spanish monarchs. See also Pauline Moffitt Watts, "Prophecy and Discovery: On the Spiritual Origins of Christopher Columbus's 'Enterprise of the Indies,'" *The American Historical Review* 90.1 (Feb., 1985), 73-102; and Djelal Kadir, *Columbus and the Ends of the Earth: Europe's Prophetic Rhetoric As Conquering Ideology* (Berkeley, 1992).

18. Lionel Cecil Jane, ed. and trans., *The Voyages of Christopher Columbus, being the Journals of his First and Third, and the Letters Concerning his First and Last Voyages* (London, 1930), pp. 142. See also Lionel Cecil Jane, ed. and trans., *Select Documents Illustrating the Four Voyages of Christopher Columbus: A History in Eight Documents*, 2 vols. (London, 1930-32). Although the original journal of the first voyage is lost, the admiral's son Ferdinand cited the journal in his life of his father; and las Casas, the Dominican historian, made an abstract of it with his own commentary and many direct quotations from Columbus's writings.

19. *The Voyages*, p. 299.

20. *Select Documents Illustrating the Four Voyages of Christopher Columbus* (1932), vol. 2, second series, No. 70, pp. 30-31. See John Noble Wilford's explanation in *The Mysterious History of Columbus: An Exploration of the Man, the Myth, the Legacy* (New York, 1991) of why Columbus, influenced by "Medieval Christian cartographers" who had placed the Earthly Paradise "at the nether end of Asia," "felt sure he had identified the the site" on the supposed Asian mainland (210). As Wilford has pointed out, Peter Martyr in 1501 claimed that Columbus had named the shores of Cipangu—supposedly Japan but really Cuba—"Alpha and Omega" because this explorer "thought that there our East ended when the sun set in that island, and our West began when the sun rose" (quoted on p. 208). Wilford in his chapter "God's Messenger" discusses too the impact of medieval millinarian notions on Columbus's outlook, both early and late. (215-34). See also Wilford's *The Mapmakers* (New York, 2000) for a review of changing cartographic perspectives.

21. *Select Documents Illustrating the Four Voyages of Columbus* (1932), vol. 2, second series, No. 70, pp. 36-38. See also. M. Cohen, *The Four Voyages of Christopher Columbus* (Harmondsworth, 1969), pp. 216-24.

22. *The Libro de las profecias of Christopher Columbus*, p. 101.

23. *Select Documents Illustrating the Four Voyages of Columbus,* vol. 2, second series, No. 70, pp. 104.

24. *The Voyages*, p. 133.

25. *Select Documents Illustrating the Four Voyages of Columbus,* vol. 2, second series, No. 70, p. 104. The reference to Joachim is to Joachim, abbot of Flores, and to his work *Oraculum Turcicum* which, however, makes no allusion to Spain. Columbus introduces the same prophecy, again mentioning Spain, in his *Libro de las Profecias*, I, ii, 83. St. Jerome while residing in the Holy Land succeeded in urging a wealthy Christian matron to make a pilgrimage from Rome to Jerusalem and Bethlehem.

26. *The Voyages*, pp. 162. See also *Select Documents Illustrating the Four Voyages*, 2 vols.

27. *The Voyages,* p. 176.

28. Valerie J. Flint, *The Imaginative Landscape of Christopher Columbus* (Princeton, 1992), pp. 25-36. Pauline Moffitt Watts, "Prophecy and Discovery: On the Spiritual Origins of Christopher Columbus's 'Enterprise of the Indies,'" pp. 75-85, presents an excellent analysis of Columbus's confusion in relying both on D'Ailly's *Imago mundi* and medieval *mappaemundi;* and she discusses also "Columbus's preoccupation with the final conversion of all races on the eve of the end of the world" (p.93). See also the account of the loss in the middle ages of Ptolomy's cartography in Peter Whitfield, *The Image of the World: 20 Centuries of World Maps* (San Francisco, 1994), pp. 10 ff. As has long been recognized, Greek and Roman geographical writings after 300 A.D. do not refer to Ptolomy. The reintroduction of Ptolomy to the West occurred after the appearance in 1406 in Florence of a Latin translation of his geographical works.

29. See Flint, *The Imaginative Landscape*, p. 152. See also the chapter "Did Columbus Believe That He Had Reached Asia on His Fourth Voyage?" in George E, Nunn, *The Geographical Conceptions of Columbus* (New York: American Geographical Society, 1924), pp. 55-90, a chapter presenting detailed reasons why Columbus on his last voyage remained strongly convinced that he had landed in Asia. Columbus, arguing the case for his supposed Asiatic landfall in his fourth voyage, continued to insist that "the world is small. The dry land is six parts of it; the seventh only is covered with water. Experience has already shown this, and I have written it in other letters and with illustration from Holy Scripture concerning the situation of the earthly paradise, as Holy Church approves. I say that the world is not as great as the vulgar believe, and that a degree from the equinoctial line is fifty-six and two-thirds miles; easily this may be proved exactly (*The Voyages*, p. 296).

30. John Dyson, with Dr. Luis Miguel Coin Cuenca, nautical researcher, and Peter Christopher, photographer, *Columbus: For Gold, God, and Glory* (New York and London, 1991), pp. 66-68. The accepted distance from Europe to Japan as established by authorities was beyond the reach of ships of that period. The land mass of Europe, according to Ptolomy, spanned 180 of the 360 degrees comprising that circumference. The remaining 180 degrees constituted 3,375 leagues (10,800 nautical miles), a span beyond the reach of ships of the period (pp. 67-68). Paolo Toscanelli, with whom Columbus corresponded in 1481 or 1482, estimated the distance across the Great Ocean to be about 4,000 miles with many islands along the way (p. 67). Columbus estimated the distance from the Canary Islands across the Atlantic at about 750 leagues (2,400 miles), well within the sailing range of a caravel. The sailors and the owner of the *Santa Maria*, Juan de la Cosa, signed on for a passage from the Canaries each way for just this distance, and then threatened mutiny on Sept. 25, 1492, when the limit appeared to be overreached. The pilots estimated that they had sailed 800 leagues, according to later evidence given at the *pleitos*. Columbus exhorted them to continue, winning their agreement to sail on for eight more days to an anticipated "mainland."

31. *The Anatomy of Melancholy,* ed. and tr. from the Latin, Floyd Dell and Paul Jordan-Smith (New York, 1955), The Second Partition, Sec. 2, Memb. 3, the "Digression on Air," pp. 412-14.

32. *A Pisgah-sight of Palestine and the Confines Thereof, with The History of the Old and New Testament Acted Thereon,* London: printed by M. F. for John Williams, 1650, Book 1, Chapter 1, p. 2.

33. *The Historie of the Holy Warre*, Cambridge: printed by Thomas Buck, 1639, Bridgewater copy, verso "To the Reader," caption on insert Palestine map.

34. *The Complete Poetry of John Donne,* ed. and notes, John Shawcross (New York, 1967), p. 281, ll. 300, 302. All line references to Donne's poetry are from this edition. For further allusions to medieval and Renaissance maps in Donne's poetry, see Robert L. Sharp, "Donne's 'Good Morrow' and Cordiform Maps," *Modern Language Notes,* 69 (1954): 275-308.

35. English Protestant travelers of the late sixteenth and seventeenth centuries repeatedly derided stories about the "star of the Nativity" as recounted by guides in Bethelehem's Church of the Nativity. In a letter from the Holy Land in *The Travels of certaine Englishmen*, London: Th. Haveland, 1609, Gvilielmus Biddulphus explains that guides in the Church of the Nativity "shewed us a hole made of purpose in the very top of the house, and told us, that thorow that hole the Starre fell downe, which directed three kings of Collen to Christ: Wherein they delivered these Untruths. (l) In saying that the starre fell downe into the roome, whereas the Scripture saith, not that it fell downe, but stood over the place where the babe was, Matth. 2" (pp. 130-131). Faynes Moryson and Thomas Fuller reported in the sixteenth century the same "false" story about this falling star.

3. HAKLUYT AND THE CONFUSION OF SOURCES

1. *Divers Voyages touching the discouerie of America, and the Island adiacent unto the same.* London, Thomas Woodcocke, 1582. Hakluyt's early nationalistic aims are very apparent in his dedication of *Divers Voyages* to Sidney. He states that he has "great hope, that the time approcheth and nowe is, that we of England may share and part stakes (if wee will our selues) both with the Spaniarde and the Portingale in part of America, and other regions as yet undiscouered. And surely if there were in vs that desire to aduance the honour of our Countrie which ought to bee in euery goodman, wee woulde not all this while haue foreslowne the possessing of those landes, whiche of equitie and right appertaine vnto vs, as by the discourses that followe shall appeare most plainely" (1, recto). See also David Armitage, *The Ideological Origins of the British Empire* (Cambridge, England, 2001), pp. 71-84, for comments on the varied sources of Hakluyt's colonial views. Armitage notes Hakluyt's nationalism and desire for colonies, but also his apparent lack of religious zeal and his Aristotelian and Thomistic interests in an "imperialism" based in part on the global exchange and distribution of goods. Richard Helgerson in "The Voyages of a Nation," *Forms of Nationhood* (Chicago and London, 1992), pp. 151-91, has also returned to the themes of nationalism and trade as central to Haklluyt's work but without reference to the pilgrimage tradition. Helgerson's stress is upon selected, so-called "corographic" English voyage narratives having ideological, nationalist overtones.

For insights into the developing outlook of Richard Hakluyt from youth to maturity, see *The Original Writings & Correspondence of the Two Richard Hakluyts,* intro. and notes, E. G. R. Taylor, 2 vols. (London, 1935, *Works Issued by the Hakluyt Society. Second Series. No. Lxxvi).*

2. Early positive assessments of Hakluyt as a compiler and cosmographer appear in Foster Watson, *Richard Hakluyt* (London, 1924); and George Bruner Parks, *Richard Hakluyt and the English Voyages,* notes and intro. James A. Williamson (New York, 1928).

The importance of Hakluyt in recording the English discoveries is discussed generally in Walter Raleigh, *The English Voyages of the Sixteenth Century*, (Glasgow, 1906), Chapter II, "Richard Hakluyt," pp. 119-47. A. L. Rowse in *The First Colonists: Hakluyt's Voyages to North America* (London, 1986), has noted, in a study generally favorable to Hakluyt, the value of the detailed compilations left by this author on colonial enterprises. See also L. E. Pennington, ed. *The Purchas Handbook*: Studies of the life, times and writings of Samuel Purchas, 1577-1626 (Cambridge, 1997), 2 vols.

3. Generally negative criticism of British and Spanish colonial activities in North America appear in Tezevtan Todorov, *The Conquest of America: The Question of the Other,* trans. Richard Howard (New York, 1984); orig. French edition 1982; Stephen Greenblatt, *Marvelous Possessions: The Wonder of the New World* (Chicago, 1991); Kirkpatrick Sale, *The Conquest of Paradise: Christopher Columbus and the Columbian Legacy* (New York, 1990); Michael Paiewonsky, *The Conquest of Eden 1493-1515.* (Rome, St. Thomas, Tortola: MAPes MONDe Editore, n.d.).

4. See the first edition of *The Principall Navigations, Voiages and Discoveries of the English nation, made by Sea or ouer Land, to the most remote and farthest distant Quarters of the earth at any time within the compasse of these 1500 yeeres: Diuided into three seuerall parts*, published in a single folio volume. London, George Bishop and Ralph Newberie, Deputies to Christopher Barker, 1589. British Library shelf mark copy C 32 m. 10; Huntington shelf mark 3437. An "epistle dedicatorie" to Sir Francis Walsingham was deleted in later editions. It is different in structure from subsequent editions because, "Diuided into three seuerall parts," it begins with overland travels to the Near East, India, and the south parts of Asia as well as to ports in Africa; next takes up voyages to the North and Northeast; and finally ends recording sea journeys to "all the corners of the vaste and new world of *America"* (title page).

5. *Herodotus,* tr. J. Enoch Powell, 2 vols. (Oxford, 1949). See also Herodotus, "Account of Egypt," tr. G. C. Macaulay, *Voyages* *and Travels: Ancient and Modern*, ed. Charles Eliot. (New York, 1910), pp. 5-9).

6. See the preface "to the Reader" in the initial second edition entitled *Principal Navigations, Voiages, Traffiques and Discoueries of the English Nation made by Sea or ouer-land, to the remote and farthest distant quarters of the Earth, at any time within th e compasse of these 1500 years: Diuided into three seuerall Volumes* (sic), London, George Bishop, Ralph Newberie and Robert Barker, 1598-1600. This edition is bound in two books with the first book divided into two "volumes" published together and dated 1598-99; and the second book containing a third "volume" dated 1600. In this initial second edition, the first part of 1598 now opens, not with Near Eastern land travels and related Asian and African land and sea discoveries, but rather with voyages North and Northeast by Sea. The second part of 1599 concerns "personall trauels, &c. of the *English*...to *Alger, Tunis*, and *Tripolis, in Barbary*, to *Syria* and *Armenia*, to *Jerusalem* and other places in *Judea;* and the third part of 1600 is a sweeping and revealing compilation of voyages to the New World and to the "backside of *America*" together with "two renowmed, and prosperous voyages of *Sir Francis Drake* and *M. Thomas Candish* round about the circumference of the whole earth." British Library shelf-mark copy 683 b 5; and Huntington shelf-mark copy 3428.

A later printing of this second edition of *The Principal Navigations, Voiages, Traffiqves and Discoveries of the English Nation*...is in three folio volumes. London: George Bishop, Ralph Newberie, 1599-1600; Huntington shelf mark 3438. The British Library shelfmark copy 212 d. 2 is from the library of King George III. In these later printings in three folio volumes, the first volume contains a changed title page omitting a reference to the supposed "victorie" of Essex at Cadiz, and omitting pages 607-619 describing this supposed "victorie."

7. See Hakluyt's positive comments, in a public letter to Walter Ralegh, printed as an introduction to the map in Petri Martyris Anglerii's *De Orbe Novo*, Paris, Gvillelmvm Avvray, 1587; unpaginated introduction with the world map on p. 1 verso.

4. WORLD HISTORY REVISED

1. See Bacon's remarks on the compatibility of religious views and the empirical knowledge of universal nature in his "A Confession of Faith" in *Francis Bacon*. ed. and notes, Brian Vickers (Oxford and New York, 1996), pp. 107-112. As Vickers points out in his notes to the "Confession," Bacon, while seeking "physical laws" freed from the notion of divine legislation, still held a theoretical concept of divine law that "is somewhat old-fashioned. It belongs more with the biblical notion of a divinely appointed cosmic order, as expressed in the Psalms or in several Old Testament books. Bacon follows the old tradition of regarding the Bible, the record of God's words and works, as a contribution to scientific knowledge" (564). But it needs to be emphasized that, while recognizing a form of "natural law," Bacon also insisted upon a special and separate category of empirical "physical laws." For an analysis of the relation of science and theology, see Paul Russell Anderson, *Science in Defense of Liberal Religion*: *A Study of Henry More's Attempt to Link Seventeenth Century Religion and Science* (New York and London, 1933).

See also Douglas Bush in his edition of *English Literature in the Earlier Seventeenth Century 1600-1660* (Oxford, 1962) who uncritically praises Thomas Browne's *Religio Medici* (1643) for treating religion and science as the same kind of knowledge and value systems. In Bush's words, "Unlike Bacon, Browne does not bow to the Deity and pass on. For him science and religion are inseparable, or rather, science is still a part of religion" (288).

2. *The Two Bookes of Francis Bacon. Of the proficience and aduancement of Learning, diuine and humane*, London at Graies Inne *Gate in Holborne*: Printed for *Henrie Fomes*, 1605; bk. 2, p. 7 verso. Bacon later greatly enlarged this work to nine books publishing *Of the Advancement and Proficience of Learning or the Partitions of Sciences*, Oxford: Printed by Leon: Lichfield, Printer to the University; for Rob Young & Ed. Forrest, 1640. See also *The Works of Francis Bacon,* ed. and trans. James Spedding,

Robert Leslie Ellis, and Douglas Heath, 15 vols. (Boston, 1863-5), vol. 8 (1863), bk. 2, p. 409.

3. *The Two Books*, bk. 2, p. 15 verso. Bacon's optimism rested on the basis of books on new voyage discoveries and navigation such as John Dee's *General and Rare Memorials Pertayning to the Perfect Arte of Navigation: Annexed to the Paradoxal Compas, in Playne:* now first published: 24 yeres, after the first Inuention thereof. London: Iohn Daye, 1577.

4. *The Works of Francis Bacon*, vol. 8, bk. 1, xix., p. 7. On the issue of Bacon's objectivity, Julie Robin Solomon in *Objectivity in the Making: Francis Bacon and the Politics of Inquiry* (Baltimore and London, 1998) argues that mercantile and royalist interests underlie Bacon's scientific program. In a qualified reading that neglects the theme of historicist methodology in Purchas, she claims that Bacon's "self-distancing" in the *Novum Organum* does not derive fundamentally from a deep aversion to the supposed biases of Aristotle and the schoolmen, but derives rather from "the lived experience of traders, factors, and vocational travelers who sought their ways in a growing commercial society." She adds, however, that Bacon's desire to overcome bias in the *Novum Organum* and elsewhere, "when not viewed as paradox," "delineates a cognitive stance that transcends all conditions of nature, nurture, class, nation, and history" and so comprises "an early modern form of what we now call scientific objectivity" (110).

See also F. J. Levy, "Francis Bacon and the Style of Politics," *Renaissance Historicism: Selections from "English Literary Renaissance,"* ed. Arthur F. Kinney and Dan S. Collins, (Amherst, 1987): 146-167. Levy points out that Bacon, in the light of his extensive but troubled political experience in the English court, employed suggestive aphorisms, rather than more exacting language, to stir originality and flexibility in political as well as scientific thinking. Levy's essay appears in an anthology centered on varied critical approaches to English literary history and its relation in particular to Renaissance culture.

5. Perez Zagorin's *Francis Bacon,* (Princeton, 1998), rightly notes, however, that Bacon in "the establishment of axioms by induction" included "the requirement that they must extend beyond the particulars from which they were derived, so as to indicate new particulars that served to confirm them. This statement is one of a number suggesting quite clearly that Bacon's understanding of an axiom included the concept of a theory or hypothesis to be tested and corroborated by its prediction and discovery of new facts and observations" (87-88). Zagorin points out that with the work left incomplete, Bacon failed to "include a number of additional topics as helps to induction" (90). Writing before the time of David Hume, Bacon had "no reason to doubt the validity of induction in establishing the empirical generalizations and axioms he desired in natural philosophy" (92). Bacon, Zagorin continues, nevertheless "failed to see that no inductive conclusion, however well supported could be made invulnerable against the future possibility of falsification by a contradictory instance" (101).

6. Martin Elsky, *Authorizing Words: Speech, Writing, and Print in the English Renaissance* (Ithaca, 1984), maintains that George Herbert's hieroglyphic poems, "which project themselves both aurally and visually, occupy a textual space made possible by print and Renaissance Hebraicism, a space in which the human voice and divine writing intersect." Elsky compares "this tension between speech and writing in Herbert to Bacon's articulation of the artificial written sign to be used in scientific communication; Bacon's artificial language would consist of signs divorced both from the humanistic touchstone of social consensus and from the Hebraicist totem of divine writing" (7). It should be noted, however, that Bacon considered the new scientific language, not as "artificial," but rather as more objectively and specifically related to external things than either religious or general social language. Bacon wanted this scientific language stabilized, as Elsky observes, in printed books for transmission to others.

7. Peter Novick, *That Noble Dream*: "The Objective Question and the American Historical Profession." (Cambridge and New York, 1988), pp. 34-39.

8. Blunderville, *The true order and Methode of wryting and reading Histories, Huntington Library Quarterly*, 2 (Jan., 1940): 164ff.; and *Blvnderville His Exercises*, London, William Stansby, 1622. See also Harris Francis Fletcher, *The Intellectual Development of John Milton,* 2 vols. (Urbana, 1956-61), vol. 2 (1961), Chapter 17, "The Study of History," pp. 322-36; and Chapter 18, "Cosmography and Geography," 337-50. Fletcher confesses surprise that "Not much attention has been paid elsewhere to the manner of Milton's beginnings in such studies, and so far as I know, none at all to how he carried them on at Cambridge" (337). He notes that such studies began with Aristotle's *Physics,* and he confirms that geographical works by Ortelius and Peter Heylyn were also used and appear listed in Joseph Mede's account books (347).

9. Abraham Ortelius. *Theatrvm Orbis Terrarvm: The Theatre of the Whole World*, London, John Norton, 1606. In his preface "to the courteus Reader," the author calls the world "our Theater" (unpaginated). Ortelius's work was first published under the title *Theatrum orbis terrarum,* Coppenium Diefth, Antverpiae, 1570; and republished under the same title in 1595 and in 1601. A condensed version of the work appeared as *Abraham Ortelius His Epitome of The Theater of the Worlde...*Micheal Coignet. London: Ieames Shawe, 1603. See also the bibliographical information on early editions of *Theatrum orbis terrarum* by Riet van Alkemade under *Ortelius,* Abraham, in Cornelius Koeman's, *Atlantes Neerlandici* (Amsterdam, 1967-70), vol. 3, 1969, pp. 27-83.

10. Comenius. *The Great Didactic of John Amos Comenius* intro. and tr. M. W. Keatinge. London: Adam and Charles Black, 1896, section 8, p. 434. See also the seventeenth-century Latin text, *Opera Didactical Omnia,* ab anno 1627 ad 1657 continuata, Amsterdami, Anno 1657. Comenius produced an illustrated book of worldly types entitled *Orbis Sensualium Pictus...A Picture-and Nomenclature of all the chief Things that are in the world, and of Mens Employments therein.* Trans. Charles Hoole (teacher of a Private Grammer-School in Lothbury, London) from Latin and High Dutch. London: Printed for J. Kirton, 1659.

5. SKEPTICISM AND FAITH

1. *Pvrchas his pilgrim. Microcosmvs, or, The Historie Of Man. Relating the Wonders of his Generation, Vanities in his Degeneration, Necessity of his Regeneration. Meditated on the words of David. Psal. 39.5. Verily, euery Man at his best state is altogether Vanity. Selah,* London, Printed by W. S. for H. Fetherstone, 1619.

2. *Haklvytvs posthumus or Pvrchas his pilgrimes. Contayning a History of the World, in sea voyages. & lande Trauells, by Englishmen & others. Wherein Gods Wonders in Nature & Prouidence, The actes, Arts, Varieties, & Vanities of Men, wth a world of the Worlds Rarities, are by a world of Eywitnesse Authors Related...In fower parts, each containing fiue Bookes,* London, Printed by W. Stansby for Henry Fetherstone, 1625.

3. See the remarks of Douglas Bush, *English Literature* (Oxford, 1952), pp. 179-80.

4. F. Smith Fussner, *The Historical Revolution* (London, 1962), p. 57.

5. Baker, *The Race of Time Three Lectures on Renaissance Historiography* (Toronto, 1967). See by contrast E. G. R. Taylor, *Late Tudor and Stuart Geography: 1583-1650* (New York, 1968), reprinted from the 1934 edition), who presents a positive view of Purchas's aims and editorial techniques, and includes an extensive list of English manuscripts on geography for the period cited, with 150 of them showing relationships to Purchas's work.

James A. Boon, *Other tribes, other scribes: Symbolic anthropology in the comparative study of cultures, histories, religions and texts* (Cambridge, 1982), argues that Purchas's representation of native Americans were colored by his views of monarchy and vagrancy, and not rationalizations for colonizing American lands. West Indians, Boon believes, were associated by Purchas with Jacobean "vagrants" and so were depicted negatively, whereas East Indians were seen as having monarchical governments and so were depicted positively. See also Francis Jennings, *The Invasion of America: Indians, Colonialism, and the*

198

Cant of Conquest (Chapel Hill, 1975), pp. 77-82, who maintains that Purchas remarks in "Virginias Verger" show him as racist and anti-Indian. Ronald Sanders, *Lost Tribes and Promised Lands: The Origins of American Racism* (Boston, 1978) also contends that Purchas displays anti-Indian racism, and that he became estranged from Hakluyt because he made available to Captain John Smith manuscripts loaned by Hakluyt. Maxwell Ford Taylor, Jr., however, in "The influence of religion on white attitudes toward Indians in the early settlement of Virginia, (unpublished doctoral dissertation, Emory University, 1970), pp. 145-51, 220-23, argues that Purchas favored peaceful missionary work with the Indians from about 1607 through 1622, and then after 1622 favored forceful measures.

6. See *Compassing the vaste globe of the earth: studies in the history of the Hakluyt Society, 1846-1996,* ed. R. C. Bridges and P. E. H. Hair (London, 1996). Among Hakluyt Society publications is the excellent *The Purchas Handbook: Studies of the life, times and writings of Samuel Purchas, 1577-1626,* ed. L. E. Pennington, 2 vols. (London, 1997), which includes an excellent bibliography of articles and books on Purchas. See also discussions of voyages in Walter Raleigh, *The English Voyages of the Sixteenth Century.* (Glasgow, 1906); and Robert Brandon, *Making It Explicit: Reasoning, Representing, and Discursive Commitment* (Cambridge, Mass., 1994).

7. *Purchas his pilgrimage, or, Relations of the world and the religions observed in all ages and places discouered...In foure partes. This first containeth a theologicall and geographicall historie of Asia, Africa, and America, with the ilands adiacent,* London, Printed by W. Stansby, for H. Fetherstone, 1613. See "The primary Purchas bibliography" by P. A. Neville-Sington of the printings of all editions of *Purchas his pilgrimage,* under this title and variations of the title, in *The Purchas Handbook,* ed. L. E. Pennington (London, 1997), vol. 2, pp. 465–571. The bibliography is organized by international library holdings, rather than the dates of publication, and so tends to obscure Purchas's developing views.

See also in vol. 2, "A secondary Purchas bibliography" by L. E. and G. Z. Pennington, pp. 574–743.

The second edition of 1614 held to the original organizational plan, with further travel materials added: *Purchas his Pilgrimage. Or, Relations of the world and the religions observed in all ages and places discouered, from the Creation vnto this Present. In Fovre parts...The second Edition, much enlarged with Additions through the whole Worke*, London, Printed by W. Stansby for H. Fetherstone, 1614.

8. The third edition of 1617 again follows the original organizational plan: *Purchas his pilgrimage, or Relations of the world and the religions observed in al ages and places discouered, from creation unto this present. In foure parts,* London, Printed by W. Stansby for H. Fetherstone, 1617.

9. "Preface to the Reader," *Purchas his Pilgrim: Microcosmus, or The Historie Of Man,* London: Printed by W. S. for *Henry Fetherstone,* 1619, unpaginated. The full subtitle is printed as follows:

Wonders of his Generation,

Relating the *Vanities in his* Degeneration,

Necessity of his Regeneration.

Meditated on the words of David. Psal. 39.5

Verily euery Man at his best state is altogether Vanitie. Selah.

10. Donne, *Pseudo Martyr, Selected Prose,* selected by Evelyn Simpson, eds. Helen Gardner and Timothy Healy (Oxford, 1947), PP. 41-65.

11. *Metempsycosis* in *The Complete Poetry of John Donne,* ed. John Shawcross (New York, 1967), stanza 7, p. 313.

12. *Conversations with Drummond* in *Ben Jonson,* eds. C. H. Herford and Percy and Evelyn Simpson (Oxford, 1925), vols. 1-2, ll. 130-37, p. 136.

13. See the *Second Anniversary* in *The Complete Poetry,* pp. 289-306.

14. Hayden White in *The Content of the Form: Narrative Discourse and Historical Representation* (Baltimore, 1987) argues in great detail that narratives by their very focus, and by exclusions resulting from that focus, misrepresent the very events they are supposed objectively to delineate. See also White's *Metahistory: The Historical Imagination in Nineteenth-Century Europe* (Baltimore, 1973). Purchas's later developing historiography, composed of often disparate and disengaged entries from an ever-increasing multitude of sources, shows some similarities with what Michel Foucault, in "Nietzsche, Genealogy, History" in *Language, Counter-Memory, Practice: Selected Essays and Interviews*, ed. D. F. Bouchard (Ithaca, 1977), pp. 139-64, terms "discontinuous," or "ruptured" history. Foucault, taking exception to so-called "continuous" narrative history, argues that "'effective' history deprives the self of the reassuring stability of life and nature, and it will not permit itself to be transported by a voiceless obstinacy toward a millenial ending" (p. 154).

6. TOWARD A HUMANIST GLOBAL HISTORICISM

1. *Haklvytvs posthumus or Pvrchas his pilgrimes. Contayning a History of the World, in sea voyages. & lande Trauells, by Englishmen & others. Wherein Gods Wonders in Nature & Prouidence, The actes, Arts, Varieties, & Vanities of Men, wth a world of the Worlds Rarities, are by a world of Eywitnesse Authors Related to the World. Some left written by Mr: Hakluyt at his death. More since added. His also perused, & perfected. All examined, abreuiated. Illustrated with Notes, Enlarged with Discourses, Adorned with pictures, and Expressed in Mapps. In fower parts, each containing fiue Bookes*, 4 folio vols., London: Printed by W. Stansby for Henry Fetherstone, 1625. The number volumes will be cited for each of Purchas's editions and publications for reasons of clarity.

2. Cawley, Robert Ralston. *Unpathed Waters: Studies in the Influence of the Voyagers on Elizabethan Literature* (Princeton, 1940), pp. 32-41, on the significance of arguments over the location of Ophir and on Purchas's discussion of this place. See also Cawley's *Milton and the Literature of Travel* (Princeton, 1951) for

a discussion of Purchas as a source for place names and descriptions in Milton's work.

3. *Pvrchas his pilgrim. Microcosmvs, or, The Historie Of Man. Relating the Wonders of his Generation, Vanities in his Degeneration, Necessity of his Regeneration. Meditated on the words of David. Psal. 39.5. Verily, euery Man at his best state is altogether Vanity. Selah,* 1 vol., London, Printed by W. S. for H. Fetherstone, 1619, pp. 59. 588.

4. *Purchas his pilgrimage, or, Relations of the world and the religions observed in all ages and places discouered...In foure partes. This first containeth a theologicall and geographicall historie of Asia, Africa, and America, with the ilands adiacent,* 4 folio vols., London, Printed by W. Stansby, for H. Fetherstone, 1613, vol. 1, unpaginated.

5. *Pvrchas his Pilgrimage. Or Relations of the world and the religions obserued in all ages and places Discouered from the Creation to unto this Present. Contayning a theologicall and geographicall historie of Asia, Africa, and America, with the ilands adiacent...4th ed., much enl. with...three whole treatises annexed, one of Russia and other north easterne regions by Sr. Ierome Horsey; the second of the Gulfe of Bengala by Master William Methold; the third of the Saracenicall Empire...*1 folio vol., London, Printed by H. Fetherstone, 1626.

6. Arnold J. Toynbee. *A Study of History,* second ed., fourth printing, 12 vols. (Oxford, 1945-61).

7. Purchas the polemicist, however, ends the fourth volume of the 1625 edition with an essay entitled "His Maiejites late care for Virginia," extolling British colonization of Virginia, and attacking the Indians as "vnneighbourly malicious Naturalls" (1.172; 1. 51). He approves of the King's sending of "a Running Armie of Souldiers to secour the Countrey of vnneighbourly malicious Naturalls, and to secure the planters from their priuie ambushments." (1.172;1.50-52). Purchas notes in volume four that he has "never trauelled two hundred miles from *Thaxted* in *Essex*"; and he chauvenistically contends that "all lines tend to this Centre," and other nations "left the knowledge of the World to the *English*"

(2.16, 20-21). David Armitage in *The Ideological Origins of the British Empire* (Cambridge, 2001), pp. 82-94, observes, however, that Purchas's arguments "deserve to be taken more seriously, not only to recover Purchas from the condescension of posterity, but also to reveal just how little part an apocalyptic conception of the British Empire would play in the future" (90). See also V. Afanasiev's comments on Purchas's negative treatment of Las Casas in "The Literary Heritage of Bartolome de las Casas" in *Bartolomé de las Casas in History: Toward an Understanding of the Man and his Work*, ed. Juan Friede and Benjamin Keen (De Kalb, 1971), pp. 539-78.

7. MILTON AND THE STRANDS OF RENAISSANCE HISTORIOGRAPHY

1. J. Milton French, "Milton as a Historian," *PMLA* 50 (June, 1935): 476-77. See also *The Life Records of John Milton*, 5 vols. (New Brunswick, 1949-58). See also very different conclusion of Stanley Fish in *How Milton Works* (Cambridge, Mass., 2001) who, in following an essentially reader-response approach to Milton, argues throughout that the poet is anti-empirical and entirely focused on God. Fish, however, gives slight attention to the range and details of Milton's prose writings on theology and history, writings that offer contextual insights into the major poetic works.
2. *Paradise Lost* in *The Riverside Milton.* ed. Roy Flannagan, (Boston and New York, 1998) 1.26, P. 355. All references to Milton's work are from this edition unless otherwise noted.
3. Joan Bennet in *Reviving Liberty; Radical Christian Humanism in Milton's Great Poems*, (Cambridge, Mass. 1989), pp. 33-58, equates Satan in a detailed analysis to both Charles I and Cromwell, and in turn discusses these two political leaders in relation to Milton's developing theology and depiction of God. Malcolm MacKenzie Ross in *Milton's Royalism: A Study of the Conflict of Symbol and Idea in the Poem*, (Ithaca, 1943), pp. 50-51, [New York: Russell & Russell, 1970] takes a strained position,

given Milton's anti-monarchist prose tracts of the middle period and the context of later writings, in arguing that ambiguous allusions in *Paradise Lost* imply the poet in his politics was a latent monarchist. Stevie Davies in *Images of Kingship in Paradise Lost* (Columbia, Mo., 1983) finds essentially anti-royalist references in Milton's epic. See also Robert Fallon's discussion in *Divided Empire: Milton's Political Imagery* (University Park, Penn., 1995), pp. 61-65, 70-71, of Satan as suggesting both Charles I and Cromwell.

4. David Quint in *Epic and Empire: Politics and Generic Form from Virgil to Milton* (Princeton, 1993), p. 410, n. 4, rightly notes that "Satan and the devils can play the roles of parliamentary debaters—as well as members of a papal conclave—in book 2." Quint adds that "attacks on the Stuart monarchy, which seem to be the dominant strain in Milton's late poetry, do not exclude retrospective criticism of aspects of the Commonwealth and Cromwellian Protectorate as well" (p. 410, n.4). See Fallon, *Divided Empire,* for comparisons of the Satanic conclave and the Commonwealth parliament. The well-known, and often repeated association between the demonic assembly in Pandemonium and a "secret conclave" of Cardinals in the Sistine Chapel rests in large measure on Milton's allusion in book 1 to the Seraphic Lords of Hell meeting in "secret conclave" (64-65).

5. J. Martin Evans, *Milton's Imperial Epic: "Paradise Lost" and the Discourse of Colonialism* (Ithaca, 1996), pp. 96-132, sees the epic focused upon the New World as the site of colonial "planting," and the work reflective of a genre of cultural imperialism having contemporary overtones. David Quint in *Epic and Empire: Politics and Generic Form from Virgil to Milton* (Princeton 1993) also regards *Paradise Lost* as to some degree a "politicization of epic poetry" under the impetus of a generic imperialism (8). Quint writes that the "romance retreat of Eden is the site—and the figure—of psychological inwardness and of contingent choices of conscience" and points to "the bourgeois novel rather than to the aristocratic romance" (323). He adds that "Milton reverses epic tradition by giving the private world of Eden prominence over a public arena of military-political exploits—a reversal so remarkable that it almost seems to create a new genre" (283). However, Quint perceptively notes that, unlike Virgil, Milton in his epic attempted "to divorce a divine, cosmogonic order from a human political order," and that the the poem's "muddle of topical reference reflects the confusion of civil war... For Milton, especially after the 1660 Restoration and the failure of his own republican hopes, this confusion has become the political condition of human history itself" (43-44). Bruce McLeod, "The 'Lordly eye': Milton and the Strategic Geography of Empire" in *Milton and the Imperial Vision*, Balachandra Rajan and Elizabeth Sauer, eds., (Pittsburgh, 1999): 48-66, 49, presents Milton as suggesting English imperialist possession of the world. "The 'Lordly eye'" of God in *Paradise Lost*, he argues in a questionable reading, "is located in England and centrifugally sweeps the globe" (57), just as Eden is supposed to reflect England because of "its clear reference to English notions of the ideal country estate, 'Lantskip' (5.142), and the 'happy Isles/ Like those Hesperian Gardens fam'd of old (3.567-68)" (61). Blair Hoxby, however, in *Mammon's Music: Literature and Economics in the Age of Milton* (New Haven and London, 2002) points out that Milton, by the time he composed *Paradise Lost*, was essentially opposed to empire and trade. Hoxby rightly notes that "in *Paradise Lost*—in which Satan is associated with grandiose mercantile ventures and imperial projects and Adam's vision from the Top of Speculation includes a disturbing panorama of global exploitation indebted to Luis Vaz de Camoës's *Os Lusiadas*—the contiguity of trade and conquest is cast in a darker light, and the Restoration ideal of an empire of trade is subverted" (12).

6. Mary Ann Radzinowicz in *Toward Samson Agonistes; The Growth of Milton's Mind* (Princeton, 1978) takes exception to the view that Milton in his last years made a "total withdrawal from public life and from patriotic concern for his nation" (115). She believes that Milton took exception to a typal "restored Davidic king" as rendered by Dryden and Cowley in their writings, and rather advanced the "imaginative portrait of the representative of the people, elected, not born, into leadership" (178). Milton turned, she believes, to individuals. "From the sight of one man freeing himself from despair taught by his own failure to achieve his political destiny, might yet come personal regeneration. Milton anticipated that other men might learn one by one to free themselves for political ends. Tragic catharsis might lead his own people into the stability of a consensus of virtuous men" (179). She observes, however, the commonplace view that Milton's "political beliefs fall into a simple rising and falling or outgoing and recoiling pattern: a period of hopefulness during which he evolved a theoretical libertarianism; a high point in *The Tenure of Kings and Magistrates* (1649) and *Areopagitica* (1644), leading to a public post; a period of slow reluctant compromise with the events, which whittled down the ideal Commonwealth to the actuality of Protectorate; and a final, total withdrawal from public life and from patriotic concern for his nation" (p. 115). See also Don M. Wolfe, *Milton in the Puritan Revolution* (London, 1963); Douglas Bush, *John Milton* (London, 1965), pp. 123-30.

   7. *The Correspondence of Henry Oldenburg*, ed. and trans. by A. Rupert Hall & Marie Boas Hall, Vol. l, 1641-1662, (Madison and Milwaukee, 1965), p. 341. The complete correspondence is published in thirteen volumes.

   8. *The Riverside Milton.* ed. Roy Flannagan, (Boston, 1998) 12, 561-54, p. 707.

   9. *History of Britain*, ed. George Philip Krapp in *The Works of John Milton*, gen. ed. Frank Allen Patterson, (New York, 1933), vol. 10, pp. 2, 128, 179-80. See also the discussion of the relation of the *History of Britain* to *A Brief History of Moscovia* in John G. Demaray, *Cosmos and Epic Representation: Dante, Spenser, Milton and the Transformation of Renaissance Heroic Poetry* (Pittsburgh, 1991), pp. 183-86.

   10. *A Brief History of Moscovia and Of other less-known Countries lying eastward of Russia as far as Cathay.* Gather'd from the Writings of several Eye-witnesses. London: Printed by *M. Flesher,* for *Brabazon Alymer* at the *Three Pigeons* against the *Royal Exchange,* 1682; pp. A2r; 274.

11. The influence of masque and sacred representational form on *Paradise Lost* appears in John G. Demaray, "The Thrones of Satan and God: Background to Divine Opposition in *Paradise Lost*," *The Huntington Library Quarterly* 31 (1967): 21-33, and "Love's Epic Revel in *Paradise Lost:* A Theatrical Vision of Marriage," *Modern Language Quarterly*, 38 (1967): 3-20. Neo-classical "disguisings" such as the poet's *A Maske* and the poet's theatrical entertainment "Arcades" (1630s) traditionally concealed or "screened" underlying social, biblical, and Hebraic-Christian meanings fully revealed in a final "unmasking." "Disguising" themes and forms were thus regularly subsumed within sacred representational and religious literary and theatrical works, a fact graphically illustrated in Milton's unfinished early poem "The Passion" (1630?) in which the narrator declaims of the Son's Crucifixion: "Oh what a Masque was there, what a disguise!" (19).

12. Stella Pruce Revard in *The War in Heaven* (Ithaca and London, 1980), pp. 87-107, traces the influence of Milton's *In Quintum Novembris* on primarily book 6 of *Paradise Lost;* David Quint in *Epic and Empire,* pp. 271-81, comments upon similarities between *In Quintum Novembris* and *Paradise Lost,* and discusses the possible influence of another poem on the gunpowder plot, Phineas Fletcher's *Locustae* or in English *The Locusts or Appollyonists* (1627), the last published the year after Milton's "epic in miniature" was written. The blending of theatrical devices with Virgilian epic form is examined in John G. Demaray, "Gunpowder and the Problem of Theatrical Heroic Form: Milton's *In Quintum Novembris*," *Urbane Milton: The Latin Poetry*, ed. James Freeman and Anthony Low (Pittsburgh, 1984): 3-19.

Milton, who by 1642 espoused theologian David Pareus's argument that parts of the Bible are of theatrical design, arranged the segments of *Paradise Lost* into their final form ultimately following the classical twelve-book model of the *Aeneid*, but with attention to internal theatrical elements and patterns. In the poet's prose tract *The Reason of Church Government* of 1642, Milton declares that "the Apocalypse of Saint *John* is the majestick image of a high and stately Tragedy, shutting up and intermingling her

Solemn Scenes and Acts with a sevenfold *Chorus* of halleluja's and harping symphonies: and this my opinion the grave authority of *Pareus* commenting that booke is sufficient to confirm," *Riverside Milton*, p. 923. Again in the preface to *Samson Agonistes* published in 1671, Milton states that "*Paraeus* commenting on the *Revelation* divides the whole Book as a Tragedy, into Acts distinguisht each by a Chorus of Heavenly Harpings and Song between," *Riverside Milton*, p.799.

Although passages in Milton's most original epic echo or imitate components in works by a host of heroic poets—among them, Homer, Ovid, Lucan, Dante, Tasso, Ariosto, Camoës, Phineas Fletcher, Spenser, Cowley, and Davenant—Milton continued to shape scriptural events by regularly representing them theatrically, in accord with the views of a reformist Renaissance historicist such as Ortelius, as unfolding in a metaphoric Renaissance Theatre of the World rather than in a relatively "fixed" iconographic book of the world. The poet begins *in medias res* with the Fall of Satan into Hell. However, a diminishment of conflict and tension occurs in the last two books centered on sequential visions and accounts of the future.

13. For an examination of the long-term invention and disposition of the epic beginning with Milton's theatrical writings and his outlines of a sacred representation on the Fall, see Allan Gilbert's examination in *On the Composition of "Paradise Lost": A Study of the Ordering and Insertion of Material* (Chapel Hill, 1947). Gilbert, citing Virgil's twelve-book *Aeneid* and other epic works, discusses Milton's merger and adjustments of theatrical and heroic genres and materials in writing the epic in segments, as internal and external evidence suggests, which were then arranged in first ten books and finally in twelve-book form. Gilbert believes the epic reflects an underlying five-act theatrical structure. See also Demaray, *Milton's Theatrical Epic: The Invention and Design of Paradise Lost* (Cambridge, Mass., 1980) on Milton's merger of theatrical and heroic materials into a masque-like sacred representational epic without act divisions which finally was given twelve-book classical form. Hugh Richmond in *John Milton's*

Drama of "Paradise Lost" (New York, 1991) has produced a "performance copy" of the epic by retaining the substantive speeches of contending characters, deleting epic commentary, and allowing action to flow between the thrones of Satan and God with Eden at the center. Richmond successfully mounted a production of the work, following many masque staging practices, at the University of California, Berkeley, in the 1980s. Barbara Lewalski in *Paradise Lost and the Rhetoric of Literary Forms* (Princeton, 1985), stresses work by Milton on the epic in his later years with attention to the political and cultural background, and the poet's incorporation of generic elements drawn from pastoral, satiric, tragic, heroic and other literary forms. The focus of the study limits insight into Milton's sequential early theatrical invention and later integral development within the work of a grand, heroic *sacre representazione* eventually given classical epic form. In *The Life of Milton* (Oxford, 2000), pp. 443-49), Lewalski suggests that a republican Milton possibly first developed the epic in ten books for a political reason: namely, because the Roman poet Lucan, who featured republican figures in his unfinished epic *Parsalia, or The Civil War*, had planned a ten-book work. For comments on theatrical and other elements and on numerological interpretations, see John M. Shawcross, *With Mortal Voice: The Creation of "Paradise Lost"* (Lexington, Kentucky, 1982); Merritt Y. Hughes's edition of *John Milton: Complete Poems and Major Prose* (Indianapolis, 1957), pp. 173-75; and Roy Flannagan's edition of *The Riverside Milton*, pp. 309-12. For relatively conventional tragic and epic devices in Milton's epic, see John M. Steadman, *Epic and Tragic Structure in "Paradise Lost"* (Chicago, 1976).

14. See Evans, *Milton's Imperial Epic*, pp. 96-132.

8. PROPHETIC UNIVERSAL HISTORY

1. *Paradise Lost* in *The Riverside Milton.* ed. Roy Flannagan, (Boston and New York, 1998) 5.564-70, p. 355.

2. Harold Bloom in *The Western Canon: The Books and School of the Ages,* (New York, 1994) appears to strain his case, however, in observing that *"Paradise Lost* reads like the most powerful science fiction. I reread the poem constantly and am moved primarily by wonder and astonishment, by the strangeness of the Miltonic achievement." Bloom then adds that "There may be no larger triumph of visionary will in Western literature" (171-72). In his consideration of the epic as "science fiction," however, Bloom gives insufficient attention to Milton's attempts directed toward depicting the world and the universe largely in accord with the "objective" discoveries of the new science. See also Victoria Silver, *Imperfect Sense: The Predicament of Milton's Irony* (Princeton, 2001), who maintains that because the Miltonic God is deeply hidden in accord with the theologies of Luther and Calvin, and because "truth" for Milton is not "self-evident and automatic, but always impending and strange" (p. 110), the poem is a linguistic construction of ambiguous ironies embracing "catacresis" as well as "paradox or absurdity" and conveying experiences of "incongruity," "injustice" and "vertigo." Silver consequently re-writes Milton's epic argument on man's first disobedience, pressing her reading to an extreme by insisting that "Milton justifies God's ways as Luther does—not to testify to the incongruities created by human sin, but to those created by the hiddenness of God. Sin would try to clear up the problem" (p. 53). She adds that because of linguistic irony "Milton's so-called heresies derive from his principled resistance to interpretive symbologies" (p. 135). Her book nonetheless captures a sense of the imaginative uniqueness of Milton's poem, substituting a theological and linguistic analysis for Bloom's partly impressionist response. It should be stressed again that Milton's God, while often hidden and remote, is also a very forcefully engaged epic character, who directly delivers theological arguments and at times is spiritually manifest in masque-like revelations.

3. See an early analysis of what is presented as Milton's later anti-trinitarianism in Denis Saurat, *Milton: Man and Thinker,* rev. ed., (North Haven, Conn., 1964). See also Maurice Kelley's application of supposed hetrodox theology in *De Doctrina* to Milton's epic in *This Great Argument: A Study of Milton's "De Doctrina Christiana" as a Gloss upon "Paradise Lost"* (Princeton, 1941), p. 105ff. C. A. Patrides in *Milton and the Christian Tradition* (Oxford, 1966) finds relatively conventional trinitarian theology in passages of *De Doctrina,* and claims that in Milton's epic the Son is shown forth rather than created. For readings of the "begot" passage in *Paradise* Lost as signifying heretical Arian subordination of the Son to the Father, see John P. Rumrich "Milton's Arianism: why it matters," *Milton and Heresy,* ed. Stephen Dobranski and John P. Rumrich (Cambridge, England, 1998), pp. 75-92. Related critical essays in this volume consider alleged heretical conclusions in passages of *De Doctrina.* On the issue of the work's authorship, William B. Hunter in *Visitation Unimplor'd: Milton and the Authorship of De Doctrina Christiana* (Pittsburgh, 1998) has recently argued that the provenance and content of *De Doctrina* shows that it was not written by Milton. A group of scholars in England—Gordon Cambell, Fiona Tweedie, David Holmes, Thomas J. Corns, and John Hale—maintain in two articles in the *Milton Quarterly,* "Milton and *De Doctrina*" vol. 30, 3 (October, 1996), electronic report pages, and "The Provenance of *De Dotrina Christiana,*" vol. 31, 3 (October, 1997): 67-110, that a computer-generated statistical study reveals that, while parts of the manuscript "show stylometric characteristics unlike Milton's; much of the manuscript probably constitutes a Miltonic appropriation and transformation" of theological writings by others ("Provenance," p. 110). Michael Lieb in "*De Doctrina Christiana* and the Question of Authorship," *Milton Studies,* XLI, ed. Albert C. Labriola (Pittsburgh, 2002), pp. 172-230, further discusses in detail questions of provenance and content, again raising questions about attributing to Milton all or parts of this unsigned work, which first came to light in 1823. See also Arthur Sewell, *A Study of Milton's "Christian Doctrine"* (London and New York, 1939), who argued that *De Doctrina* was written by Milton over many years in three drafts that contained changing views.

4. For analyses of Dante's vision of Beatrice as the "inceptive cause" of the *Commedia,* see Helen Dunbar, *Symbolism in Medieval Thought* (New York, 1961), pp. 29-30; William Anderson, *Dante the Maker* (London and Boston, 1980), pp. 335-37; Erich Auerbach, *Dante: Poet of the Secular World,* trans. Ralph Manheim (Chicago, 1961), pp. 94ff.; and Demaray, *The Invention of Dante's Commedia* (New Haven, 1970), pp. 59-63; and *Dante and the Book of the Cosmos: Architectural Typology and Structure in the Commedia* (Philadelphia, 1987), pp. 7ff.

5. See Laura Lunger Knoppers, *Historicizing Milton: Spectacle, Power, and Poetry in Restoration England* (Athens, Georgia, 1994), who in reading *Paradise Lost* centers attention upon 1660s' processional Triumphs as manifestations of the "power and problematics of monarchical spectacle in the Restoration." She argues that "*Paradise Lost* resists a central tenet of royalist ideology in Restoration England, the return of the golden age on earth, the restoration of joy" with the investiture of Charles II as king (p. 79).

6. John G. Demaray in *Milton and the Masque Tradition: The Early Poems, "Arcades," and "Comus"* (Cambridge, Mass. and Oxford, 1968), and *Milton's Theatrical Epic: The Invention and Design of Paradise Lost* (Cambridge, Mass., 1980) traces the influence of the lavish royalist indoor masques upon Milton. See also Allan H. Gilbert, *On the Composition of Paradise Lost: A Study of the Ordering and Insertion of Material* (Chapel Hill, 1947) for an analysis of dramatic and theatrical elements in Milton's epic.

7. Ben Jonson captured some sense of the immediate, pleasurable reactions of masque spectators in commenting on the performance of his masque *Hymenaei* in 1606:

Such was the exquisit performance, as (beside the
pompe, splendor, or what we may call the *apparelling*
of such *Presentations*) that alone (had all else beene
absent) was of power to surprize with delight, and steale
away the *spectators* from themselues. Nor was there
wanting whatsoeuer might giue to the *furniture, or
complement;* eyther *riches*, or strangenesse of the

habites, delicacie of *daunces*, magnificence of the
scene, or diuine rapture of *musique*. Onely the enuie
was, that it lasted not still, or (now it is past) cannot
by imagination, much lesse description, be recouered
to a part of that *spirit* it had in the gliding by.

See Ben Jonson, *Ben Jonson*, ed. C. H. Herford and Percy and
Evelyn Simpson (Oxford, 1941), vol. 7, p. 229, ll. 668-70.

8. If Milton also wished to imply through the words of his
poem, using a paraphrase of the "exultation" psalm, that the Son
was "created" as well as shown forth in time in the timelessness of
eternity possibly on a cyclical as well as an epochal basis, then
such a paradoxical event of awe and wonder would be yet one
more among the many poetic paradoxes of Godhead and eternity—
whatever it might mean. Post-Cartesian analytical logic would have
to yield to the intuitive paradoxes of Renaissance literary tradition
as discussed by Rosalie Colie, *Paradoxia Epidemica: The
Renaissance Tradition of Paradox* (Princeton, 1966).

9. See the discussion of dialectics and oppositions in the light
of religious values in Hannah Disinger Demaray's "Milton and the
'Intelligible Flame': 'Sweet Converse' in Milton's Prose and Poetry,"
Renascence, vol. LIII, no. 1 (Fall, 2000): 23-42. Milton's epic is
examined as "a great dialectical construct of delicately
counterbalanced demonic pseudo-conversations of fallen angels,
heavenly "seeming" conversations actually manifesting the
paradoxical expressive silence in the substantive union of the
transcendent persons of a single God, and true conversations on
earth among separate and limited mortal and immortal beings
having a need for genuine discourse" (24).

Although the term "dialectics" is often applied to the opposed
or contrasting arguments and typology in Milton's prose and
poetry, the poet held ideological and religious views that
distinguish his outlook from the idealist and secular dialectics of
major nineteenth century theorists. Milton urged and depicted, as
the article on epic "discourse" makes clear, open trials of ideas and
values by what is contrary, trials that tested the ability of free
agents using right reason to choose from among a nuanced

hierarchy of ideas and types believed to exist on different levels of truth or falsehood in a universe created and sustained by infinite Godhead. Resolutions attained by right reason and prophetically informed knowledge are seen as rising from matter to spirit, "from shadowy types to truth," to ever higher illumination in this hierarchical scale under the transcendent, eternal, omnipotent, unified Godhead. Where oppositions are depicted in the Triumphs of the divine Son in Heaven and the antithetical pseudo-Triumph of the demonic Satan in Hell, good and evil in unequal relation are in addition given respective personalities, namely, in the sacrificial virtue of the loving Son and the opposed, malevolent will-to-power of the malicious Archfiend.

10. Hobbes, *Leviathan*, ed. Richard Tuck, (Cambridge, England, and New York, 1996). See also Stephen Fallon, *Milton among the Philosophers: Poetry and Materialism in Seventeenth-Century England* (Ithaca, N.Y., 1991) who argues that Milton was strongly influenced by the materialism of Hobbes and the new philosophers of the seventeenth century.

11. Arthur O. Lovejoy "Milton and the Paradox of the Fortunate Fall," *Essays in the History of Ideas* (Baltimore: Johns Hopkins University Press, 1948), pp. 277-95, appropriately argued that the First Parents' Fall downward into sin resulted, through the Son's Redemptive act, in their potential for being lifted spiritually higher than would otherwise have been the case. This Christian pattern of a low Fall, followed by a rise to a higher level through grace, is evident in Christian literature from Dante's *Commedia* through John Bunyan's *Pilgrims Progress* and stands in contrast to the classical pattern of virtuous adherence to a "golden mean."

12. David Lowenstein in *Milton and the Drama of History: Historical Vision, Iconoclasm, and the Literary Imagination* (Cambridge, 1990), p. 121, attributes considerable poetic and emotive force to the relatively flat masque-like "speaking pictures" in book 11 and to the Nimrod episode opening book 12, but lesser poetic power to the rising hierarchy of narrated biblical events and main masque-type Triumphs in the rest of the last book. "The poet," he observes, "responds to the bleakness and terror of events of inhuman history by interpreting them in the context of an eternal pattern. And yet despite the eschatological and typological configurations of Milton's historical account, the passages dramatizing the nightmare of history are undoubtedly among the most forceful in the last books; this suggests that critics have tended to overstress the progressive typological revelation of Michael's prophecy" (121). Such a reading, however, takes insufficient notice of the impact of the elaborate, theatrical Jubilee and main masque-type Triumphs in the first ten books. These powerfully convey eschatalogical and typological meaning, and lend dimension and significance to the necessarily brief relation of future typal epochs and future main-masque-type Triumphs in book 12. Still, critics have rightly found that both book 11 with its presentations of evils, as well as book 12 with its typology and Triumphs, to be of diminished poetic force; for the two books together contain a series of "educational" typal revelations of future history rather then episodes of sustained theatrical conflict by major actors.

13. "*Animadversions*" in *The Complete Prose Works of John Milton*, gen. ed., Don M. Wolfe, 8 vols. (New Haven and London, 1953-82), vol. 1 (1952), p. 707.

14. "Of Reformation" in *The Complete Prose Works of John Milton*, vol.. 6, p. 616.

15. *De Doctrina Christiana* in *The Complete Prose Works of John Milton*, vol. 6, pp. 615, 623-27. See the discussion of changes in Milton's views in Christopher Hill, *Milton and the English Revolution* (London, 1977), under the headings "Losing Hope," "Back to Egypt," and "The Last Years" (189-222); and the headings "The Millennium and the Chosen Nation," and "Sons and the Father" (279-96). See also Hill's *The English Bible and the Seventeenth-Century Revolution* (London, 1993).

9. AN OVERVIEW. PATTERNED FORMS OF WORLD HISTORICISM

1. Whitehead, *Science and the Modern World,* (New York, 1926), pp. 81-82.

2. See Henry More, "Psychathanasia" in *Philosophical Poems* (Cambridge, 1647), bks. 1 and 2, written under the influence of Plotinus, and *The Immortality of the Soul* (London, 1659), bk. 1 on spirit and matter, Chapter 2, sec. 10-11; and Chapters 7-9. See also A. Jacob's notes in his edition of *The Immortality of the Soul* (Dordrecht, 1987), and Paul Russell Anderson's *Science in Defense of Liberal Religion: A Study of Henry More's Attempt to Link Seventeenth Century Religion with Science* (New York, 1933), pp. 100-104.

3. Georg Wilhelm Friedrich Hegel, *The Philosophy of History,* preface Charles Hegel, trans, J. Sibree (New York, 1900), pp. 103, 442. This work by Hegel was assembled from his papers by his students. See also Carl Page, *Philosophical Historicism and the Betrayal of First Philosophy* (University Park, 1957). The lectures on Hegel given by Alexandre Kojeve, the French-Russian philosopher who taught at Ecole Pratique des Hautes Etudes in the 1930s, have been published under the title *An Introduction to the Reading of Hegel,* trans. James Nichols (New York, 1969). See also Raymond Aron, *Memoirs,* (New York and London, 1990), pp. 65-66.

4. Given his positions on English politics in prose works mainly of his middle period, Milton has been labeled on specific issues—particularly those of domestic, political, and religious liberty—an early modern liberal, a forerunner of what has been called, in controversial publications, eighteenth-century Whig liberalism. Milton's "liberalism" appears notably in his *Areopagitica, The Doctrine and Discipline of Divorce* (1643-44), *The Second Defence of the English People* (1654), and *The Ready and Easy Way to Establish a Free Commonwealth* (1660). However, the poet's later publication of *Paradise Lost*—centered on the relationship of all individuals to God and to evil in the past,

216

present, and future—has been seen to outline a divine universal history with many traditional elements.

Citing Herbert Butterfield's *The Whig Interpretation of History* (1630), William Kolbrener in chapter 7 of *Milton's Warring Angels: A Study of Critical Engagements* (Cambridge, England, 1997) has astutely observed that "many critics persist in abiding his [Butterfield's] narratives that alternately extol and deplore—but assume as given—the emergence of the modern individual in the seventeenth century" (3). Kolbrener takes mixed and complex positions, noting distinctions between so-called Early Modern Miltonic and Whig political "liberalism" in England, and its supposed contemporary democratic counterparts this in a continuing debate on the rise of the modern individual involving historians such as Quentin Skinner, J. G. A. Pocock, Blair Wordon, Conrad Russell, Kevin Sharpe, and Mark Kishlansky; and Miltonists such as Thomas Corns, Annabel Patterson and Nigel Smith.

5. *Paradise Lost*, ed. Roy Flannagan (Boston and New York, 1998), p. 335, PL, 1.26. All references to Milton's work are from this edition unless otherwise noted.

6. Friedrich Engels, "Socialism: Utopian and Scientific," reprint of the 1892 authorized English edition in *The Marx-Engels Reader,* ed. Robert C. Tucker (New York, 1963), p. 620.

7. Engels, "Speech at the Graveside of Karl Marx," *The Marx-Engels Reader,* pp. 603–04.

8. Engels, "Socialism: Utopian and Scientific," reprint of the 1892 authorized English edition in *The Marx-Engels Reader,* p. 615. Later revisionist materialist Marxists strongly influenced by Hegelian conceptions of historicist total "form," if not by Hegelian philosophic idealism, have in effect revived Hegel through continuing attempts to apply metaphysical dialectics to phenomenological historicist issues.

Forty years after Marx's death, the Hungarian Marxist Gyorg Lukács in *History and Class Consciousness* (1923), without access at the time to Marx's as yet unpublished *Economic and Philosophical Papers* and *The German Ideology,* detected and discussed Marx's strong early debts to Hegel while also advancing sharp criticisms of the then-dominant Marxist "Enlightenment-Utilitarian" conception of science—outlooks resulting in Lukács's being labeled a Marxist deviationist. In the 1930s Marx's *Economic and Philosophical Papers* and *The German Ideology* were published and provided support for Lukas's assessment of the early Marx.

For examples of subsequent Marxist revisionist theory, see Max Horkheimer and Theodor W. Adorno's *Dialectic of Enlightenment*, tr. John Cumming [1944] (New York, 1972) containing an ideological attack upon eighteenth-century Enlightenment utilitarian science which is alleged to have corrupted Western culture and fostered twentieth-century fascism. The authors' abstract dialectic counterpoises imagination, critical reason, and empathy for nature against scientific technology employed for mastery over nature and human society. They argue that Enlightenment thought, because dedicated in a supposedly exclusive way to the utilitarian subjugation and domination of nature through science, "radiates disaster triumphant" (3). "For the Enlightenment," they write, "whatever does not conform to the rule of computation and utility is suspect" (6). In applying their dialectic to the West in the mid twentieth century, they contend with a paucity of specific documentation, that the Enlightenment was largely responsible for a separation of individuals from nature and society, a decline in the quality of mass culture, and a political climate cultivating fascism.

See also Theodor W. Adorno, *Negative Dialectics*, tr. E. B. Ashton [1966] (New York, 1997), who, disillusioned by Nazi aggression and the Second World War, grew doubtful of Marxist teleological belief in an end-of-history classless society. Adorno observes that "after the catastrophes that have happened, and in view of the catastrophes to come, it would be cynical to say that a plan for a better world is manifested in history and unites it." Adorno addresses history by way of abstruse dialectics leavened by forays into theoretical and rhetorical comments on class and economics. "History," he writes, "is the unity of continuity and discontinuity. Society stays alive, not despite its antagonism, but by means of it; the profit interest and thus the class relationship make up the objective motor of the production process, which the life of all men hangs by, and the primacy of which has its vanishing point in the death of all. This also implies the reconciling side of the irreconcilable" (320).

It should be noted that Jacques Maritain in *On the Philosophy of History*, ed. J. W. Evans (London, 1959), in analyzing dialectical-metaphysical historicism, is one among a number of philosophers who have strongly criticised Hegel's dialectical philosophy of history and its influence. Maritain writes with emphasis, "Once again, the philosophy of history is no part of metaphysics, as Hegel believed. It pertains to moral philosophy, for it has to do with human actions considered in the evolution of mankind" (133). As a French Neo-Scholastic, Maritain argues that, for a philosopher using "natural reason" alone, "the philosophy of history is bound either to fail in its own expectations, or to risk mystification, for in order to get at some level of real depth and significance it inevitably requires prophetic data" (31).

9. Robert Owen, *The Book of the New Moral World* (London, 1836), Section 14, p. 40. See also Owen's *The Marriage System of the New Moral World* (Leeds, 1839) and John Finch, ed. Robert Owen, *Moral Code of the New Moral World, or Rational State of Society* (Liverpool, 1840). Echoes of Milton's poetry appear in Robert Owen's *New View of Society* (New York, 1972), "Mr. Owen's Address Delivered at the adjourned Meeting at the City of London Tavern, August 21, 1817," pp. 50-63. Owen is quoted as saying, "Why so many people living in wretchedness and ignorance?...hitherto you have been prevented from even knowing what happiness really is, solely in consequence or the errors—gross errors—that have been combined with the fundamental notions of every religion that has hitherto been taught to men. And, in consequence, they have made man the most inconsistent and the most miserable being in existence. By the errors of these systems, he has been made a weak, imbecile animal; a furious bigot and fanatic; or a miserable hypocrite; and should these qualities be carried, not only into the projected villages, but "into Paradise itself, a Paradise would be no longer found" (p. 59).

10. *Letters to the Human Race* (London, 1850), p. 130. Quoted from Ernest Lee Tuveson, "The Millenarian Structure of *The Communist Manifesto," The Apocalypse in English Renaissance Thought and Literature: Patterns, Antecedents, and Repercussions*, eds. C. A. Patrides and Joseph Wittreich (Manchester, 1984), p. 331.

11. Marx and Engels, "The Communist Manifesto," *The Marx-Engels Reader*, pp. 335–36.

12. Marx, *The Poverty of Philosophy*, intro. edited by Friedrich Engels (New York, 1971), pp. 174–75. This edition is based on the French edition of 1847, and includes later corrections by Marx and Engels written just before they composed *The Communist Manifesto*. See David McLellan, *Karl Marx: His Life and Thought* (London, 1973), p. 131. See also Ernest Lee Tuveson, "The Millenarian Structure of *The Communist Manifesto," The Apocalypse in English Renaissance Thought and Literature*, pp. 323–41; and Tuveson's *Millennium and Utopia: A Study in the Background of the Idea of Progress* (Berkeley, 1949).

13. The death of Marx is recounted in detail from primary sources in David McLellan, *Karl Marx: His Life and Thought* (London, 1973), pp. 450–51.

14. Francis Fukuyama, "An Idea for a Universal History," *The End of History and the Last Man* (New York, 1992), pp. 5-81. Fukuyama favorably cites Immanuel Kant as noting, in an essay reprinted in *On History* (Indianapolis, 1993) that, "The History of the world is none other than the progress of the consciousness of Freedom" (60). Fukuyama also favorably cites views paraphrased from Hegel's *The Philosophy of History*, observing that "for Hegel, the embodiment of human freedom was the modern constitutional state, or again, what we have called liberal democracy. The Universal History of mankind was nothing other than man's progressive rise to full nationality, and to a self-conscious awareness of how that rationality expresses itself in liberal self-government" (19).

15. In contrast to Fukuyama's views, see also Michael Hardt and Antonio Negri, *Empire* (Cambridge, Mass., 2000) for a militant, manifesto-like statement demanding a political revolution to transform an alleged exploitative yet vaguely defined global capitalist empire—a statement of abstract analysis, italicized passages, and strong demands having contexts in but deviating from positions taken by Hegel and Marx. The authors propose that a "new proletariat" comprised of all those "exploited by capital, the entire cooperating multitude" around the world, join in altering the capitalist "empire" by demanding, among other things, *"a social wage and a guaranteed income for all"* and the *"right to reappropriation"* of the means of production and public informational exchanges (402-06). "The multitude," the authors insist in a loose and wavering argument, "is a biopolitical self-organization"; still, the authors await "the construction, or rather the insurgence, of a powerful organization" involving the multitude, an organization "with a form that has yet to emerge." *"Reality is not dialectical, colonialism is,"* the authors dogmatically declare, and they contend that the transformation of the empire by the multitude will dissolve such antitheses (128).

16. In recalling a conversation on historicism, Felipe Fernández-Armesto in *Millennium: A History of the Last Thousand Years* (New York, London, Toronto, 1995), composed prior to his *Civilizations* discussed later in this chapter, records the following exchange: "When I confessed...that I was striving to write a history of the world, a colleague I admire told me there was no such thing—'only the histories of parts of it'" (19). Some recently published global historicist works confirm that such wide ranging studies, however much needed, remain in a discipline without an agreed upon form.

See David Fromkin's *The Way of the World: From the Dawn of Civilization to the Eve of the Twenty-First Century* (New York, 1998) which seeks to define evolutionary stages in historical development; namely, the emergence of the huminoid line, and with it in further stages, of agriculture, cities, political organizations, religions, and moral systems. Subsequent speculations focus on topics such as the future of world population growth, future anticipated conflicts between global governing bodies and nation states, and future possible attempts to colonize planets. See also the lucidly written and popular world cultural history—Will Durant's *The Story of Civilization* vols. 1-6, with Ariel Durant, vols. 7-11 (New York, 1935-75)—which adopts an openly "narrative" approach and a period-thematic type structure. This ambitious work, inspired by Enlightenment values derived largely from Voltaire, examines arts, sciences, politics, humanities, and societies, and is laced with witty and revealing observations, but it has attracted criticism from experts in specific areas and lacks comparative critical assessments of differing civilizations. See also Crane Brinton, John B. Christopher, Robert Lee Wolff, *A History of Civilization*, 5th ed. (Englewood Cliffs, N. J., 1976) for an insightful but condensed critique of world civilizations. For an excellent comparative cultural study with rich and incisive commentary, see Jacques Barzun's *From Dawn to Decadence: 500 Years of Cultural Triumph and Defeat*, 1500 to the Present (New York, 2000).

17. Voltaire, *Essai sur les moeurs et l'esprit des nations et sur les principaux faits de l'histoire depius Charlemagne jusqu'a Louis XIII* (Paris, 1963).

18. Auguste Comte. *Cours de philosophie positive,* trans. Harriet Martineau (New York, 1855).

19. Herbert Spencer, *Synthetic Philosophy*, 8 vols. (New York, 1884-87).

20. H. G. Wells, *The Outline of History* (New York, 1931).

21. Giambattista Vico, *Principi di una scienza nuova,* (Ithaca, 1968).

22. Gibbons, *The Decline and Fall of the Roman Empire,* 4 vols. (1776-88), quoted here from the "verbatim reprint" (London, 1893-92). Spengler, *The Decline of the West* (1918-22), trans. Charles Francis Atkinson, 2 vols. (New York, 1957). As an offshoot of the cyclical mode, see also other works which, by comparing historical cultural trends of the present to those of the past, have sought to show a decline in Western civilization. Among these works are Max Nordau's *fin de siècle* psychological study of alleged history and decay in nineteenth-century literature and art entitled *Degeneration* (New York, 1895); and Pitrim Sorokin's sociological analysis of a supposed six-hundred-year-old "sick" and increasingly "sensate" Western civilization, yet one having some hope of reprise, in *The Crises of Our Age* (New York, 1941).

23. Toynbee, *A Study of History* second ed., fourth printing, 12 vols. (Oxford, 1945-61). Toynbee in vol. 12 (1961), p. 663, for example, states in a "meta-history" segment that "Religion is Man's attempt to get in touch with absolute spiritual Reality behind the phenomena of the Universe, and, having made contact with It, to live in harmony with It." See also the author's comments on changes in his approach to history in chapter 1, "My View of History"; and chapter 3, "Does History Repeat Itself?" in *Civilization on Trial* (New York, 1948).

24. In reviewing the work Hans Kohn, in *The Journal of Philosophy* (28 Aug., 1947): 499, associating Hegel's philosophic idealism with Toynbee's religious stance, takes the strongest exception to the use by Toynbee of idealistic faith-based values in making qualitative assessments of civilizations: "as Hegel before him, so Toynbee undertakes to rewrite Saint Augustine's principal work by interpreting the City of Man as the City of God *in statu nacendi*." However, Crane Brinton in *The Virginia Quarterly Review* (Summer, 1956): 361-75, while also critical of Toynbee's overall approach, notes the strong anthropocentric and humanist currents underlying evaluations in much of the study: "It is surely a theodicy; but, if we think of Milton, or Leibnitz, or Joseph de Maistre, or even the author of the Book of Job, it is a vague and imprecise theodicy. Indeed at times so great is Toynbee's insistence on the freedom of the human spirit, his work sounds more like an 'anthropodicy.'"

25. *Civilizations* (London, 2000), p. xii.

SELECTIVE BIBLIOGRAPHY

PRIMARY RENAISSANCE SOURCES

Bacon, Francis. *Of the Advancement and Proficience of Learning or the Partitions of Sciences.* Enlarged to nine books. Oxford: Printed by Leon Lichfield, Printer to the University for Rob Young & Ed. Forrest, 1640.

——. *The Two Bookes of Francis Bacon. Of the proficience and aduancement of Learning, diuine and humane.* London at Graies Inne Gate in Holborne: Printed for *Henrie Fomes*, 1605.

——. *The Novum Organum. Or A True Guide to the Interpretation of Nature.* By Francis Bacon, Lord Verulam, Lord Chancellor of England. Tr. G. W. Kitchin. Oxford University Press, 1855. Francis Bacon: Selections. Ed. Brian Vickers. Oxford: Oxford University Press, 1996.

——. *The Works of Francis Bacon.* Eds. James Spedding, Robert Leslie Ellis and Douglas Denon Heath. 15 vols. Boston: Brown and Taggard, 1860-64.

——. *Biblia pauperum.* English and Latin facsimile edition. Tr. and commentary, Albert C. Labriola and John W. Smeltz. Pittsburgh: Duquesne University Press, 1990.

Blunderville. *Blvnderville His Exercises.* London: William Stansby, 1622.

Botero, Giovanni. *Relations of the most famovs kingdomes and Common-wealths thorowout the world: Didscoursing of their Situation, Religions, Languages, Manners, Customes, Strengths, Greatnesse and Policies.* Tr. R. I. London: Printed by John Haviland, sold by John Partridge, 1630.

——. *The Travellers Breviat, or A historical description of the most famous kingdomes in the world.* London: Imprinted by Edm. Bollifant, for John Iaggard, 1601.

Burton, Robert. *The Anatomy of Melancholy.* Ed. and tr. Floyd Dell and Paul Jordan-Smith. New York: Tudor Publishing Co., 1955.

Columbus, Christopher. *Select Documents Illustrating the Four Voyages of Christopher Columbus, A History in Eight Documents.* Ed. and tr. Lionel Cecil Jane. 2 vols. London: Hakluyt Society, 1930-32.

——. *The Journal of Christopher Columbus.* Ed. and tr. Lionel Cecil Jane. London: Blond & the Orion Press, 1960.

————. *The Voyages of Christopher Columbus, being the Journals of his First and Third, and the Letters Concerning his First and Last Voyages.* Ed. and trans., Lionel Cecil Jane. London: Argonaut Press, 1930.

————. *Christopher Columbus's Book of Prophecies, Reproduction of the Original Manuscript with English Translation.* Ed. and tr. Kay Brigham. Barcelona: M.C. E. Horeb and TSELF Inc., 1991.

————. *The Libro de las profecias of Christopher Columbus, An en face* edition. Tr. and commentary by Delno C. West and August Kling. Gainesville: University of Florida Press, 1991.

Columbus, Ferdinand. *The Life of the Admiral Christopher Columbus by His Son Ferdinand.* Tr., intro. Benjamin Keen. New Brunswick: Rutgers University Press, 1959.

Comenius, John [or Johann] Amos. *Opera Didactical Omnia,* ad anno 1627 ad 1657 continuata. Amsterdam: Anno 1657.

————. *Analytical Didactic.* Tr., intro. and notes Vladimir Jelinek. Chicago: University of Chicago Press, 1953.

————. *The Great Didactic of John Amos Comenius.* Intro. and t. W. Keatinge. London: Adam and Charles Black, 1896.

————. *Orbis Sensualium Pictu...A Picture and Nomenclature of all the chief Things that are in the world, and of Mens Employments therein.* Tr. Charles Hoole from Latin and High Dutch. London: Printed for J. Kirton, 1659.

Conway, Countess Anne. *The Principles of the most Ancient and Modern Philosophy.* Amsterdam: Printed by M. Brown, 1690. Reprinted, London, 1692.

Dee, John. *General and Rare Memorials Pertayning to the Perfect Arte of Navigation: Annexed to the Paradoxal Compas, in Playne:* now first published: 24 yeres, after the first Inuention thereof. London: Iohn Daye, 1577. One hundred copies printed.

Donne, John. *The Complete English Poems of John Donne.* Ed. and notes C. A. Patrides. London: J. M. Dent and Sons, 1985.

————. *The Complete Poetry of John Donne.* Ed. and notes John Shawcross. New York: Doubleday, 1967.

————. *Selected Prose.* Selected by Evelyn Simpson, eds. Helen Gardner and Timothy Healy. Oxford: Clarendon Press, 1967.

Fuller, Thomas. *A Pisgah-sight of Palestine and the Confines Thereof, with The History of the Old and New Testament Acted Thereon.* London: Printed for J. F. for John Williams, 1650.

————. *The Historie of the Holy Warre.* Cambridge: Printed by Thomas Buck, 1639.

Grafton, Richard. *A chronicle at large, and meere history of the affayres of Englande.* London: H. Danhan, 1569.

Hakluyt, Richard. *Divers Voyages touching the discouerie of America, and the Island adiacent unto the same.* London: Thomas Woodcocke, 1582.

————. *The Principall Navigations, Voiages and Discoveries of the English nation, made by Sea or ouer Land, to the most remote and farthest distant Quarters of the earth at any time within the compasse of these 1500 yeeres: Diuided into three seuerall parts....* First ed. 1 vol. London: George Bishop, Ralph Newberie, 1589. The "epistle dedicatorie," deleted in later editions, is to Sir Francis Walsingham. The edition is "Diuided into three seuerall parts." British Library shelf mark copy C 32 m. 10; Huntington Library shelf mark 3437.

————. *Principal Navigations, Voiages Traffiques and Discoueries...within the compasse of these 1500 years.* 2 printed books, the first divided into 2 vols. and the second consisting of a third vol. London: George Bishop, Ralph Newberie, and Robert Barker, 1598-1600. British Library shelf mark copy 683 b 5; Huntington Library shelf mark 3428.

————. *The Principal Navigations, Voiages, Traffiqves and Discoueries of the English Nation, made by Sea or ouerland, to the remote and farthest distant quaters of the Earth, at any time within the compasse of these 1600 years: Diuided into three seuerall Volumes, according to the positions of the Regions, where unto they were directed.* 3 vols. London: George Bishop, Ralph Newberie, and Robert Barker, 1599-1600, with 1589 insertions; Huntington Library shelf mark 3438. The British Library shelf mark copy 212 d. 2 is from the library of King George III.

Hakluyt, Richard, Jr. and Sr. *The Original Writings & Correspondence of the Two Richard Hakluyts.* Intro. and notes, E. G. R. Taylor. 2 vols. London: W. Lewis for the Hakluyt Society, 1935. In *Works Issued by the Hakluyt Society, Second Series, No. 71.*

Holinshed, Raphael. *The First volume of the Chronicles of England, Scotland, and Irelande.* London: George Bishop, 1577.

Jonson, Ben. *Ben Jonson.* Ed. C. H. Herford and Percy and Evelyn Simpson. 11 vols. Oxford: Oxford University Press, 1924-52.

Lanquet. Thomas. *An Epitome of Chronicles.* Enlarged first by Thomas Cooper and then brought to completion to the time of Elizabeth I by Robert Crowley. London: no listed printer, 1559.

Milton, John. *A Brief History of Moscovia and of other less-known Countries lying eastward of Russia as far as Cathay.* Gather'd from the Writings of several Eye-witnesses. London: Printed by *M. Flesher,* for *Brabazon Alymer* at the *Three Pigeons* against the *Royal Exchange,* 1682.

————. *History of Britain,* ed. George Philip Krapp in *The Works of John Milton.* Gen. ed. Frank Allen Patterson. New York: Columbia University Press, vol. 10, 1933.

————. *Milton's Complete Poetical Works Reproduced in Photographic Facsimile.* Ed. Francis Harris Fletcher. 4 vols. Urbana: University of Illinois Press, 1943-48.

————. *The Works of John Milton.* Gen. ed. Frank Allen Patterson. 21 vols. New York: Columbia University Press, 1931-38.

————. *The Complete Prose Works of John Milton.* Gen. ed. Don M. Wolfe, Douglas Bush, J. Milton French, et al. 8 vols. New Haven: Yale University Press, 1953-82.

————. *The Riverside Milton.* Ed. Roy Flannagan. Boston: Houghton Mifflin Company, 1998.

————. *The Poetical Works of John Milton.* Ed. John Henry Todd. 6 vols. London: Bye and Law, 1801. Enlarged 2nd ed. 7 vols. London: Bye and Law, 1809.

————. *John Milton: Complete Poetry and Major Prose.* Ed. Merritt Y. Hughes. Indianapolis: Odyssey Press, 1947.

More, Henry. *Democritus Platonissans or An Essay upon the Infinity of Worlds out of Platonick Principles.* Herento is annexed *Cupids Conflict* together with *The Philosophers Devotions.* Cambridge: Printed by Roger Daniel, 1646.

————. *The Immortality of the Soul,* in *A Collection of Several Philosophical Writings.* London: Printed by James Flesher, for William Morden, 1662.

————. *The Immortality of the Soul.* Ed. A. Jacob. Dordrecht: Martinus Nijhoff Publishers, 1987.

————. *Philosophical Writings of Henry More.* Ed. with intro. and notes, Flora Isabel Mackinnon. London: Oxford University Press, 1925.

Ortelius, Abraham. *Theatrum orbis terrarum.* Coppenium Dieft: Antverpiae, 1570. Reprints 1595 and 1601.

————. *Abraham Ortelius His Epitome of The Theater of the Worlde.* Ed. Micheal Coignet. London: Ieames Shawe, 1603.

————. *Theatrum Orbis Terrarum. The Theatre of the Whole World.* London: John Norton, 1606. Huntington 62823.

Purchas, Samuel. *Purchas his pilgrimage, or, Relations of the world and the religions observed in all ages and places discouered...In foure partes. This first containeth a theologicall and geographicall historie of Asia, Africa, and America, with the ilands adiacent.* 1st ed. 4 vols. London: Printed by W. Stansby for H. Fetherstone, 1613.

————. *Purchas his Pilgrimage. Or, Relations of the world and the religions observed in all ages and places discouered, from the Creation vnto this Present.* In Fovre parts...The second Edition, much enlarged with Additions through the whole Worke. 2nd ed. 4 vols. London: Printed by W. Stansby for H. Fetherstone, 1614.

————. *Purchas his pilgrimage, or Relations of the world and the religions observed in all ages and places discovered, from the creation unto this present. In fovre parts. The first contayneth a theologicall and geogrphicall historie of Asia, Africa, and America, with the ilands adiacent. Declaring the ancient religions before the flovd, the heathenish, Jewish, Saracenicall in all ages since...much enl. with additions through the whole worke.* 3rd ed. 4 vols. London: Printed by W. Stansby for H. Fetherstone, 1617.

————. *Pvrchas his pilgrim. Microcosmvs, or, The Historie Of Man. Relating the Wonders of his Generation, Vanities in his Degeneration, Necessity of his Regeneration. Meditated on the words of David. Psal. 39.5. Verily, euery Man at his best state is altogether Vanity. Selah.* London, Printed by W. S. for H. Fetherstone, 1619. 1 vol. of meditations and commentary. Not printed as an "edition."

————. *Haklvytvs posthumus or Pvrchas his pilgrimes. Contayning a History of the World, in sea voyages. & lande Trauells, by Englishmen & others. Wherein Gods Wonders in Nature & Prouidence, The actes, Arts, Varieties, & Vanities of Men, with a world of the Worlds Rarities, are by a world of Eywitnesse Authors Related to the World. Some left written by Mr. Hakluyt at his death. More since added. His also perused, & perfected. All examined, abreuiated. Illustrated with Notes, Enlarged with Discourses, Adorned with pictures, and Expressed in Mapps. In fower parts, each containing fiue Bookes.* 4 vols. Not printed as an "edition." London: Printed by W. Stansby for Henry Fetherstone, 1625.

————. *Pvrchas his Pilgrimage. Or Relations of the world and the religions obserued in all ages and places discouere...Contayning a theologicall and geographicall historie of Asia, Africa, and America, with the ilands adiacent...4th ed., much enl. With...three whole treatises annexed, one of Russia and other north easterne regions by Sr. Ierome Horsey; the second of the Gulfe of Bengala by Master William Methold; the third of the Saracenicall Empire.* 1 vol. London: Printed by H. Fetherstone, 1626.

Ralegh, Walter. *The Pilgrimage. Written by Sir Walter Ralegh, Knight, After his Condemnation,* The Day before his Death. London: Printed by George Larkin, 1681.

————. *The Discoverie of the large and bewtiful Empire of Guiana, with a relation of the great and Golden Citie of Manoa (which the Spanyards call El Dorado) And of the Prouinces of Emeria, Arromaia. Amapaia, and other Countries, with their riuers, adioyning.* London: Robert Robinson, 1596.

————. *The History of the World.* London: Printed for Walter Bvrre, 1614. Huntington shelfmark 289707.

————. *The Historie of the World. In Five Bookes.* London: Printed for Walter Bvrre in 1634, but with a 1614 title page. Huntington shelfmark 21776.

Ross, Alexander. *Arcana Microcosmi: Or, The hid Secrets of Man's Body discovered; In an Anatomical Duel between Aristotle and Galen concerning the Parts thereof:* As also, By Discovery of the strange and marveilous Diseases, Symptomes & Accidents of Man's Body. With A Refutation of Doctor Brown's *Vulgar Errors,* The Lord Bacon's *Natural History,* and Doctor Harvy's Book *De Generatione,* Comenius, and Others. London: Theo Newcomb, 1652.

————. *Mystagogvs Poeticus, or The Muses Interpreter: Explaining The Historical Mysteries, and mysticall Histories of the ancient Greek and Latine Poets.* Here Apollo's Temple is again opened, the *Muses* Treasurers the second time discovered, and the Gardens of Parnassus disclosed more fully whence many flowers of usefull, delightfull, and rare Observations, never touched by any other Mythologist are collected. 2nd ed. London: T. W. for Thomas Whitaker, 1643.

————. *The Marrow of History: Or, an Epitome Of all Historical Passages from the Creation, to the end of the last Macedonian War.* First set out at large by Sir Walter Rawleigh, and now Abbreviated by A.R. 2nd ed. London: Printed by John Place and William Place, 1662.

————. *A View of all Religions of the World, From the Creation, to these time together with A Discovery of all known Heresies in all Ages and Places.* London: Printed for Iohn Saywell, 1653.

————. *Arcana Microcosmi: Or, The hid Secrets of Man's Body discovered; In an Anatomical Duel between Aristotle and Galen concerning the Parts thereof.* London: Theo Newcomb, 1652.

————. *A View of all Religions of the World, From the Creation, to these times together with A Discovery of all known Heresies in all Ages and Places.* London: Printed for Iohn Saywell, 1653.

————. *Orbis Sensualium Pictus...A Picture and Nomenclature of all the chief Things that are in the world, and of Mens Employments therein.* Tr. Charles Hoole (from Latin and High Dutch. London: Printed for J. Kirton, 1659.

————. *Mystagogvs Poeticus, or The Muses Interpreter: Explaining The Historical Mysteries, and mysticall Histories of the ancient Greek and Latine Poets.* 2nd ed. London: T. W. for Thomas Whitaker, 1643.

Stow, John. *A Summarie of Englyshe Chronicles.* London: Thomas Marshe, 1565.

MEDIEVAL PILGRIMAGE: TEXTS AND CRITICISM

Anonymous Pilgrims I-VIII. *Itinerary from Anonymous Pilgrims I-VIII.* Tr. Aubrey Stewart. London: Hanover Square, 1894. Stewart's translation is based upon the text published in *Oesterreichischer Vierteljahreschrift für Katholische Theologie*, notes V. Newmann. Vienna, 1868, 1870.

Arculfus. *Arculf's Narrative about the Holy Places, Written by Adamnan.* Tr. and notes, James Rose Macpherson. London: Hanover Square, 1895.

Benini, Rodolfo. "Il grande Sion, il Sinai, e il piccolo Sion," *Rendiconti della Reale Accademia dei Lincei*, 5th ser. 23 (Roma, 1915): 1-27.

Bernard the Wise. *The Itinerary of Bernard the Wise.* Tr. J. H. Bernard. London: Hanover Square, 1893.

Beazley, C. Raymond. *The Dawn of Modern Geography.* 3 vols. Oxford: Oxford University Press, 1906.

Biddulphus, Gviliemus. *The Travels of certaine Englishmen.* London: Th. Haveland, 1609.

Bordeaux Pilgrim. *Itinerary from Bordeaux to Jerusalem.* Tr. Aubrey Stewart; notes C. W. Wilson. London: Adelphi, 1887.

Demaray, John G. "Patterns of Earthly Pilgrimage in Dante's Commedia: Palmers, Romers, and the Great Circle Journey," *Romance Philology* (November, 1970): 239-58.

————. "Pilgrim Text Models for Dante's Purgatorio," *Studies in Philology* (January, 1969): 1-24.

————. "The Pilgrim Texts and Dante's Three Beasts, Inferno I," *Italica* (Autumn, 1967): 233-41.

————. *Cosmos and Epic Representation: Dante, Spenser, Milton and the Transformation of Renaissance Heroic Poetry*. Pittsburgh: Duquesne University Press, 1991.

————. *The Invention of Dante's Commedia*. New Haven: Yale University Press, 1974.

Etheria, see Silvia, St. under "Pilgrimage Materials."

Fetellus. *Description of Jerusalem and the Holy Land*. Tr. James Rose MacPherson. London: Hanover Square, 1896.

Hoade, Fr. Eugene, ed. *Western Pilgrims*. Jerusalem: Franciscan Press, 1952. Contains a bibliography of English pilgrim texts of the fourth through the seventeenth centuries, pp. 80-114.

Holloway, Julia Bolton. "Dante's Commedia: Egyptian Spoils, Roman Jubilee, and Florence's Patron," *Studies in Medieval Culture* 12 (1978): 97-104.

————. "The Vita Nuova: Paradigms of Pilgrimage," *Jerusalem: Essays on Pilgrimage and Literature*. New York: AMS Press, 1998, pp. 101-20.

————. *The Pilgrim and the Book: A Study of Dante, Langland, and Chaucer*. Berne and New York: P. Lang, 1987.

Howard, Donald Roy. *Writers and Pilgrims: Medieval Pilgrimage Narratives and Their Posterity*. Berkeley: University of California Press, 1980.

Khitrowo, B., ed. *Itinéraires Russes en Orient*. Osnabrück: Zeller, 1966.

Labib, Mahfouz. *Pèlerins et Voyageurs au Mont Sinai*. Cairo: French Oriental Institute, 1961.

Leonardo Frescobaldi, Georgio Gucci, and Simone Sigoli: *Visit to the Holy Places*. Tr. Fr. Theophilus Bellorini and Fr. Eugene Hoade; Preface and notes Fr. Bellarmino Baggatti. Jerusalem: Franciscan Press, 1948.

Maundeville, John, [also called Mandeville] attributed to Jean de Bourgogne and Jean d'Outremeuse. *The Bodley Version of Mandeville's Travels*. Ed. M. C. Seymour. London: Oxford University Press, 1963.

————. "The Book of Sir John Maundeville," *Early Travels in Palestine*, pp. 127-282. Ed. Thomas Wright. London: Henry G. Bohn, 1848.

————. *The Voyages and Trauailes of Sir John Mandeuile Knight.* London, Thomas Snodham, 1625. Huntington shelf mark 62427.

————. *The Buke of John Maundeuill.* Ed. George F. Warner. British Museum, Egerton Ms. 1982 together with French text, notes, and intro. Illustrations, British Museum Ms. 24,198. Westminster: Nichols and Sons for the Rorburghe Club, 1889.

Michelant, Henri and Gaston Raynaud, eds. *Itinéraires à Jérusalem et Descriptions de la Terra Sainte.* Geneve: Jules Giullaume, 1882. Reprint, Osnabrück, Zeller, 1966.

Migne, Jacques-Paul. *Patrologiae cursus completus.* Series Graeca. 161 vols. in 166 books. Paris, 1857-1866.

———— Series secunda Latin. 221 vols. Paris, 1844-1855.

Nicollo of Poggibonsi. *A Voyage Beyond the Seas.* Tr. Fr. Theophilus Bellorini and Fr. Eugene Hoade; Intro. Fr. Bellarmino Bagatti. Jerusalem: Franciscan Press, 1954.

The Palestine Pilgrims' Text Society. 14 vols. London: Adelphi and Hanover Square, 1887-97. Reprint, *The Library of the Palestine Pilgrims' Text Society.* 13 vols. New York: AMS Press, 1971.

Rohicht, Reinhold, ed. *Deutsche Pilgerreisen nach dem Heiligen Lande.* Aalen: Scientia Vertag, 1967.

Silvia, St. (also called Etheria). *The Pilgrimage of St. Silvia of Aquitania to the Holy Places.* Intro, notes, tr. John H. Bernard; Appendix, C. W. Wilson. London: Adelphi, 1887.

Suger, Abbot. *Abbot Suger on the Abbey Church of St-Denis and its art treasures.* Ed., trans., annotated Edwin Panofsky. 2nd ed., Gerda Panofsky-Soergel. Princeton: Princeton University Press, 1979.

Tobler, Titus and Augustus Molinier, eds. *Itinera Hierosolymitana et Descriptiones Terrae Sanctae.* Osnabrück: Zeller, 1966.

Wright, Thomas. *Early Travels in Palestine.* London: Henry G. Bohn, 1848.

Zacher, Christian K. *Curiosity and Pilgrimage.* Baltimore: Johns Hopkins University Press, 1976.

EDITIONS

Arnold, Mathew. *On Classical Tradition*, Ed. R. H. Super. Ann Arbor: University of Michigan Press, 1960

Carew, Thomas. *The Poems of Thomas Carew.* Ed. W. Carew Hazlett. London: Chiswick Press, 1870.

Casas, Bartolomé de las. *History of the Indies.* Tr. and ed. Andrée Collard. New York: Harper & Row, 1971.

Cicero, Marcus Tullius. *De oratore.* Tr. E.W. Sutton. Cambridge, Mass.: Harvard University Press; London: W. Heinemann, 1942.

Comte, Auguste. *Cours de philosophie positive.* Tr. Harriet Martineau. New York: Calvin Blanchard, 1855.

Gibbon, Edward. *The Decline and Fall of the Roman Empire*; "verbatim reprint." 4 vols. London: Frederick Warne, 1892-93.

Hegel, Georg Wilhelm Friedrich. *The Philosophy of History.* Preface Charles Hegel, tr. J. Sibree. New York: Colonial Press, 1900.

Herodotus. *Herodotus.* Tr. J. Enoch Powell. 2 vols. Oxford: The Clarendon Press, 1949.

―――. "Account of Egypt," Tr. G. C. Macaulay in *Voyages and Travels: Ancient and Modern.* Ed. Charles Eliot. New York: P. F. Collier, 1910.

Jones, Inigo. *Designs by Inigo Jones for Masques and Plays at Court.* Intro. and notes by Percy Simpson and C. F. Ball. Oxford: Oxford University Press, 1924.

Marx, Karl and Friedrich Engels. *The Marx-Engels Reader.* Ed. Robert C. Tucker. 1st ed. New York: Norton, 1972.

Marx, Karl. *Die deutsche Ideologie.* Wien: Verlag für Literatur und Politik, 1932.

―――. *Early texts.* Tr. David McLellan. Oxford: Blackwell, 1971.

―――. *The Poverty of Philosophy.* Intro., ed. Friedrich Engels. Tr. from the first French edition of 1847 with corrections by Marx in 1876 and by Engels for the second French edition and the German editions of 1885 and 1892. New York: International Publishers, 1971.

Oldenburg, Henry. *The Correspondence of Henry Oldenburg.* Ed. and tr. A. Rupert Hall & Marie Boas Hall. 13 vols. Madison: University of Wisconsin Press, 1941-62.

Owen, Robert. *The Book of the New Moral World.* London: Effingham Wilson, 1836.

――――. *The Marriage System of the New Moral World.* Leeds, n. p., 1839.

―――. and John Finch. *Moral Code of the New Moral World, or Rational State of Society.* Liverpool, 1840.

233

————. *New View of Society*. 3rd ed. London: Printed for Longman, Hurst, Orme, and Brown et al., 1817.

———— *Letters to the Human Race*....London: n. p., 1850.

Paris, Mathieu. *Grande chronique de Mathieu Paris*. Tr. en francias, Huillard-Breholles. Paris: Paulin, 1840-44.

Raleigh, Walter. [See also, Ralegh, Walter.] *The Poems of Sir Walter Raleigh*. Ed. and intro. Agnes Latham. Cambridge: Harvard University Press, 1962.

————. *Selected Writings: Sir Walter Raleigh*. Ed. Gerald Hammand. Manchester: Carcanet, 1984.

Spencer, Herbert. *Synthetic Philosophy*, 8 vols. New York: D. Appleton, 1884-97.

Spengler, Oswald. *The Decline of the West*. Tr. and notes Charles Francis Atkenson. 2 vols. New York: Alfred A. Knopf, 1957.

Vico, Giambattista (Gianni Battista). *Principi di una scienza nuova*. Tr. Thomas Bergin and Max Fisch. Ithaca: Cornell University Press, 1968.

Voltaire, François Marie Arouet de. *Le Philosophie de l'Histoire*. Unnamed tr. London: Printed for I. Allcock, near St. Pauls, 1766.

————. *The Philosophy of History*, Intro. and tr. Thomas Kiernan. New York: Philosophical Library, 1965, from the 1st edition published in London, 1766.

————. *Essai sur les moeurs et l'espirit des nations et sur les principaux faits de l'histoire depius Charlemagne jusqu'a Louis XIII*. Paris: Garnier frères, 1963.

GENERAL WORKS

Adorno, Theodor A. *Negative Dialectics*. Tr. E. B. Ashton. New York: Continuum, 1997. Original edition: *Negative Dialektik*. Frankfurt am Main: Suhrkamp Verlag, 1966.

Anderson, Paul Russell. *Science in Defense of Liberal Religion: A Study of Henry More's Attempt to Link Seventeenth Century Religion and Science*. New York: G. P. Putnam's Sons, 1933.

Anderson, William. *Dante the Maker*. London: Routledge and Kegan Paul, 1979.

Armitage, David. *The Ideological Origins of the British Empire*. Cambridge: Cambridge University Press, 2001.

Aron, Raymond. *Memoirs*. New York: Holmes and Meier, 1990.

Auerbach, Erich. *Dante, Poet of the Secular World.* Trans. Ralph Manheim. Chicago: University of Chicago Press, 1961.

Bagrow, Leo. *History of Cartography.* Rev. and enl. R. A. Skelton, tr. D. L. Paisey. Cambridge: Harvard University Press, 1964.

Baker, Herschel Clay. *The Race of Time: Three Lectures on Renaissance Historiography.* Toronto: University of Toronto Press, 1967.

Bartolomé de las Casas in History: Toward an understanding of the man and his work. Ed. Juan Friede and Benjamin Keen De Kalb: Northern Illinois University Press, 1971.

Barzon, Jacques. *From Dawn to Decadence: 500 years of western cultural life.* New York: Harper Collins, 2000.

Bennet, Joan. *Reviving Liberty; Radical Christian Humanism in Milton's Great Poems.* Cambridge: Harvard University Press, 1989.

Bloom, Harold. *The Western Canon: the books and school of the ages.* New York: Harcourt Brace, 1994.

Blunderville. *"The true order and Methode of wryting and reading Histories,"* Huntington Library Quarterly, 2 (Jan., 1940): 164ff.

Boon, James A. *Other tribes, other scribes: Symbolic anthropology in the comparative study of cultures, histories, religions and texts.* Cambridge: Cambridge University Press, 1982

Brandon, Robert. *Making It Explicit: Reasoning, Representing, and Discursive Commitment.* Cambridge: Harvard University Press, 1994.

Braudel, Fernand. *Civilta e impere del Meditterraneo nell eta di Filippo II.* New ed. Torino: G. Einaudi, 1976.

Bridges, R. C., and Hair, P.E. H., eds. *Compassing the vaste globe of the earth: studies in the history of the Hakluyt Society, 1846-1996.* London: the Hakluyt Society, 1996.

Brinton, Crane, with John B. Christopher and Robert Lee Wolff. *A History of Civilization.* 5th ed. Englewood Cliffs, N. J.: Prentice-Hall, 1976.

―――. *Civilization in the West.* Englewood Cliffs, N. J.: Prentice-Hall, 1973.

Bush, Douglas. *English Literature in the Earlier Seventeenth Century,* Oxford: Clarendon Press, 1962. First published, 1946.

―――. *John Milton.* London: Weidenfeld & Nicolson, 1965.

Cambel, Ali Bülent. *Applied Chaos Theory: A Paradigm for Complexity.* Boston: Academic Press, 1992.

Carrad, Phillipe. *Poetics of the New History*: French Historical Discourse from Braudel to Chartier. Baltimore: The Johns Hopkins University Press, 1992.

Cawley, Robert Ralston. *Milton and the Literature of Travel.* Princeton: Princeton University Press, 1951.

————. *Unpathed waters: Studies in the influence of the voyagers on Elizabethan literature.* Princeton: Princeton University Press, 1940.

Cerny, Jaroslav. *Ancient Egyptian Religion.* London: Hutchinson's University Library, 1952.

Cohn, Norman. *The Pursuit of the Millennium.* 2nd ed. New York: Harper and Brothers, 1961.

Collingwood, R. G. *The Idea of History.* Rev. ed. with Lectures 1926-1928. Ed. Jan Van Der Dussen. Oxford: Oxford University Press, 1993.

Crone, G. R. *The World Map by Richard of Haldingham in Hereford Cathedral.* London: Royal Geographical Society, 1954.

Davies, Stevie. *Images of Kingship in Paradise Lost.* Columbia: University of Missouri Press, 1983.

Demaray, Hannah Disinger. "Milton and the 'Intelligible Flame': 'Sweet Converse' in Milton's Prose and Poetry," *Renascence*, vol. 53, no. 1 (Fall, 2000): 23-42.

Demaray, John G. *Milton and the Masque Tradition: The Early Poems, "Arcades," and "Comus."* Cambridge: Harvard University Press, 1968.

————. *Dante and the Book of the Cosmos: Architectural Typology and Structure in the "Commedia."* Independence Square, Philadelphia: American Philosophical Society, 1987.

————. *Milton's Theatrical Epic: The Invention and Design of "Paradise Lost".* Cambridge: Harvard University Press, 1980.

————. *Shakespeare and the Spectacles of Strangeness: "The Tempest" and the Transformation of Renaissance Theatrical Forms.* Pittsburgh: Duquesne University Press, 1998.

————. "The Temple of the Mind: Cosmic Iconography in Milton's *"A Mask."* *"Comus" Contexts*: *Medieval and Renaissance Texts and Studies.* Ed. Roy Flannagan. Binghamton, 1987: 59-76.

————. "Gunpowder and the Problem of Theatrical Heroic Form: Milton's *In Quintum Novembris*," *Urbane Milton: The Latin Poetry.* Ed. James Freeman and Anthony Low. Pittsburgh: Duquesne University Press, 1984: 3-19.

————. "Love's Epic Revel in *Paradise Lost:* A Theatrical Vision of Marriage," *Modern Language Quarterly*, 38 (1967): 3-20.

————. "Milton's *Comus:* The Sequel to a Masque of Circe," *The Huntington Library Quarterly* (May, 1966): 245-54.

————. "The Thrones of Satan and God: Background to Divine Opposition in *Paradise Lost,*" *Huntington Library Quarterly* 31 (1967): 21-33.

Destombes, Marcel. *Mappaemondes: A.D. 1200-1500.* Amsterdam: N. Israel, 1964.

Dobranski, Stephen and John P. Rumrich, eds. *Milton and Heresy.* Cambridge: Cambridge University Press, 1998.

Durant, Will. *The Story of Civilization.* Vols. 1-6. vols. 7-11 with Ariel Durant. New York: Simon and Schuster, 1935-75.

Dyson, John with Luis Miguel Coin Cuenca and Peter Christopher. *Columbus: For Gold, God, and Glory.* New York: Simon and Schuster, 1991.

Elton. G. R. *Return to Essentials: Some Reflections on the Present State of Historical Study.* Cambridge: Cambridge University Press, 1991.

Engels, Friedrich. "Socialism: Utopian and Scientific," reprint of the 1892 authorized English edition in *The Marx-Engels Reader.* Ed. Robert C. Tucker. New York: W. W. Norton, 1963.

Evans, J. Martin. *Milton's Imperial Epic: "Paradise Lost" and the Discourse of Colonialism.* Ithaca: Cornell University Press, 1996.

Fallon, Robert. *Divided Empire: Milton's Political Imagery.* University Park: Pennsylvania State University Press, 1995.

————. *Milton among the Philosophers: Poetry and Materialism in Seventeenth-Century England.* Ithaca: Cornell University Press, 1991.

Fernández-Armesto, Felipe. *Millennium: A History of the Last Thousand Years.* New York: Scribner, 1995.

————. *Civilization.* London: Macmillan, 2000.

Fletcher, Harris Francis. *The Intellectual Development of John Milton.* 2 vols. Urbana: University of Illinois Press, 1956-61.

Flint, Valerie I. J. *The Imaginative Landscape of Christopher Columbus.* Princeton: Princeton University Press, 1992.

————. *Ideas in the Medieval West: Texts and their Contexts.* London: Variorum Reprints, 1988.

Foucault, Michel. *Language, Counter-Memory, Practice: Selected Essays and Interviews.* Ed. and intro. Donald F. Bouchard; tr. Donald F. Bouchard and Sherry Simon. Ithaca: Connell University Press, 1977.

Frankfort, Henri. *Ancient Egyptian Religion.* New York: Harper and Row, 1948.

French, J. Milton. "Milton as a Historian," *PMLA* 50 (June, 1935): 469-79.

———. *The Life Records of John Milton.* 5 vols. New Brunswick: Rutgers University Press, 1949-58.

Fromkin, David. *The Way of the World: From the Dawn of Civilization to the Eve of the Twenty-first Century.* New York: Alfred A. Knopf, 1998.

Fukuyama, Francis. *The End of History and the Last Man.* New York: Maxwell Macmillan, 1992.

Fussner, F. Smith. *The Historical Revolution: English Historical Writing and Thought, 1580-1640.* London: Routledge and Paul, 1962.

———. *Tutor History and the Historians.* New York: Basic Books, 1970.

Gilbert, Allan H. *On the Composition of "Paradise Lost": A Study of the Ordering and Insertion of Material.* Chapel Hill: University of North Carolina Press, 1947.

———. *A Geographical Dictionary of Milton.* New Haven: Yale University Press, 1919.

Glacken, Clarence J. *Traces on the Rhodian Shore: nature and culture in Western thought from ancient times to the end of the eighteenth century.* Berkeley: University of California Press, 1967.

Greenblatt, Stephen. *Marvelous Possessions: The Wonder of the New World.* Chicago: University of Chicago Press, 1991.

———. *Sir Walter Ralegh: The Renaissance Man and his Roles.* New Haven: Yale University Press, 1973.

Hardt, Michael and Antonio Negri. *Empire.* Cambridge: Harvard University Press, 2000.

Helgerson, Richard. *Forms of Nationhood: The Elizabethan Writing of England.* Chicago: University of Chicago, 1992.

Hopkins, A. G., ed. *Globalization in World History.* London: Pimlico, 2002.

Himmelfarb, Gertrude. *On Looking into the Abyss.* New York: Alfred A. Knopf, 1994.

Hill, Christopher. *Intellectual Origins of the English Revolution.* Oxford: Oxford University Press, 1965.

———. *Milton and the English Revolution.* London: Faber & Faber, 1977.

————. *The English Bible and the Seventeenth-Century Revolution.* London: The Penguin Press, 1993.

Holloway, Julia Bolton. *Jerusalem: Essays on Pilgrimage and Literature.* AMS Press, 1998.

Horkheimer, Max and Theodor W. Adorno. *Dialectic of Enlightenment.* Tr. John Cumming. New York: Herder and Herder, 1972. Original edition: *Dialektik der Aufklärung.* New York: Social Studies Association, 1944.

Hoxby, Blair. *Mammon's Music: Literature and Economics in the Age of Milton.* New Haven: Yale University Press, 2002.

Hunter, William B. *Visitation Unimplor'd: Milton and the Authorship of De Doctrina Christiana.* Pittsburgh: Duquesne University Press, 1998.

Jennings, Francis. *The Invasion of America: Indians, colonialism, and the cant of conquest.* Chapel Hill: University of North Carolina Press, 1975.

Kadir, Djelal. *Columbus and the Ends of the Earth: Europe's Prophetic Rhetoric As Conquering Ideology.* Berkeley: University of California Press, 1992.

Kelley, Maurice. *This Great Argument: A Study of Milton's "De Doctrina Christiana" as a Gloss upon "Paradise Lost."* Princeton: Princeton University Press, 1941.

Kingsford, Charles L. *English Historical Literature in the Fifteenth Century.* Oxford: Oxford University Press, 1913.

Kinney, Arthur F. and Dan S. Collins, eds. *Renaissance Historicism: Selections from "English Literary Renaissance."* Amherst: University of Massachusetts Press, 1987.

Knoppers, Laura Lunger. *Historicizing Milton: Spectacle: Power, and Poetry in Restoration England.* Athens: University of Georgia Press, 1994.

Kolbrener, William. *Milton's Warring Angels: A Study of Critical Engagements.* Cambridge: Cambridge University Press, 1997.

Kojeve, Alexandre. *An Introduction to the Reading of Hegel.* Tr. James Nichols. New York: Basic Books, 1969.

Lefranc, Pierre. *Sir Walter Raleigh, écrivain, l'oeuvre et les idées.* Paris: A. Colin; Quebec: les Presses de l'Université Laval, 1968.

Levy, F. J. *Tutor Historical Thought.* San Marino: Huntington Library Press, 1967.

Lewalski, Barbara. *The Life of John Milton.* Oxford: Blackwell, 2000.

————. *"Paradise Lost" and the Rhetoric of Literary Forms.* Princeton: Princeton University Press, 1985.

Lieb, Michael. "De Doctrina Christiana and the Question of Authorship," *Milton Studies* 41. Ed. Albert C. Labriola. (Pittsburgh: 2002):172-230.

Lovejoy, Arthur O. "Milton and the Paradox of the Fortunate Fall," *Essays in the History of Ideas.* Baltimore: Johns Hopkins University Press, 1948, pp. 277-95.

Lowenstein, David. *Milton and the Drama of History: Historical Vision, Iconoclasm, and the Literary Imagination.* Cambridge: Cambridge University Press, 1990.

Lukács, Gyorg. *Essays on Realism.* Trans. David Fernbach, ed. Rodney Livingston. Cambridge: M. I. T. Press, 1980. Original edition, 1971.

————. *History and Class Consciousness: Studies in Marxist Dialectics.* Ed. and intro. R. Pascal; tr. Rodney Livingston. London: Merlin Press, 1971. Original edition, 1923.

Lupton, Julia Reinhard. *Afterlives of the Saints: Hagiography, Typology, and Renaissance Literature.* Stanford: Stanford University Press, 1996.

MacKenzie Ross, Malcolm. *Milton's Royalism: A Study of the Conflict of Symbol and Idea in the Poem.* Ithaca: Cornell University Press, 1943. Reprinted, New York: Russell & Russell, 1970.

Maritain, Jacques. *On the Philosophy of History.* Ed. Joseph W. Evans. London: Geoffrey Bles, 1959.

Martin Elsky. *Authorizing Words: Speech, Writing, and Print in the English Renaissance.* Ithaca: Cornell University Press, 1984.

Mason, Henry. *Toynbee's Approach to World Politics.* New Orleans: Tulane University Press, 1958.

Martland, Peter, ed. *The Future of the Past: The Big Questions in History.* London: Pimlico, 2002.

McKisack, May. *Medieval History in the Tudor Age.* Oxford: Clarendon Press, 1971.

McLellan, David. *Karl Marx: His Life and Thought.* London: Macmillan, 1973.

Milhou, Alain. *Colón y su Mentalidad Mesiánica en el Ambiente Franciscanista Español.* Valladolid: Casa-Museo de Colon, Seminario Americanista de la Universidad de Valladolid, 1983.

Morison, Samuel Eliot. *Admiral of the Ocean Sea: A Life of Christopher Columbus.* 2 vols., Boston: Little, Brown & Co., 1942. Reprinted: New York: Doubleday, 1967.

Neri, Damiano. *Il S. Sepolcro riprodotto in Occidente.* Jerusalem: Franciscan Press, 1971.

Nicoll, Allardyce. *Stuart Masques and the Renaissance Stage.* New York: Harcourt Brace, 1938.

Nicolson, Majorie Hope. *The Breaking of the Circle: studies in the effect of the "new science" upon seventeenth-century poetry.* New York: Columbia University Press, 1960.

————. *Mountain Gloom and Mountain Glory: the development of the aesthetics of the infinite.* Ithaca: Cornell University Press, 1959.

————. *Newton Demands the Muse: Newton's Opticks and the eighteenth century poets.* Princeton: Princeton University Press, 1946.

————. *Voyages to the Moon.* New York: Macmillan, 1948.

Nordau, Max. *Degeneration.* New York: D. Appleton, 1895.

Novick, Peter. *That Noble Dream: The Objective Question and the American Historical Profession.* Cambridge: Cambridge University Press, 1988.

Nunn, George E. *The Geographical Conceptions of Columbus.* New York: American Geographical Society, 1924.

Page, Carl. *Philosophical Historicism and the Betrayal of First Philosophy.* University Park: Pennsylvania State University Press, 1957.

Paiewonsky, Michael. *The Conquest of Eden, 1493-1515.* Rome, St. Thomas, Tortola: MAPes MONDe Editore, undated.

Palmer, Bryan D. *Descent into Discourse: The Reification of Language and the Writing of Social History.* Philadelphia: Temple University Press, 1990.

Panofsky, Erwin. *Gothic architecture and scholasticism.* Latrobe, Pa.: Archabbey Press, 1951.

————. *Meaning in the visual arts; papers in and on art history.* Garden City: Doubleday, 1955.

Parks, George Bruner. *Richard Hakluyt and the English Voyages.* Notes and intro. James A. Williamson. New York: American Geographical Society, 1928.

Patrides, C. A. *Milton and the Christian Tradition.* Oxford: The Clarendon Press, 1966.

————. *The Grand Design of God: The Literary Form of the Christian view of History.* London: Routledge & Kegan Paul, 1972.

————. *The Phoenix and the Ladder*: the rise and decline of the Christian view of history. Berkeley: University of California Press, 1974.

———— with Joseph Wittreich eds. *The Apocallypse in English Renaissance Thought and Literature: Patterns, Antecedents and Repercussions*. Manchester: Manchester University Press, 1984,

———— with William B. Hunter and J. H. Adamson, eds. *Bright Essence: Studies in Milton's Theology*. Salt Lake City: University of Utah Press, 1971.

Patterson, Annabel M. *Early Modern Liberalism*. Cambridge: Cambridge University Press, 1997.

————. *Nobody's Perfect*. New Haven: Yale University Press, 2002.

D. Pennington, L. E. ed. *The Purchas Handbook*: *Studies of the life, times and writings of Samuel Purchas, 1577-1626*. 2 vols. London: The Hakluyt Society, printed at Cambridge University Press, 1997.

Phelan, John Leddy. *The Millennial Kingdom of the Franciscans in the New World*. 2nd ed. Berkeley: University of California Press, 1970.

Pocock, J. G. A. *The Ancient Constitution and Feudal Law: A Study of Historical Thought*. Cambridge; Cambridge University Press, 1957.

Quint, David. *Epic and Empire: Politics and Generic Form from Virgil to Milton*. Princeton: Princeton University Press, 1993.

Radzinowicz, Mary Ann. *Toward Samson Agonistes; The Growth of Milton's Mind*. Princeton: Princeton University Press, 1978.

Rajan, Balachandra, and Sauer, Elizabeth, eds. *Milton and the Imperial Vision*. Pittsburgh: Duquesne University Press, 1999.

Raleigh, Walter. *The English Voyages of the Sixteenth Century*. Glasgow: James MacLehose and Sons, 1906.

Revard, Stella Pruce. *The War in Heaven*. Ithaca: Cornell University Press, 1980.

Randall, Jr., John Herman. *Religion and the Modern World*. New York: Frederick A. Stokes, 1929.

Richmond, Hugh M. *John Milton's drama of "Paradise Lost."* New York: Peter Lang, 1991.

Rowse, A. L. *The First Colonists*: *Hakluyt's Voyages to North America*. London: Alden Press for the Folio Society, 1986.

Sale, Kirkpatrick. *The Conquest of Paradise: Christopher Columbus and the Columbian Legacy*. New York: Alfred A. Knopf, 1990.

Sanders, Ronald. *Lost tribes and promised lands: The origins of American racism.* Boston: Little, Brown, 1978.

Saurat, Denis. *Milton: Man and Thinker.* Rev. ed. North Haven, CT: Archon Press, 1964.

Sewell, Arthur. *A Study of Milton's "Christian Doctrine."* London: Oxford University Press, 1939.

Sharp, Robert L. "Donne's 'Good Morrow' and Cordiform Maps," *Modern Language Notes* 69 (1954): 275-308.

Silver, Victoria. *Imperfect Sense: The Predicament of Milton's Irony.* Princeton: Princeton University Press, 2001.

Solomon, Julie Robin. *Objectivity in the Making: Francis Bacon and the Politics of Inquiry.* Baltimore and London: John Hopkins University Press, 1998.

Singleton, Charles S. "In Exitu Israel de Aegypto," *Seventy-Eighth Annual Report of the Dante Society* (Boston, 1960): 1-24.

———. *Dante Studies I: "Commedia" Elements of Structure.* Cambridge: Harvard University Press, 1954.

———. *Dante Studies II: Journey to Beatrice.* Cambridge: Harvard University Press, 1958.

Sorokin, Pitrim. *The Crises of Our Age.* New York: E. P. Dutton, 1941.

Southern, R. W. *Western Views of Islam in the Middle Ages* Cambridge: Harvard University Press, 1962.

Todorov, Tezevtan. *The Conquest of America: The Question of the Other.* Tr. Richard Howard. New York: Harper & Row, 1984; orig. French edition, 1982.

Toynbee, Arnold. *A Study of History.* 2nd ed., 4th printing. 12 vols. Oxford: Oxford University Press, 1945-61.

———. *An Historian's Approach to Religion.* Oxford: Oxford University Press, 1956.

———. *Civilization on Trial.* New York: Oxford University Press, 1948.

Trevelyan, Raleigh. *Sir Walter Raleigh.* New York: Henry Holt, 2003.

Tuveson, Ernest Lee. *Millennium and Utopia: A Study in the Background of the Idea of Progress.* Berkeley and Los Angeles: University of California Press, 1949.

———. "The Millenarian Structure of *The Communist Manifesto*," *The Apocalypse in English Renaissance Thought and Literature:*

Patterns, Antecedents, and Repercussions. C. A. Patrides and Joseph Wittreich, eds. Manchester: Manchester University Press, 1984.

Vickers, Brian, ed. and notes. "A Confession of Faith" (1641) in *Francis Bacon.* Oxford: Oxford University Press, 1996.

Watson, Foster. *Richard Hakluyt.* London: Sheldon Press, 1924.

Watts, Pauline Moffitt. "Prophecy and Discovery: On the Spiritual Origins of Christopher Columbus's 'Enterprise of the Indies,'" *The American Historical Review* 90.1 (Feb., 1985): 73-102.

Wells, H. G. (Herbert George). *An Outline of History, Being a Plain History of Life and Mankind.* New York: Macmillan, 1926.

————. *The Outline of History.* Rev. ed. Garden City: Garden City Publishing Co., 1931.

White, Hayden. *Metahistory: The Historical Imagination in Nineteenth-Century Europe.* Baltimore: Johns Hopkins University Press, 1973.

————. *The Content of the Form: Narrative Discourse and Historical Representation.* Baltimore: Johns Hopkins University Press, 1987.

Whitehead, Alfred North. *Science and the Modern World.* New York: Macmillan, 1926.

Whitfield, Peter. *The Image of the World: 20 Centuries of World Maps.* San Francisco: Pomegranate Artbooks in association with the British Library, 1994.

Wilford, John Noble. *The Mapmakers.* New York: Alfred A. Knopf, 2000.

————. *The Mysterious History of Columbus: An exploration of the Man, the Myth, the Legacy.* New York: Alfred A. Knopf, 1991.

Wolfe, Don M. *Milton in the Puritan Revolution.* London: Cohen and West, 1963.

Zagorin, Perez. *Francis Bacon.* Princeton: Princeton University Press, 1998.

INDEX